Runaway
Waltz

A Memoir from Vienna to New York

Frederic Morton

SIMON & SCHUSTER

New York • *London* • *Toronto* • *Sydney*

SIMON & SCHUSTER
Rockefeller Center
1230 Avenue of the Americas
New York, NY 10020

Parts of this book appeared,
in altered form, in
Harper's and
The Atlantic Monthly.

SIMON & SCHUSTER and colophon are
registered trademarks of Simon & Schuster, Inc.

For information about special discounts for bulk purchases,
please contact Simon & Schuster Special Sales at
1-800-456-6798 or business@simonandschuster.com.

Designed by Dana Sloan

Manufactured in the United States of America

10 9 8 7 6 5 4 3 2 1

Library of Congress Cataloging-in-Publication Data

Morton, Frederic.
    Runaway Waltz / Frederic Morton.
        p. cm.
    1. Morton, Frederic. 2. Authors, American—20th century—Biography. 3. Refugees,
Jewish—United States—Biography. 4. Jews—United States—Biography. 5. Austrian
Americans—Biography. 6. Vienna (Austria)—Biography. 7. New York (N.Y.)—Biography.
I. Title.

PS3525.O825Z47 2005
813 '.54—dc22

                                                            2005042493

ISBN 0-7432-2539-2

In memory of M.C.M.
and
For Rebecca

Contents

Vienna 1936: *Austerlitz and I*   1

1939: *Vienna to London—the Day I Became a Refugee*   9

1942: *Manhattan Nocturne*   23

1945: *The Bride in the Gym*   39

1949: *Rendezvous at Salt Lake City*   69

May 1955: *Best Man on the Baltic*   88

1960: *Christmas with the Rothschilds*   104

March 1967: *St. Moritz Blues*   134

1972: *Miami, Mutti, and Morton Rampant*   159

September 1994: *Vienna, Bald Starlet*   192

Acknowledgments   213

Runaway
Waltz

Vienna 1936

Austerlitz and I

He will arrive as He should arrive—eventually, in due time. His slowness is part of the thrill. So is the slight shock against my skin as I sit down to await Him. Against my back tingles wood as hard and cold and electric as I've known only in the seats of the Lux Movie Theater in our outer district in Vienna, in the midthirties.

The fans won't start revolving until everybody has settled down. Overhead the three bulbs, already burned out last time, still haven't been replaced. Three chandelier arms still curve lightless, naked, sooty. This will make the transition from present dreariness to His radiance all the more exciting. Actually, the less illumination right now, the better. I'm less exposed to people staring at my clothes.

In the Lux Movie Theater almost all other kids my age wear rough loden jackets and manly weathered leather shorts. I must sit there in a sissy sailor suit. Those staring kids have no knowledge, of course, of my own leather shorts, which are as toughly weathered as any of theirs. They have no idea that the sailor suit is the fault of the Café Landtmann; that I'm allowed movies only right after our family hot chocolate at the flossy Landtmann downtown, where men's cuff links gleam up during hand kissing and where I must scrawl on some fringed paper napkin examples of my penmanship for Aunt Emma. The Lux kids don't know that her jokes about my Chinese letters always go on and

on, followed by Uncle Karl's endless, nervous, underbreath interpreta-
tions of the latest speech from Berlin. Nor do the Lux kids know or care
that that's how I'm kept captive until after 4 PM, which means no
chance to change into my leather shorts: I have barely two and a half
hours for Him at the Lux, including travel time: I must be home again,
ready for the supper table, hands washed, at 7 PM sharp—in fact, earlier these days, when the sun sets sooner. My father, having caught
Uncle Karl's nervousness, has decreed that in such times as ours I can't
be out after dark. Therefore, to make His five o'clock showing I must
rush like mad from Landtmann to the Lux, still imprisoned in my hor-
rid sailor suit.

How explain all that to the starers? Or explain further that I'm sitting
almost alone in this expensive row up front only because even with my
glasses I'd be unable to see Him clearly farther back? Since my bond
with Him would be less special if I gave it away, I never mention Him to
my mother in any emphatic way. I just remind her of the headache I get
from eyestrain—presto! she coughs up the extra fifty groschen for a seat
nearer the screen. And she's always good for the thirty groschen more
that buy the program on which only very few others in the audience have
splurged. To me the program is vital, brimming with portraits and revela-
tions of Him. To my father this is just the sort of indulgence that will
spoil a child. Still, my mother always prevails with her theory about my
film program collecting: it may not be as constructive as stamp collecting, but at least it does encourage the discipline I badly need if I am ever
to improve my grades.

Grades, study habits, politics . . . all that fuss recedes, now that the
chandelier is dimming. At the same time pictures begin to glimmer up
across the speckles of the screen. They are His vanguard, even though
they are just hand-painted lantern slides advertising local stores.

Two identical loden jackets appear; one coffee-stained and dotted by
the little spots of the screen; the other with the stain removed but of
course still screen-mottled—A. Lazar, the neighborhood cleaner. Cher-
ries, mottled and voluptuously lipstick red—the greengrocer Peter Ze-
leny. The locksmith Alois Matuschek, with a big mottled, mustached
grin, holding aloft a big mottled lock.

After Matuschek the house grows quite dark. The ceiling fans have begun to rotate: propellers that will soon fly the Lux Theater across the Atlantic. Their low whir mingles with the hiss of an air-freshening spray. The sprayer is the usher, who has as his badge of office a World War I sergeant's cap. A flashlight fixed to his visor, he bestrides the aisle, hissing aroma into the air, holding the spray can aloft like an annunciatory trumpet.

However, it's not He who responds to the fanfare—not yet. It's more commercials. Still, these are no longer crude daubs but photographs, quite polished ones, and therefore already approximations of Him. There is the cravated lady-killer, sporting a patent-leather forelock and a silver cigarette case from which he extracts with knowing gusto a Jonny smoke, his dash mottled by the screen's rash. A pretty lady, mysteriously smiling, mottled from gamine bangs to stiletto heels, caresses her Odol toothpaste tube. No less mottled are the muscles of a runner in a relay race, handing along a bottle of Obi apple juice.

Out in the ordinary world the mottles might be blemishes. In the Lux they are the hallmark of a prelude like no other. They spice my expectation. They warm the slick pages of the program in my hand. It's too dark to read it yet another time, but my fingers can feel its centerfold illustration: Him, leaping high in black-tie glory.

Meanwhile, drums and woodwinds surge from the loudspeakers. The newsreels thunder onto the screen. No longer still photographs but moving pictures, they are yet stronger prophecies of Him. Great personages begin to loom. Unlike Him they have no personal connection to me. Yet their eminence points toward His ultimate peak.

The king of England, affable, breast handkerchief folded like a crown, pushes an amputee's wheelchair into the hospital he has just opened. In compassionate shirtsleeves the president of Mexico hugs a wizened peasant next to an adobe hut ruined by an earthquake. Our Austrian chancellor, standing in St. Stephen's Square, hair ruffled by September winds, inaugurates the annual charity campaign by shaking a coin box at the camera. Only the German part of the newsreel seems, at least for a moment, aimed in my direction: the Reich Leader performs a hearty handshake with the chairman of the committee organizing the Winter

Olympics scheduled in Bavaria—but just before he turns away his eyes glare at me—me the big-nosed fancypants sitting in an expensive row on the Austrian side of the border. Yet even his ominous face is spotted with the same screen measles shared by the Austrian chancellor, the English majesty, the Mexican excellency, the lady-killer smoker, our neighborhood cleaner A. Lazar, etc. They have all merged into the parade of preliminaries to His main event.

Whose coming is still delayed, even after the newsreels. For now Mickey Mouse jumps into the picture. Here he is a hapless elevator operator in a hotel a zillion stories high. This means that Mickey Mouse lives somewhere in my god's skyscraper latitudes; in other words, Mickey brings His presence still closer. And indeed Mickey Country seems like a mottled fun house antechamber to the Real Thing which I can only reach after laughing my way through an infinity of pratfalls.

And so I chortle along with all the others at Mickey's inspired ineptitudes. The mouse is as nervous as Uncle Karl, but his anxiety is a lot more fun since it's not Germany that rattles him but his elevator. He simply can't keep the contraption from running amok. Going down, he crashes beyond the basement into Hell. Going up, he splinters through the roof into Heaven. Angels and devils tumble into his cabin, tripping over annoyed hotel guests. All passengers, winged, goat-footed, or luggage-burdened, are mottled, all furious at Mickey. Finally he fumbles his elevator into a tilt, sliding his tormentors into the hotel pool, thus finagling a happy end.

Only this, of course, is not the end.

It is the start of the beginning. At last the time has come for Him.

Loudspeaker explosions, drumbeats, cymbals. Orchestral fireworks launch the feature. Ready for this moment, my right hand (the one not clutching the program) has been curled around the wrapped lozenge in my pocket. Off with the paper, into my mouth, with this genuine imported American chiclet. Never mind what it has done to my pocket money. Even my mother refuses to fund "such American craziness" with an extra subsidy. The seventy groschen nearly kill my weekly allowance. Yet this Yankee chewing gum is much more pungently mint-flavored than the feeble Austrian sort. It spreads on my tongue the very flavor of His New World aura about to unfold on the screen.

The usher celebrates His advent with yet another air-freshening strut down the aisle. The spraying tempo joins the rhythm of the title-and-credits music—puffs and sound track accelerate together into a simultaneous crescendo.

And, yes, there He is!

There He materializes on the screen, ambling down a street. Mind you, He is still mottled. He is still not the god, though all of us in the audience know that soon he will assume an unearthly grace. But only I am alert to that quick glance He shoots me as He rounds the corner: I am His kind. None of the differences between us really matter. True, He is a New York boulevardier striding along an avenue aroar with cars bigger and faster than anything seen by the Danube. I'm just a Viennese grade school slacker, all agog in my wooden seat. Yet proof of our kinship is spelled out in rotogravure print under His leaping picture in the program. I know His capsule biography there by heart: regardless of what He may be called in any film—Bob or Dick or Jim or whatever American word, His real first name, the one He was born with, is exactly the same as my own. *Fritz*. And His real last name, *Austerlitz* (disclosing His Austrian parentage) contains not only the same number of syllables but also the same number of letters as my own: *Mandelbaum*.

Indeed as Fritz Mandelbaum watches Fritz Austerlitz, the other links between us come alive again. While Fritz Austerlitz is too big to be a problem child, He is certainly a problem person. For one thing, He is overdressed like me. A carnation flashes out of His buttonhole; tassels drip from His loafers. And He gets into hot water fast.

In this film, too, His trouble seems related to His objectionable way of talking, though in His case it's not that He keeps lapsing into raw Viennese dialect, which upsets my mother even more than my father and which raises teachers' eyebrows heavenward and which I love because the brawny street sounds make up for the sailor-suit self forced on me one way or another. No, His speech is nonslang, but far from good mellow Austrian German; it's German German of the Reich sort, with consonants as jagged as the Leader's glare at me a few minutes ago. What's more, this German German twists unnaturally out of His mouth, blur-

ring and rasping, and, especially at the beginning of the action, anything
He says has the wrong effect.

This is true once more here, in this film on that crowded New York
sidewalk, where He tries to approach a fast-walking lady. Each time He
catches up with her, He addresses her so awkwardly that she huffs off in
contempt. To get away from him, she crosses the street while the light
changes. He jaywalks after her right through the screaming of many
brakes. A policeman (similar to the one who confiscated the soccer ball I
kicked into the traffic last week) writes Him up because He answers
back so badly. Immediately afterward He rushes into the building into
which the lady vanished. She turns out to be a teacher in a dancing
school, and it's a disaster when He enrolls as her pupil.

Austerlitz is as bad a student as Mandelbaum. During a fox-trot lesson
He keeps sweet-talking her clumsily, pays no attention to her instructions, and, in a catastrophic stumble, sprawls on the floor, dragging her
down with Him.

But it is at this very point that the transfiguration comes to pass. It is
here that He, all aflounder on the parquet, wincing at the young
woman's fury, turns wondrous. He sorcers his blunder into a masterful
joke.

Music flows into his limbs. With superb suppleness He rises from
the floor, suddenly commanding a language as new as His voice. This
new voice is marvelously unblurred, untwisted, fitting his lip movements since it is no longer dubbed. That I don't understand His words
only enhances their mystery: in contrast to His spoken German, he
sings His limpid English. His cry, melodious beyond my comprehen-
sion . . .

You're lovely to look at, delightful to know, and heaven to kiss!

. . . frees Him from the gravity pulling down sodden mortals. Fritz
Austerlitz soars into Fred Astaire.

Being Fred Astaire, he needs only to touch the woman to render her
weightless as Himself. Instantly she lilts off the floor. Together they start
gliding on violin wings, vaulting, swaying, pirouetting. Mellifluously in-

tertwined, their momentum sweeps away all her anger. The whole world, until now so nasty to Him, so flyspecked, unmottles and melts into sheer elan and elegance and amorousness.

As for me in my wooden seat, my tongue can't speak the language danced on the screen, but my mouth can move to it. Between my teeth the gum floats to the beat of his legs. The rhythm effervesces down my body; it tickles my feet with the promise that some such wizardry, invoked in English, will lift me into the lightning ease of the planet's greatest soccer center forward. And just as His carnation is no longer foppishness but a prodigy's blazon, so the sailor suit will be the heraldic costume in which to kick in my world championship goal . . .

I must go before it's over. I must be home in time. Not that it's so terrible to miss the end. The end usually has Him in a static clinch with her, mouthing muzzy earthbound German. Better to walk up the dark aisle now, between rapt faces, and look back for a last glimpse of Him, slim-tuxedoed in mid-dance, levitating above a champagne goblet, smiling as though he'd never ever need to touch the ground again.

Today, though, I seem to have left Him too soon. The best time to relinquish His spell, to descend once more into ordinariness, is at the onset of twilight: early enough for me to reach our house before real night yet dusky enough, the city already obscure enough, that I can confuse, at least for a little while, my Vienna with His Manhattan.

But coming out of the dream-womb darkness, I am almost blinded by the Neulerchenfelderstrasse. Too much bruising harsh gray left over from the afternoon. The streetlamps are not yet switched on. In the day's unmerciful dregs they look so rusty and ungainly compared to the sleek lights of New York from which I've just parted. I close my eyes halfway to preserve inside my head His Broadway glow. With eyelids lowered I keep walking until I reach A. Lazar's Cleaner Store.

It is locked on Sunday, of course. But I know that if I press my spectacles against my nose and peer hard through the glass door, I'll be able to spot, far back in the dimness, leaning against the counter, the poster which weekdays stands in front of the store and whose picture of the two jackets, one stained, one cleaned, started the Lux magic culminating in

Him. And I raise my eyelids to find again, through the poster, the promise of Him coming again.

What I see is nothing of the sort.

I don't even see any glass door—just ugly ash-colored, wrinkled metal. Just another of those corrugated iron shutters sprouting lately all over town as protection. But they didn't protect A. Lazar against the bloodred words newly smeared across the corrugations—a wet crimson curse screamed against the Lazars, the Mandelbaums, and their likes.

Quickly I shut my eyes against it. But paint sticks to my right index finger. Ugly, viscous, somehow hot, it burns away all pulsing echoes of His feet. And I no longer even care. Feet are no longer there for dancing, only for running. Running, running hard, I spit out my Yankee gum. Anything to breathe better as I tear down the five blocks home.

1939

Vienna to London—
the Day I Became a Refugee

In the weeks after I had passed fourteen, hardly a day went by in which my parents didn't remind me that soon I would be a refugee. The word became part of parental rhetoric in the house. Perhaps my father and mother pronounced it so often in order to familiarize themselves with it—to develop, perhaps, some mental calluses against the word, or to domesticate it as one domesticates and warms, by frequent use and comfortable complaint, a frost-haunted idea such as Old Age.

But the word would not yield. We were members of the condemned race in the Vienna of 1939. When my mother left for the hairdresser or I for school, we always kissed each other without admitting why. Each time might be the last. We lived from breath to breath. The supreme sound in the world was the footstep on the stairs. Outside, in the fine spring sun, troops of apple-cheeked young men marched through the city and sang "The Song of the Long Knives."

These dangers were bright and lethal and intimate. My father had been swallowed up by them in Dachau and emerged again. But "refugee" was, for all of us, strangely beyond the imagination. I knew it had to do with being poor, with learning English and studying the mazed map of

London. But none of these things plumbed the depth of the word. It became less fathomable the more quickly we approached it.

Our British visas arrived. The "Aryanization" of family properties was completed. My father decided to travel with my uncle and myself and to let my mother, my brother, and my aunt follow a few days later (the smaller the party, the less the danger). Clothing, books, dishes, the whole vocabulary of our daily existence, vanished into trunks. The great change was at hand.

It was barely dawn when my father, my uncle, and I walked to the taxi that would drive us out of our native street forever. Inside the cab my father slipped a heavy gold ring onto my finger. The ring, I understood, had a sober purpose. As refugees in London we would have to live on what we brought, and we were permitted one piece of jewelry each. Yet the massive yellow band bedizened me. Its heavy gleam on my finger kindled the whole day into flamboyance. Our concierge, who must have discovered our departure after all, ran out of the house and to our surprise—for we had thought her sympathies uncertain—wept into a huge red-checkered handkerchief. A pebble hit the side of the car, an urchin's voice pelted us with "Drive 'em all the way to Palestine!," and as the taxi turned the corner and my childhood bumped out of view, my father covered our heads and prayed for a safe journey.

Abruptly the station seized us, all color and fever. Tiers of soldiers, helmets polished by the sun, marched to a train, singing. Song also came from a group of Hitler Youth with their black velvet shorts and snow white shirts, entraining, I think, for a picnic in the Vienna Woods. Great garish posters pulsed down from the walls, and beyond the glass walls of the station, on the rooftops all about us, a hundred ebony swastikas on a hundred crimson flags flared and fountained in the breeze.

But I who stood in line with my father and my uncle; I who plucked at the tightness of my blue beret and who saw the officer with the Death's-Head visor at the end of the queue (*Judenpässe*—Jews' passports—it said above his desk); I who knew that such officers could give or withhold our traveling documents, could destroy, deliver, or—most usually—extort as they pleased; I, who was terribly afraid, didn't feel a bit like a refugee. I felt closer than ever to the city, curiously fascinated by its glittering menace. I had never been in so clear and shiny and frank a Vienna; I thought I understood for the first time its cobbly twists, its baroque flourishes, and the gargoyles crouching in its nooks.

I even saw my father, with a definition newly drawn out of the pressure, the dazzle of that morning. In "peacetime," as my parents had come to call the days before the *Anschluss,* he had been a stern pin-striped presence at the dinner table; true, weekends in the coffeehouse, he'd playfully debate soccer with his son but soon withdrew behind newspapers to take "one glance at the situation." Now, while we inched toward the Death's Head, my father was quite changed. His deep tan from outdoor work at Dachau had not yet faded. The seven weeks of starving there still pinched his jaw into bold angles. This, together with his shaven skull, gave him the profile of a Red Indian. He was the last person I would have expected to be touched by the gusts of James Fenimore Cooper, my great boyhood author. Yet here he loomed up next to me, gaunt, wild, even a little absurd, wearing the black loden coat he had worn ever since he had brought it back from the camp, and which he would not go without even now, in the July heat. He glanced carelessly at the station clock, and as he stepped up to the desk of the Death's Head and barked out in the prescribed Prussian manner our names, passport numbers, and destinations, I became, in the middle of my fear, astonished at something perverse, something oddly eager in my father's eyes.

The Death's Head listened with half-closed eyes. He pulled out a file, dozed over documents. With the lazy disgust of a man who decides to wave away a mosquito before slapping it, he remarked that we owed the Greater German Reich the sum of ninety thousand reichsmarks.

"Beg to point out, my tax clearance is here," my father said.

"You didn't hear me," the Death's Head said sleepily.

"Beg to report, my family has been living on soup kitchen tickets for the last ten weeks." My father produced three depleted ticket booklets. I had never been in a soup kitchen nor seen the booklets, but I recognized the insignia of the Jewish Welfare Board, on which my father had served for many years.

The Death's Head frowned at the evidence. His black sleeve swung toward my father's face. My uncle cried out, but my father stood straight and keen. The Death's Head marked a small *x* on his forehead. Then I felt crayon on my skin, and my uncle submitted to it. We were passed baggage. The Death's Head stamp pounced three times on our three open passports, leaving pitch-black scars next to our green precious, life-saving British visas. My father caught the sheaf of documents thrown at him, and suddenly we were running to catch our train, tearing at our heavy bags; and while we heaved through the crowd and the engine blasted white impatience through the blue air, I heard my father's cackle. It was really a cackle, a prankster's giggle at having pulled a mad trick. It came out of a grimace that revealed in my father's mouth two front teeth whose length and wolfishness I had not previously noticed.

The sight and sound infected me. We scurried so ridiculously; we staggered so drunkenly with the heaviness of our bags. It was all so funny and crazy and desperate. And again I felt that this reeling of ours through the crowded platform, this tripping over valises and stumbling across children, was truer than all the sedate promenading we had done in Vienna; truer than the many days when we had been deferred to, flattered yet not tolerated, when lips had smiled yet curled all around us. All those "peace years" had been polite fake. They'd had to be sat through as rough boys have to sit through the last school hour. Now the bell had rung release. The city came down on us, one giant and garlanded bully. And we ran for our lives with the exhilaration of our pursuers; we ran those last few yards of native soil in mischievous hysteria, pulling and panting, scrambling through farewell wishings and raised-hand hailings, through jeers and jokes and through the throwing of a tomato that splattered the suitcase of my father just as we climbed the platform of a third-class carriage.

There we rested. The palpitation of my heart became the palpitation of the wheels. For a moment I wondered if I shouldn't be conscious of being a refugee now. Vienna was rolling away underneath. Tomorrow, if all went well, we would step out of the train into a fresh universe. Still I could summon no solemn sense of metamorphosis or liberation.

I was glad when my father beckoned and the heavy suitcase handle yanked me back into his frantic spoof. It seemed logical, it was excellent, that instead of wiping away the tomato splotch he should put out a tasting finger. And after we had toiled our luggage across a giddy connection bridge onto a carpeted corridor, it seemed right that the first-class conductor should wear spectacles of an immense steel-rimmed dignity ill supported by a clownish pygmy of a pink nose. He threw his head back in anger and asked what we thought we were doing. With another head toss he refuted my father's tickets: we had no reservations; the whole matter was typically disorderly ("typically" in such cases always referred to our race); we had better report to the trainmaster.

And then it seemed quite natural that my father should affect obedience—that he should lead us slowly in the direction of the conductorial forefinger until the pink pygmy nose was out of sight and that he should then, suddenly, with another cackle, swerve into a first-class compartment where sat a one-eyed major of the Wehrmacht.

My father brought his heels together, bowed, rapped out, "Permission?"

The major turned his head slowly from the book he was reading. I remember him well. His peaked cap lengthened his long head and conspired with his long, flat nostrils to suggest a pale and precise stallion. His black eye patch made him look like one of those piebalds that are spotted over one eye. He took us in for two full seconds. He didn't say a word. His head began to move back to the book again, but just when I considered ourselves cast out, his hand reached for the wine bottle in the middle of the compartment table and pulled it back toward his side. We were admitted.

My father clicked, "Thank you." My uncle and I stowed luggage. And as soon as we were ensconced, the door burst open with the conductor's indignation. "This is incredible!"

"We have the Herr Major's permission," my father said politely, securing a loose window shade.

"Really!" said the conductor. The major, deaf, read his book and sipped his wine. The conductor cleared his throat officially. Perhaps to gain time, he asked for the ticket of the Herr Offizier. The major reached promptly into his coat pocket and with a small thud unfolded his billet. An instant later my father presented our tickets with the same promptness and unfolded them with an identical thud. The exact repetition created a mirage of solidarity between the major and my father. It reduced the conductor to a sardonic *"Ja so?"* The bite of his puncher into our tickets intended viciousness but sounded impotent, like a foot stamp. He didn't counterattack until he strutted out, and then only with a long, sardonically drawn out *"Interessant!"* which intimated that the matter was far from settled.

Today you may find cunning in my father's behavior. For us then it was sheer sudden mania, yet a madness wonderfully armed against the madness all around us. He sat on the scarlet plush in his black coat. More than ever he looked like a stoic, savage Cherokee. The unreason that lived in his eyes was like a talisman to us. He proposed we practice English. My uncle began to drill me in auxiliary verbs. The mystery of "refugee" rose as usual out of the print smell of my primer. But it couldn't fasten on my mind though with each bend of the Danube the known world fell still further behind. The stampede of landscapes seemed as insubstantial as the conjugation of "I am," "I can," "I have." Only the bright cushions of our coupé were real. I felt snug among its prodigies and perils.

And so Upper Austria floated away in green waves toward the horizon. The sun crawled up the window like a fabulous insect. I became hungry. I watched the wine level dropping in the bottle of the one-eyed major, who read and sipped, silent and steady, one knee folded neat above the other, the book held before his face like a mask, half Buddha, half spotted horse. I had a marvelous sense of closeness with whatever was to come.

The Bavarian hills welled up, subsided. In Franconia the dining room steward wove chanting through the length of the train. The officer rose to an unsuspected height, deposited his cap, disclosed crushed blond curls, and, walking out, compressed himself into what seemed not only a stoop but a bow. I was hungry; I resented so prosaic a need in the middle of the dark wonders of our voyage. But I was so hungry. I watched everybody stream past our compartment toward the sign that ornamented the diner entrance at the end of the car. The sign said, with beautifully curlicued Gothic letters, *Juden Verboten*. JEWS FORBIDDEN. A candy vendor shouted his way through the aisle. My heart hoped, my stomach prayed, my father was already poised. But the conductor materialized, whispered into the vendor's ears, pointed at us through the glass door. The vendor went on.

And then the train pulled into Nuremberg. "Watch," my father said. He pulled the curtain down the door. And before I saw how, he had put on the major's cap and greatcoat. Again it wasn't the foolhardiness of his action that struck me but the fact that this grinning desperado, who even took time out to mock the goose step, had once been my pin-striped "peacetime" father. A moment later he leaned out the window with a Prussian thrust, waving a bill and bellowing at platform concessionaires. Then the major's cap and greatcoat were in place again and we had six steaming sausages, six hunks of black bread, and six mounts of mustard, and were munching away.

By the time the major returned I was once more lazing over English participles. He rolled the door open with such a bang that I sat up in terror. I thought our bootlegged feast had been discovered. But the major, as if to make up for his explosive entrance, resumed his seat in silence and with a curious stiff gravity. He placed a white paper bag on the table, for some reason closer to me than to himself. He had also brought a new wine bottle, already half empty and growing emptier still as he took stately sips. He fixed me, *me* specifically, with his concentrated glance and then sank back and appeared to fall asleep.

But I didn't believe him. I didn't like the way he had stared at me. His middle finger kept tapping slowly against his knee. I had the shuddery intuition that the moment his "good" eye had closed, the other one had started to see. The black eye patch became a huge fierce pupil which drilled right through my skin. I tried to escape. But no matter in which direction I twisted, his head seemed to follow me. I tried to find refuge in the window. The gingerbread scenery of Franconia hastened away from a livid sunset, much too busy to give me relief. My father sat stoic and soundless. My uncle didn't rescue me with a grammatical challenge though we hadn't yet covered irregular verbs. The compartment grew dusky to the wheels' metallic, monotonous excitement. I was delivered to the persecution of the Cyclopean eye. And then the other eye sprung alive, as I'd known it would. The officer impaled me on his single prong, said in a high-pitched North German accent:

"A young man who lets his ice cream melt is nothing but a brat."

I was stunned. My father, though, snapped to. He lifted a big soggy ice-cream cup out of the white bag.

"Eat the ice cream the Herr Major brought!"

"A wooden spoon is attached for the convenience of our young wastrel," the major said bitterly at the liquid mess.

I used the spoon. I ate. With the monoglance still leveled at me, I tasted no flavor, only wetness. I licked steadily while the major, ceremonious and somnambulistic, his visible lid closed, took sip after sip. It was the most fathomless ice-cream cup I have ever encountered.

"Opportunities must be taken to the fullest," the major said, a shade less implacable, "especially by people who need them."

"Yes, sir," my father said.

"Our side is taking *our* opportunity to the fullest."

"Yes, sir."

"I therefore expect the other side to take its opportunity to the fullest."

"Yes, sir."

"Then there can be fairness. Because fairness is possible."

"Yes, sir."

All of a sudden the major stood up. "One can drink to that!" He reached behind him into a leather bag and with three categorical gestures produced three glasses for us.

"I am entitled to drink to that with intelligent persons no matter who," he said, icy, to an invisible heckler, poured the last of the bottle into the new glasses, and threw it, with a fine shocking curve, into the streets of Frankfurt that had begun to flank us.

"A toast to fairness," he said, lifting his glass.

"Thank you, sir," my father said, and imitated him along with my uncle.

"No one is too young to lift his glass to that!" the major thundered, for the childhood taboo against "intoxicants" had made me hesitate for a second.

"We have the honor to toast fairness!" the major proclaimed from his impressive altitude. "To decency! To honest opportunities! To no hard feelings!"

With each exclamation his arm rose higher. It must have been a strange spectacle, our disparate foursome performing a rite in a side-shaking coupé. I didn't see its end because I closed my eyes before the unknown impact of alcohol.

Something formidably tart bit my mouth and stung me. At the same time the train jumped to a halt. Perhaps the major's glass was jolted out of his hand, perhaps he threw it down to observe the custom. At any rate there was a silver splintering, a great shouting of "Frankfurt!," a banging of doors, and a wildness of porters, and almost instantly the evening sagged soft, heavy, wayward, into my life's first tipsiness. The hours that followed held danger and significance, but I can't give a responsible account of them since my own experience didn't happen to me but disported itself at a certain frivolous distance in the form of errant masks and jumbled pageants.

A gnomelike orderly, for example, flashed up and vanished with all the major's belongings and, so it appeared, with even the major himself on his back. A big woman with a fur piece gaped and dissolved. The conductor came, his puncher gnashing at our tickets; a horde of other travelers, tramping, intruding, disintegrating—and then nothing. The clatter of wheels again, like distant hooves in the abrupt night, blackness, and my father huddled in the shadow of his loden coat; a huge jagged ghost afloat in the dark, probably the cathedral in Cologne. Resumption of darkness, of the hooves, and—of a sudden—our coupé blinding bright, littered with the contents of our luggage, and a man with a gray uniform and a red mustache grubbing into our bags like a mole, plowing up heaps of trousers, shirts, soaps, books. The conductor leaning by the door, his glasses aglint and agloat. And the conductor leaping to hold up a little jewel box. Here my memory comes alive with sound. The Red Mustache, a portentous bass, blared that the smuggling of jewels by Jews meant automatic arrest, forfeiture of passports. My father had to fish out a key. The little box snapped open. An Iron Cross lay on blue velvet. My father cackled a cough, explained that this was his cousin's decoration, awarded posthumously during the Great War, for heroic resistance

against the Russians. He begged permission to take it with him. The Red
Mustache became thoughtful even though there was no such cousin.
And the cross looked like one of the many medals my father had produced at his plant. While my thoughts floundered over such contradic-
tions, the Red Mustache was succeeded by a pink-cheeked man in a
green uniform. The train rolled again. My father pulled down the door
shade, took out his jackknife; with a grin he scratched into the Iron
Cross a gleaming crevice of gold. And only then did I realize that my father had perpetrated another grotesque hoax—and that we had done it,
we had passed the border, we had actually passed the German border,
we were in Holland. Now we must truly be refugees.

During the rest of the journey my lame brain wrestled with that realization. I recall mistily that the electric luggage van on the Hook of Holland transferred not only our bags but also myself, and that this caused
amusement around me. Later, on the boat, the salted Channel wind
blew some alertness into my mind, but I still couldn't focus on a sense of
relaxation or relief or of entering a new existence. On the contrary, the
highly varnished blue gold dome of the summer sea morning closed over
my head with a resonant chaos remarkably like the oceanic station hall in
Vienna of the day before. The same sun which had glittered on the
swastikas now bounced off the white lifeboats of the ferry. The world
swung above whitecaps, dipped below gull cries. Loudspeakers cho-
rused, "Roll out the barrel . . ." Floods of French tourists clattered and
chattered down on us. They screamed with each pitch of the boat, as on
a roller coaster in an amusement park, and asked my father (my uncle
being busily seasick) to snap them against life preservers. My father
complied. Then he anchored himself on a valise, watchful as ever in his
loden, waiting.

Waiting for what? For the soil of England, which felt gratifying solid
but no different from the one we had fled? For the old lady in the train
compartment who knitted black wool and whose pensive pale-nosed silence created in my groggy mind the mad fancy that she was making an
extra eye patch for the major? For the unending succession of red roofs
and green hedges which hypnotized me to sleep again? For London's
dun-colored clangor, which burst my eyelids open. The taxi that brought

us through a hazy, veering street hive to the flat my uncle's "contact" had secured for us? Or for the room into which we were finally led by a seventeen-year-old girl with a pink strap falling down her bare arm?

My father had, of course, been waiting for that room. We all had. That room triumphed over my hangover. It swept aside even the pink strap which, to my fourteen-year-old sheltered self, was an enormity. The room contained, even if it didn't immediately offer, the final truth of our journey.

It was a huge room. "A suitable two-fam'ly room," as the girl said, waving at the curtain that ran through the middle. It was a room into which, she promised, "the Mum" would enter in a moment to greet us. It was a room dark, low, breathtakingly dusty. Dust festooned the paper lampshades with its flakes; dust made the sunken armchairs look like scaly hippos; dust covered the unwashed dishes in the sink and hung from the wall phone. Dust slept on the room's lumpy landscape like snow and lent it the air and mood of dream. The room was in many ways the most startling marvel of our trip.

My father took one of the slipcovers that lay, for some reason, stripped next to an easy chair and applied it against a wall. A small avalanche of flakes fell; a white spot showed up. My father, abstracted, produced white spots all over the wall. From corner to corner he walked, poising the slipcover. My uncle and I watched him and strolled tranced among the furniture like sightseers among famous ruins.

And then "the Mum" came down on us. She screamed even before she entered, as if she had just been violated in the hallway. She was a ruddy, chunky creature with a florid badge-of-office housecoat that swarmed behind her as she ran up to the slipcover my father had used. She picked up the dust-smudged cloth to cry, "My best! If it isn't my best! *Ja!*" Against the gray dunes of the room she stood like a pagan priestess in her purple gown, holding the smudged slipcover aloft with one flaring sleeve, pointing with the other in declamatory pantomime at a number of objects and pouring out geysers of what sounded to me like a forgotten heathen language.

And not until she strode away in a ferocious hiss of skirts, not until she removed the key from the door with a mighty yank and streamed out of sight and down the stairs with a rumble and a mutter, not till then did I understand what she had meant. She had meant that she had given us her foremost, her largest room; the one, as she had pointed out, with the extension phone on the wall here; the one with the hassock there; the one with these, her best slipcovers, which she had been about to put on the chairs. And we had befouled her offering by befouling her slipcovers. We had ruined them beyond bleaching. And she had made them herself. Not if she were down to her last farthing did she want to be dependent on such guests. We were finished. We were evicted before we moved in.

We stood dazed in the dusk of the room. My father whispered. He held an accounting consultation with my uncle, of which the conclusion was that an "adjustment" would be cheaper than finding a new place by means of a new taxi. He held a spelling consultation with my uncle and on one of the parchment envelopes from our escritoire wrote FOR DAMAGES. Into it he folded a ten-shilling bill. Cackling again, he gave it to me together with a clap on the shoulder.

"Give it to her," he said.

And I went forth with a certain goose-pimpled keenness. I wonder now if I wasn't hoarding my goose pimples. Perhaps I had already discovered that terror successfully survived becomes adventure and that all our Nazi suffering would someday become an unadmitted treasure. I do remember stepping down the stair carpet, whose mousy gentility was rained on by chipped plaster from the wall, and I remember listening with curious contentment to each gaudy squeak my footsteps made, smelling the sweetish stale scent the whole house exhaled at each pressure of my foot as though it were one gigantic and mildewed perfume atomizer. At the first landing I met the girl, her strap brash as ever. I hid my piquant paralysis behind a lack of language. "Mum?" I asked, indicating curves of housecoat. She gestured back: thumbed downward and raised two exquisite and slightly soiled fingers. I thanked her with an almost Continental bow and went down for two more stories until I reached an open door.

Behind it, talking into a telephone, was "the Mum." From the wrought-up cascades of her gown, I knew she was speaking to my father.

One nod of hers at my envelope brought me inside the hall and had me deposit my burden on a table next to a sleeping cat as dusty as anything else in the house. Another nod dismissed me.

And so I walked upstairs again. This time I didn't have to cope with a pink strap. But suddenly I became aware of sounds which I had heard but not understood on my way down—the code, the language, new to me, of a building with thin walls. Coughs, groans, passions, secrets, even boredoms rode the air. And it seemed to me, climbing through the many-tongued twilight of the staircase, that I had been traveling the whole past day through a long tunnel that had begun at our house in Vienna, and along whose windings there still stirred in niches the Death's Head with the crayon, the bespectacled conductor, the one-eyed major, the customs-inspector mole, the Frenchmen on the boat crying *"Voulez-vous . . . ,"* the English lady knitting a black silence—a tunnel that had finally widened into the musky murmurous grotto of this London house and ended before the askew bronze knocker and mottled green paint of a door.

I opened the door. I entered our room again. And the moment I did, our whole journey fell away from me. The tunnel died. I saw that we were staying. My uncle was unpacking. We had been pardoned by "the Mum"; we had arrived. My father was washing dishes in the sink. He actually washed dishes, and it was a heartbreakingly small and mean action for a man who had done such deeds on our voyage. Yet here he was, his black loden coat doffed, his Red Indian self dead—crumpled on a sooty chair. He stood bent behind the sink, fumbling wetly.

And I believed it. I saw, for the first time, that my father's hair was beginning to grow back except for a bald spot in the middle. I saw it because the electricity had been turned on, a weak watery yellow that drizzled down from a nude lightbulb—a light that rinsed fantasy from all the dust and left only its drabness. I saw tacked on the coarse wood of the dresser the address of the Rescue Committee, where my father and my uncle would go tomorrow in the hopes of finding a job. I heard the vast impassive roar of the foreign city all around us, and I stood still, barely beyond the threshold of the room. I put my hands in my pockets because I felt so frozen. I believed it all, and my heart shivered as your heart shivers when you must leave the theater after the show and walk in the hard cold streets that you must live in, must believe in all the days of your life. The magic and the madness were over.

I took my hands out of my pockets and stripped off the gold ring even before being asked. I knew the ring would have to be sold. It had come upon us. I was a refugee.

1942

Manhattan Nocturne

The first thing to do after climbing down into the bakery cellar is to look at the worksheet Mr. Frosch has hung on the wall for us. I always wince a little in advance. But today I am not prepared for what Mr. Frosch has scrawled on the bottom of a list already heavy with Saturday orders: "15 doz jel donuts (8th ave street fare tomorrow)."

Never mind that his misspelled street fair parenthesis may be a sort of saying "sorry" for such an infliction. Fifteen dozen jelly doughnuts on top of our normal weekend workload! At the end of tonight's shift, the pile that will be facing me in the sink! Not only the mixing bowls, the cupcake forms, the cake rings, the pie molds to scrape and scrub and rinse and dry; now I shall also have to scrape clean that huge vat encrusted with doughnut frying oil.

As for my boss, Bert, the doughnuts threaten his political agenda because of the extra heat involved. So he tries to handle the threat by making them first.

In vain. Hours after we have finished the doughnuts, the sultriness of their frying persists and combines with the oven's torrid breath. Steam fogs my glasses. We are soaking in our undershirts. Only the fan keeps us from suffocation. But since the fan is fascist Bert cannot admit he needs it, too.

That's why he starts to curse Mr. Frosch. Saddling him with child labor! Bad enough to hire a kid sixteen, worse yet to pick an outlander like me, a greenhorn not used to crazy New York summers, let alone to one hundred goddamn degrees in this crummy cellar! And no, no goddamn use my protesting I don't feel any worse than him—something ever happens to me, on whose goddamn head will it be? His, Bert's! No, tonight, on this goddamn doughnut night, he'll have to wait until the apricot tarts (our final batch) are done before killing the fascist fan.

This fan swings from the ceiling (no other room for it in our cramped cave), cruises through the air like a winged meat slicer, ready to lop off any arm raised too high. And it really is reactionary: its static jams the progressive potential of our radio's shortwave band; yet it never disturbs a single capitalist commercial of any local station on the AM dial. And on this doughtnut-ridden night Bert, stuck with fragile child labor, me, will have to leave the fan on as long as the oven is on.

Right into a critical broadcasting period. Instead of Moscow's shortwave program, our wireless set (which looks so class-conscious sooty) gives off the bourgeois sounds of WNEW's *Melody Lane Hour*. Bert must put up with all that mooning and crooning and Pepsi-Cola jingling until all the apricot tarts are baked through.

Now the fruit flavor of these tarts is a deliciously nuanced sweet/sour. A dainty scalloping of crust wreathes the filling. They are the most popular pastry in the neighborhood and Mr. Frosch gets away with charging more for them than for éclairs with more expensive ingredients. These tarts are Bert's pride; therefore he bakes them at the end of the shift so they will be Frosch's freshest offering in the morning. Yet tonight they bedevil him because they take forever in the oven.

Typically enough, that becomes more and more my fault. After a while Bert gets no relief from blasting Mr. Frosch who is sleeping out of earshot, in plutocratic comfort, three floors up. I make a much more satisfying target, being physically available and, after all, it is my presence that's lousing up Moscow. Not that Bert would ever blame a toiling minor for being frail. But what he can do is show impatience with a dawdler and a bungler: Look at me, greasing tart forms slow-motion, like some gentleman of leisure! . . . Am I dreaming by the apricot filler? . . . Obviously I'm trying to save Mr. Frosch money, brushing far too little melted butter on the pastry shells—why else are the fuckers browning so slowly even at 400 degrees?

Not a word of truth in any of this, of course. If anything, I have used an excess of Mr. Frosch's butter, my one way of getting even with him for the doughnut trouble. It's not because of me that the apricot tarts don't ripen into the right deep-gold pastry color until way after 10:30 PM. In fact when Bert peels the last tart tin out of the oven, it is almost eleven. Only then can be kick shut the oven's gas-heat lever while reaching up to kill the fan. Instantly—undawdlingly—I push the shortwave button on the radio.

Too late.

Melody Lane's sign-off at WNEW, Bing Crosby warbling "There'll be blue birds over, the white cliffs of Dover . . ." changes to *"Völker, höret die Signale, auf zum letzten Gefecht . . ."* a Teutonic chorus of *Die Internationale* introducing Moscow's German-language news. We have just missed the English program.

Nothing could frustrate Bert more on a Saturday night. This is the night he has to listen extra carefully to the Russian truth enunciated in the King's English; when he, having finished his shift but still sweaty, leaning forward rapt from his perch on a flour sack, pad at the ready, pencil in his moist hand, jots down facts fortifying his letter to the editor; his weekly protest against the unheard-of manner in which the *Daily News* disregards the Soviet contribution to the Allied war effort.

But tonight the German gutturals coming out of Russia don't help him at all. Suddenly he tells me I better translate what the hell they are saying.

"What?" I ask.

My sharp italics are my only defense against this imposition. As if I weren't already busy enough, transferring with clumsy asbestos gloves endless tarts out of their sizzling tins into the display trays.

"You understand them," Bert says, pencil stabbing at his pad. "You're German!"

I am Austrian, but one can't talk to him when he is in that mood. I can't waste my breath with arguments, drudging stooped over the tarts when I am frantic mentally as well, trying to sum up each German bulletin in English in time to absorb the next German one. Under the pressure I deform a number of Bert's exquisitely shaped tart shells—serves him right if he gets bawled out by Mr. Frosch.

My resentment even colors the news the wrong way. Very wrong because the concentration camp still lives under my father's scalp; his black hair, shaved off by the SS, has grown back gray in New York. Yet tonight—shameful to say—I can't truly enjoy a Nazi setback. Bert doesn't deserve the glad tidings that at Stalingrad the Red Army has captured a Wehrmacht general.

I relate the coup in indifferent tones. Just the same, Bert starts to smile as he scribbles. Indeed he says, "Thank you" when the broadcast is over. I give a brief nod. Before changing into his street clothes Bert switches the fan back on and points it helpfully at me. I am too busy to notice, slaving so hard and so stooped. This pushes Bert halfway toward an apology, into a sheepish stutter.

Uh, a Nazi general captured, he says, such great stuff, he should put it into really good language, so the goddamn editor will have to publish the letter this time for sure, so the dictionary in my locker where I get all my big words, how about borrowing it? Just for one day?

"At your disposal," I say, not looking up from the tarts.

"You'll have it back Monday, guaranteed."

I give another mute, stooped nod.

Whereupon he mutters something about all the stuff I have to lug up to the store tonight, so since he's on his way out up the stairs anyways, he might as well take along one of the tart trays.

This is an unprecedented gesture.

Now I do look at him (and see that he is already holding my Webster's dictionary). I may even be smiling.

"Don't trouble," I say. "You need both hands for a tray. You already carry the big dictionary."

"You sure? Loads of trays tonight."

"It is okay."

Only after we have waved a friends-again so long, do I realize the foreignness of "It is okay." "It's okay" would have been the correct nonoutlander phrase.

But it really is okay, bringing up the finished baked goods, entering from the back stairs the locked, empty store, no displays in the window, nothing to block my view of the street. Because at this hour I love to watch Eighth Avenue for those long automobiles with curtained windows, limousines that come from the direction of Fifth Avenue. They may not be faster than ordinary cars, yet the speed with which they glide toward the West Side Highway is supernatural. They are extraterrestrial vehicles issuing from America.

Mr. Frosch's bakery is simply not in America. Proof of that right now (as I am bringing up the first tray) is Jimmy, Mr. Frosch's security guard. He is standing flush against the glass door, up to one of his favorite tricks. He knocks against the glass until the slit-skirted woman lounging on the sidewalk turns around; he lip-purses a kiss at her, working the key in the lock with one hand while flashing a big ten-dollar bill with the other. And when the woman comes right up and can't rattle open the door Jimmy has left locked after all and sees him bent over with mean laughter, all she can do is spit. Such things don't happen in America—neither Jimmy's leering cackle nor the whore's saliva dribbling down the outside of the pane. None of messy Eighth Avenue is anywhere near America. Nor is Washington Heights uptown, where I live with my parents and where on our special occasions out my mother takes along the white combed-cotton napkins saved from Vienna and spreads them on the cracked plastic table of the Three Star Diner so that the hamburgers will have some sort of resemblance to the *Tafelspitz florentine* once served ceremoniously at the Café Restaurant Landtmann.

Nor is downtown in America, and that includes Thirteenth Street. There I attend Food Trades Vocational High School, whose baking department has found me this summer job. True, Food Trades' baking oven (donated by the Wonder Bread Company) gleams with chrome and is much newer than Mr. Frosch's. But America itself gleams nowhere in the school: its library—two shelves squeezed into a corner of the assistant principal's office—consists of a dog-eared *Encyclopedia of the Culinary Arts* from which two middle volumes are missing, with not a single dictionary to make up for it.

None of the Food Trades kids are in America, though most are born New Yorkers. This they never let me forget during my first semester, saying frequently, "Kraut, get the shit outta here!" But after I gave Haber a puffy eye and kicked Palusso into a limp (suffering a lip my mother, thank God, mistook for a blister)—after that they let me have the out-field at the parking lot games. Now and then soccer reflexes still louse up my stickball moves, but even so I have proved that I am faster than just about any of them. They still say "Get the shit outta here!" to me, but no more often than to each other.

However, they can say that with flawless vowels and crisp consonants that define them, in contrast to me, as Americans. Even this does not sit-uate them in America, though the superiority of their speech indicates that someday they might well attain it.

Sounding like them has become crucial to me. I have spent ninety cents of my first Frosch earnings on a dictionary, a used one but sizable, no fewer than eighty thousand entries; expanding my vocabulary might diminish my accent somehow, perhaps by diluting it among a greater number of words. The closer I get to the native tone, the better my chances to arrive in America.

And as a matter of fact, working at Frosch's has helped me track down America's whereabouts. Not the real live movie America, but at least the site where America hibernates, the way a rocket hibernates on its launching pad.

Each afternoon at 5 PM or so when I climb out of the Sixth Avenue sub-way station on Fiftieth Street and start walking west toward Frosch's, I am already on that launching pad: it stretches in this area from Fifth Avenue to Seventh. I walk on a carpet of special smooth asphalt soon to be touched by patent-leather shoes and fantastically high heels, but now still largely empty. I walk under sumptuous silken canopies which lead to pan-eled restaurant doors still shut, locked tight against me. I pass nightclub entrances, guarded by silver posts with red velvet ropes festooned be-tween them. Guarded against what? What fabulous ghosts? There is no-body on the sidewalk—no diners, no dancers, no revelers, no bouncers even. There is just me, shuffling in my brogues toward Mr. Frosch's cellar.

But I know that within a couple of hours the transformation will come to pass. About the time I am greasing cupcake forms for Bert, the true America on that takeoff ramp will zoom into lustrous orbit. And when I am walking home again at 3 AM, nothing will be left of that soaring glam-our except debris: thick cigar butts on the curb; perfumed lipsticked crumpled tissues; the dull glint of a dime in the gutter—dregs of some magnificent tip.

No, I can't penetrate America during the hours when it stirs miraculously alive. And yet it is at Frosch's that I get a daily clue to just how America lives. And I get it from, of all people, Jimmy, who keeps vigil in the nocturnal store.

Jimmy mustn't ever know that, of course. Let him find out he is doing me a favor—it is good-bye, favor. A toothpick keeps dangling from his mouth, pulling his face into a remarkable variety of sneers; all of them come into play in the course of his diverse functions, all of which involve some cunning dodge. He is Mr. Frosch's night watchman, payroll master, garbage disposal manager, and tricky delivery specialist. On the tray I am carrying up from the cellar now sits a basket with twenty of Bert's renowned apricot tarts. Jimmy will bring them to the Pink Banana Club on Fifty-second Street, where the tarts will be devoured for free by any cop checking if the Pink Banana really does serve warm meals till closing, as required by its late-hours liquor license.

This lowdown Jimmy once revealed to me with the bottomless smirk of an insider who has the dirt on the entire universe.

But only very rarely does Jimmy favor me with such privileged information. As a rule I am treated like some juvenile barbarian, there to be jeered at. Handing me my Saturday pay envelope now, he says—toothpick jerking derisively between smoke-stained teeth—"Sorry, Fritz, it's Hun money. Ain't legal to pay you in dollars till you're a citizen."

"Ha. Ha. Ha," I say slowly, in counterderision. Which doesn't stop him from the next jeer. He points to the *Daily Mirror* on the counter.

"There. Roast a nice rat for me."

That crack refers to my final chore each night. After I have cleaned the whole cellar and washed the pile in the sink, I take the newspaper, twist its sheets into three sausages; stuff them into the three mouse holes in our storage room; put a match to them, and have the broom ready for the kill. But before that, the *Mirror* serves a very different purpose of mine, one of which Jimmy doesn't have the faintest idea.

And so I don't even bother to answer him, just grab the paper and run out of his sight down the stairs. In the cellar I riffle through the pages on the kneading bench. Naturally the sports section is missing because Jimmy keeps the horse race listing he has marked up. But the most important part of the paper is intact. On page ten the column glows with bulletins from the real America, printed in a magic language fit for a magic planet:

Ann Sheridan oozing ooooomph all over El Morocco . . . "Oklahoma!" top-boffo again on the Rialto . . . The Franklin Delano Roosevelt Jr.'s infanticipating? . . . Robert Taylor and Barbara Stanwyck one hundred percent guaranteed pffft . . .

And then the jolt. The three dots after *pffft* . . . lead to the bombshell:

Hoofer of hoofers, Fred Astaire, raising major moolah for needy terpsichoreans at "21" tonight . . .

Is it possible? Truly true?

Sweat drops smudge Walter Winchell. Flour has clouded my glasses. I wipe them before rereading the item.

True!

But is it graspable? This key inhabitant of the elusive, authentic America, this film god of my Vienna childhood, live, in the undubbed flesh, just a few hundred yards away? Right now, tonight? So close, at the "21" restaurant on West Fifty-second Street while I am on West Fifty-first? And the Pink Banana Club even closer, on West Fifty-second itself!

I am less aware of the plan just formed than of the electric energy driving my limbs to effect it. I rush up to the store with a tray of still-hot apricot tarts, snatch a small cake carton, fold it into a box, select from among Bert's most beautiful tarts two of the very best, nestle them into the box, close the top, shear off a generous slice from the gift-paper roll, drape the red-and-white-striped wrapping lavishly around the box—then can't find any Scotch tape with which to hold it together.

That stops me for a moment. But only for a moment: I rush downstairs for the rubber bands Bert taught me to use as slingshots against cockroaches. They tie the gift wrapping very nicely. Then—stroke of genius—I rip the work sheet pad off the wall together with the string-attached pencil with which Mr. Frosch wrote the abominable doughnut order. Who ever said you have to have a pen for an autograph?

Upstairs again, I sober up, Slow myself down. Now comes the tough part. Jimmy. At the moment he is not even approachable, being busy outside the store he has temporarily unlocked, doing the weekly garbage thing. And this is good. It gives me a chance to collect my wits.

I have a minute while he extends his hand to the municipal sanitation foreman meeting him in the street.

"Hey, Big Joe!" I hear him say. "Your nose still in the trash? Lost the Sweepstakes again? Where's the luck of the Irish?"

"Well, you sure ain't got it, wop son of a bitch!" says the foreman, joining Jimmy's laughter as their palms slap together.

When their handshake is over, the ten-note Jimmy got from Mr. Frosch (the one he baited the hooker with) is gone from inside his fingers. The foreman's hand sinks closed into his pants pocket. His men are already scraping the metal cans with our bakery trash across the sidewalk toward the truck. That ten-note saves Mr. Frosch the expense of commercial garbage haulers for the entire week. And Jimmy, smirking his way back to the store, comes within reach of the move I must make now.

"Jimmy," I say. "Listen, I will do the delivery to the Pink Banana for you."

The toothpick in his mouth freezes at a suspicious angle.

"Yeah? How come?"

"I just—just want some fresh air before I finish up downstairs."

"Cost you two bucks."

Sheer extortion!

"You jest," I say. He hates hearing words he does not quite understand, especially if they are spoken by a foreigner.

"Highfalutin, huh? Keep it up, I'll make it three bucks."

I realize I am in no position to rile him.

"Come on, Jimmy, I am doing you a favor!"

"I lose the buck tip I get at the Pink Banana."

"All right," I say. "I will give you a dollar."

"Plus another buck I lose, not getting reward money from the FBI."

"What?"

"Not tellin' 'em a little Nazi spy like you is loose in the streets."

His mouth distends into a grin. The toothpick moves with evil amusement. But his hand comes at me palm upward, dead serious. I have to peel off two bills from my pay envelope.

A minute later I am out on Eighth Avenue, half running, Pink Banana bound. My right hand holds the basket with the cop-bribing tarts; my left shelters, under my apron, the gift-wrapped box for Mr. Astaire. The clatter and screech from the garbage trucks seem to have chased away pedestrians and limousines. It is still quite a bit before midnight, but the light from the street lamps trickles down humid, groggy, late—not too late, I hope, for Him at "21."

The Pink Banana Club is still very alive, with a small spotlight glaring at the exclamation on a poster:

JUANA LINU-LINU

THE BALINESE SPICE SENSATION!

"Delivery from the Frosch Bakery," I say to the giant with a black-dyed goatee and a blue turban. He stands inside the sequined curtain serving as a door. He takes the basket.

"Where's Jimmy?" he asks, not waiting for an answer but handing me, as if in logical exchange for the basket, a flowered platter with a coffeepot, a cup, and a saucer on which he drops one of the tarts from my basket.

"Okay, kiddo. That way. Up the stairs."

"Up the stairs?"

I am dumbfounded by the sudden platter in my hands.

"Her door's to the right."

"But—Jimmy never mentioned anything about any coffee up the stairs."

"Oh, Jimmy's gonna eat his heart out when you tell him."

"Jimmy said there will be a dollar tip," I say out of sheer confusion.

"Sure, she'll give it to you upstairs. Plus a free look at her tits."

"But I have to go somewhere else now, another delivery."

"Kiddo, this you don't want to miss. Just knock on the door and say 'Compliments of the management.' Only takes a minute."

There is not even a place to put down the platter. That is one reason why I do go to the stairs, though they are detour from Him, at "21." Another reason is that making Jimmy eat his heart out may be worth a minute's delay. But mostly it is the prospect of that free look. For what if the turban is not lying? What if a freely offered look at a pair of naked breasts—legend of my top secret dreams—is waiting for me at the top of the stairs? Every other whisper in the Food Trades locker room rubs in the fact that I am the only fellow in school who has never laid eyes on such a thing.

Abruptly, midway on the steep climb up, the red carpet gives out. The steps become bare wood, dim and creaking. To the right of the even creakier landing is the door with a golden paper star glued over golden paper letters saying JUANA.

The Astaire gift box I hold in my right hand I now must put on the platter I am holding with my left, in order to have my right free for knocking.

"Open," says the husky voice. "Open, open."

In the cubicle a woman sits slumped before a mirror framed with lightbulbs, of which half are burned out. Her bathrobe has come apart at the top, but stingily, showing only the middle of a black bra.

"Well, look what's come in!" she says.

At least she is interesting in the sense that one side of her face is Asiatic, the other European; the skin around one eye is pulled back into an oriental slant; but a clamp hangs down from her other ear, leaving the other brown eye round.

"Compliments of the management," I say.

"No kiddin'!"

Suddenly she has lurched up from her stool, reached out. I pull back, but not fast enough to keep her from grabbing the Astaire gift box on the platter.

"No!" I say.

She presses the box against that stingy little bit of visible black bra. Long green fingernails close around the bright wrapping.

"No! Please!"

"What's the matter, honey?"

I put the platter down on her mirror table between a cosmetic jar brimming with cigarette butts and a tall glass smelling of whiskey.

"*This* tart here and the coffee—*this* is compliments of the management!"

"Aaaah, they just wanna sober me up for the last show."

"Please return the box!"

"It's so pretty! 's not for me?"

"It is for someone else."

"Your cutie?"

"I just very much need it back!"

"You sound kinda funny. You from the other side?"

"From Vienna, But I really need—"

"Vienna! Wow! Why'd you leave a beautiful place like that?"

"It became too dangerous. But please—"

"Oh yeah, all them canals sinking into the sea."

"You have to give back the box!"

She leans back, box still pressed against her bra, and crosses a fishnet leg high enough to show a garter in midthigh.

"I'm not as cute as your cutie?"

"That cake box is for Fred Astaire!"

"Ha ha!" She tosses the box up in the air. "And me, I'm Ginger Rogers!"

"I mean it! He is in the '21' restaurant. Just two blocks down!"

She sits up, uncrosses her legs, thigh and garter vanishing into the robe.

"On the level?"

"It is in Walter Winchell!"

"No kiddin'? Fred's expecting this?"

"*Fred!*" Her impudence frees me from any obligation to tell her the truth.

"Yes, he is expecting it! A special order! You have to give it back!"

But she holds on to the box and, worse, I see that her tossing it has snapped both rubber bands. The gift paper has come apart, down to the bare cardboard box—which she now actually dares to open.

"Hey, just a couple of apricot tarts," she says.

"You have hurt the wrapping!"

"Same as my tart here. How do you like that? Him and me, same thing."

Her oriental eye remains an impassive slit, but the round European one is utterly delighted, like her smile. At my expense.

"You should not have opened that! You spoiled it!"

"Hey, Vienna, easy." She leans forward, still smiling, her European eye giving me a long-lashed wink. "I'll fix it for you."

"You even tore the rubber bands!"

"So what? Give you somethin' better."

She reaches for a pink band hanging from one of the dead bulbs of her mirror and stretches it around the box on her lap. It is a garter like the one on her thigh, but it doesn't hide the damage.

"The gift wrapping is all crumpled!"

"Oh never fear, Juana's here."

She pulls a drawer of her mirror table, finds a photograph, slides it under the garter, holds up the box for my inspection with a roguish sideward inclination of her head.

"Little better?"

Covering the wrinkled wrapping is a glossy picture of herself in a short skirt made of bananas, a skimpy halter composed of apples, torso sinuously curved as she bows a violin with slit-eyed passion.

"Okay?"

At last she hands back the box.

"Tell Fred that's with *my* compliments!"

Her own joke shakes her with such abrupt, vehement laughter, that she nearly topples from her stool. To steady herself, she holds on to my arm. A moment later her hand slides up to my shoulder, pats my cheek.

"Go on, Vienna—run along! Catch Fred!"

Outside her door I don't get rid of the photo right away. Perhaps it's the touch of her hand somehow still lingering on my cheek together with a whiff of musk and whiskey. Also it comes to me that when school starts again, a photo like that could make quite a trophy. Passing the turban downstairs, I let him have a glimpse of it and nod a "Yeah, some tits!" grin.

Back on the street I do yank the picture out from under the garter but refrain from throwing it away. I drop it into the pouch of my apron for its locker room value. Then I start running to make up for the delay.

Not until the traffic on Sixth Avenue brings me to a stop do the brighter lamps of the crossing light up what I myself have done: yanking away the photo has made Juana's damage even worse. I've shredded the gift wrapping into a completely sleazy mess. No choice but to discard it into a trash basket. Yet this disaster has given her garter a possible value—could its rosy quilted velvet pass as a decorative ribbon? I decide to leave it in place; it might maintain the gift character of the box—a hope dying at the sight of the additional blemish I discover only now: the horrible little grease stain on the box top!

Rush back to the bakery for a new box and a new gift wrap?

No, I am too time-pressed. I must keep going. Walking fast, I take her photo out of my apron pocket, slide it back under her garter on the box top, but slide it down much farther than before, bending it over the edges of the box so that some of the fishnet scandal of her legs vanishes under the box bottom yet enough of her picture is left on top to cover the grease stain with her artistic violin—

"Yes?"

A deep voice jars me out of the box top problem.

I am already there. Before the iron gate of "21." The doorman here isn't quite as tall as the Pink Banana's but much more elegant, with two rows of gold buttons glinting down a dark blue jacket and a slender blond mustache under an admiral's cap.

"Yes?" he asks again.

The question catches me idiotically unprepared.

"This—it is a delivery."

"At this hour?"

Am I too late for America alive?

I see just one car by the curb here, but it has a long black smart hood and a visored man behind the wheel, leafing slowly through a magazine—no doubt waiting for Him.

I hold up the cake box.

"This is for Mr. Fred Astaire."

But the doorman doesn't even hear. He has turned away; attends a couple flowing out of the restaurant door some inner gatekeeper has opened; the gentleman with a short silver beard matching the silver band of his black fedora; the lady lifting her long silk gown slightly to step up to the street level; both flowing in a brief detour around me and my soiled apron; then flowing into the taxi the doorman conjures out of nowhere, simply by bowing to them, finger against cap.

After the taxi pulls away, I hold up the cake box again.

"This is for Mr. Fred Astaire," I say again.

"Over there." The doorman points to a smaller gate in the iron railing, some twenty feet down. "Service entrance."

"But this is personal. A gift—"

"You can't keep standing here."

"I have to give it to him in person!"

"All right, let's have it."

He reaches for the box much more slowly than Juana but with an authority that can't be resisted. I have to yield it up.

"Please—I would like a personal answer!"

He nods, points once more.

"Wait at the service entrance."

And then he himself is gone, gone together with the cake box into the restaurant.

There is nothing for it but the service entrance. It leads into an alley flanked by two trash cans the like of which I have never seen before—so new and clean, they gleam like platinum pillars. A miniature streetlamp illuminates them, also revealing a bicycle leaning against a wall, a multispeed one I hope to afford one day. But then the light fades. I can barely make out a door, locked, as it turns out. Something like a pearl hovers in the murk. It is a white doorbell button, obviously to be pressed. I press it and take out the work-sheet pad for the autograph.

Nothing happens except the pounding of my heart. I press again. Nothing happens except more pounding. Suddenly a soft purr of a buzz swings the door slowly open into yet another alley . . . a very short passageway ending in another dim door.

This door, though, opens promptly.

So strong a shaft of light dazzles me that I, blinking in the dark, can at first comprehend no more than a black silhouette in a forked cape. Then, gaining focus, the fork defines itself as tails—white tie and tails—*Him!* But in the very next moment a belly bulges the white dress shirt . . . Has he grown fat? . . . No, worse yet, it isn't Him at all. This is a chubby red-haired waiter, a napkin on his arm.

"You the baker boy?" says his munching mouth. "Tasty tart."

This is unbelievable.

"*You* are eating that! That is for Fred Astaire!"

"Oh he's in dreamland back at the hotel."

"It is a gift! What hotel?"

"Wouldn't do you any good to know. Here."

The arm with a napkin on it holds out a bill. A thousand-dollar note could not redeem those jowls chomping my gift for Him.

"No!"

"Not enough? Tell you what. The babe in the photo, you write her number on your pad there. Gets you another buck from the guys in the kitchen."

His chewing grin, his fat shirtfront, my foolishness, my futility—enormous anger flares in my chest, boils up my throat, booms out of my mouth—

"*Fuck you!*"

I turn away. I tear up the work-sheet pad, all the pages left in it. I fling the pieces down together with the pencil, I litter the "21" restaurant, be it only the service entrance, litter it in revenge for I am not quite sure what, and kick the multispeed bicycle on my way back out of the alley.

But then, back on the street again (the street empty now, even that one waiting limousine gone), walking slowly toward an enormous filthy pile in a cellar sink, I feel a flicker of belonging; as if I had connected for a moment to some mainstream running underground across the country, even under the flash of Mr. Astaire's feet—and the connection was my shout.

"*Fuck you!*"

Me, crying out the two most American of all words. Without any accent whatsoever.

1945

The Bride in the Gym

That Warren of all people would throw a fit—and what's more, throw it while our dinner guest—who would have thought? Certainly not Papa, who's taken to him so quickly, overcoming that first encounter. But an initial awkwardness was inevitable. Just consider the cultural chasm involved.

Warren happens to be one of the neighborhood's exotica: the rare "real" American living in Washington Heights, also known as the Fourth Reich because we German and Austrian Jews walking its streets are all refugees from the Third. There wasn't a single native resident in our building before Warren and his mother came along; they moved in so recently that Papa probably never even glimpsed either one in the elevator. Then Warren made his somewhat drastic entrance into our family life. And by "drastic" I mean drastically American in a way that had to affect Papa, who is laboring under an America complex.

Granted: I once suffered from one myself. But with three college years under my belt, I've come intellectually of age on these oversold shores. Having duly seen all these Yankee wonders, I've learned how to see through them.

Papa can't. This accounts for Warren's impact on him. Incidentally— or rather not so incidentally—it also accounts for my difficulties with my father. Now, I do try to make allowances: tell myself that the man is a bourgeois generation older. Inevitably his America complex is middle aged, middle class, Middle European. In the old world he was a manufacturer of beautifully enameled ladies' shoe buckles. But assume he'd been a mere mechanic in his factory; someone of his energy would have been a guild comrade, an engaged proletarian playing a distinct and spirited role in the social arena.

But who is he here? Here, where the proletariat consists of masses of millionaires manqués? Here he is some underpaid foreman of some small workshop stringing together fake pearl earrings. In brief, here he is one of a million motes tossed about daily in the subway rush. His wonderful America has reduced him to a nobodyness never experienced in what he must now consider his awful Nazi homeland. It's a humiliation he can't very well acknowledge, least of all to himself. Yet it lives in the deep breath which is really a concealed sigh and which accompanies his frown as he drops his lunch box on the kitchen table when he returns from his job; the frown has carved new lines running from the fresh gray on his temples across his high, still boyish cheekbones, to the weighed-down corners of his mouth.

And will he ever let me tell him that the problem is not really his? That it's built into the vaunted American way of life? That a star-spangled illusion has pulled him into the numberless army of losers embattled coast to coast on a continent mercilessly premised on success?

No, he won't hear of it. Every time I try to discuss the matter, he cuts me off: enough of these immature Communist college-boy ideas!

I'm mentioning all this because it has to be factored into the Papa–Warren chemistry. Now, a simple reason brought my new friend into our apartment for the first time. Returning to our building with me from the tennis courts, he discovered that he'd lost his keys; so I suggested he wait in our place until his mother came home.

As a result there bared itself (in Papa's mind) our shame to Warren's Yankee eyes: our living room in all its rank un-American inadequacy. Like the faux Directoire coffee table with cracks in two corners (exactly what had made it a bargain at Ernie's Used Furniture Emporium). Or the sofa with its beige taffeta upholstery which would look quite presentable except for the brown scorch marks blemishing the blond legs (evidence of my attempts to burn out the bedbugs as I had once burned the mice out of their holes in the Frosch bakery cellar). Or the rust on the iron window frames, spoiling the splendidly American view of the Hudson River. This view makes the apartment so expensive that Papa has to stint on the furnishings for the sake of the rent.

But our visitor didn't seem particularly struck by any of that. When Papa walked in shortly after we did, Warren noticed something else—right away: Papa's three-piece suit from Vienna; Papa wears it to work as though he were still going to his old office there; never mind that at Koster Co. he must put over it a plebeian smock.

"Wow!" Warren said. "A ten-button waistcoat! You only see that in Brooks Brothers ads!"

"Papa," I said hastily, "this is Warren from 6A. He's been locked out."

Papa, a bit ambushed, stood by the door, key still in his hand.

"Good evening," he said.

"Oh yeah, good evening," Warren said. "But that's some garment you got there, sir!"

"Thank you, how do you do," Papa said. After all, he hadn't been properly introduced. "I am the father, Frank Morton."

"Morton?" Warren says, blatantly astonished by the contrast between that Anglo-Saxon word and Papa's heavy accent. He didn't even know my last name before. Though we're both chem majors at City College, we've never been in a class together and so, American fashion, know each other only as Warren and Fred. A Fred whose speech has become quite an indigenously nasal New Yorkese.

"I mean, Morton," Warren now adds fast, "Morton, that's nice, that's a very good name."

Papa looks down at the key in his hand. "It was not possible to keep the normal name," he says; pockets the key; walks to the bedroom and leaves it to me to explain the abnormality to Warren.

With his "normal" name it would not have been possible for Papa to get a job at the Koster Co. Like other costume jewelry makers, Koster is a closed shop, employing only members of the International Brotherhood of Ornament Crafters. When Papa applied, the union chapter head shook his head: Franz Mandel—*what?* No dice. Not with that moniker.

Never, with the Admission Committee when they see it on the list. But, say, Frank Moran, or Frank Morton—different story. And better make it legal for Social Security.

I imagine that's how the conversation went. Or maybe it was more overtly anti-Semitic and therefore even more jarring to a concentration camp alumnus like my father who very much needs to be flawlessly grateful to America as his ultimate refuge. No doubt that need led him to screen out the nastiness behind the demise of "Mandelbaum." When he came home with the news he kept emphasizing, over and over again, how "Morton" would simplify spelling problems with all the authorities here.

You see, exonerating America is for him a serious daily business and that is probably why he's become more serious, graver, here than I remember him being under the swastika in Austria or during our starveling stopover in England. In fact, he'll exonerate America at all costs, even to the extent of incriminating himself. This I say out of the suspicion that for him the loss of his "normal" name is a penalty imposed for leading a life so drab, so disgracefully limited in the Eden of unlimited opportunities. He'll deny it, of course (should I ever summon the nerve to ask him), but somewhere deep down he feels that he has failed America; *ergo* America has the right to to fail him back. Had his name been Rothschild, he wouldn't be punished by being renamed, say, Rowson. It's part of his America Complex.

"Mr. Morton!" Warren said to my father, returning from the bedroom. "Freddy here just told me. Great choice! Morton's much better than Moran. Morton like in Jelly Roll Morton!"

"Jelly? . . ." Papa said. "I am not familiar."

"No? So you did it on instinct! Shows you got great instinct! Jelly Roll Morton—one of the jazz greats!"

Papa's upper lip, once covered by the opulent mustache he's shaved off to look less foreign—that bald upper lip tightened.

"Jazz," he said. "I am sorry, I am also not familiar."

"Well, let me tell you!" Warren said, enthusiasm undampened. "You and Jelly Roll, you got a lot in common! He was a Negro, and you, I mean, you're from abroad. But he had an instinct like you have an instinct! Boy, could he make the piano smoke! You know something? I'll get you one of his records tomorrow!"

Now, if Warren had thrown a fit right then and there, Papa would not have been as surprised as he was to be later, when he'd gotten to like him—which actually happened sooner rather than later. For reasons that eluded me at first, Papa assimilated Warren's peculiarities quite fast. Or, to put it more precisely, he assimilated himself to them.

For this he's had ample occasion because Warren has been around the house a good deal. He and I have made it a posttennis habit to spend another hour together, which, like our sports time, is mutually educational. In the apartment afterward, we sit by my desk, a gift of my Uncle Max, the one family member who's been able to save some furniture from Vienna. This desk was once the appointment secretary's in his fancy dental office. Now its snow white varnish, trimmed round with golden scrollwork, is a blur of penciled lilies that have been erased, repenciled, re-erased. I can't stop myself from drawing petals while sweating over titration ratios in Physical Chemistry.

Over these tortured doodles Warren and I spread the paperwork of our little mutual aid society. Two semesters ahead of me, he must make postgraduate plans, and I, dictionary-crazed Anglicist that I've become, I help him with letters of application to master's degree studies at MIT and the tech faculties at Columbia and Cornell. I vet his unpunctuated overeagerness as well as the spelling of some of his favorite words, such as "conscientious" and "commitment." In return he gives me a hand in my calculus homework, especially the square roots of derivative variable functions—God, the sheer sight of that term on the textbook page drills pain into my right temple.

Anyway, the two of us are huddled together behind this ex-white, ex-dental desk, and it happens again and again that we hear the repeated clearing of a throat. We look up—and there's Papa, leaning against the doorjamb of my room in what he must consider an American slouching angle. (Often he's mused aloud to me, in a tone that tries to cover the underlying irritation with friendly curiosity, how interesting that young Americans seem to be absolutely unable to stand up straight.) So, artificially slouching like that against the very grain of his nature, having cleared his throat for our attention, he says, "Excuse me, Mister Warren, but what is the news with my famous Morton cousin?"

And after a moment, Warren says, "Oh—Jelly Roll! Cousin Jelly Roll!" And he collapses with laughter, and we have to start on the damn derivative variable functions all over again.

Of course I know what's really behind Papa's banter: reminding Warren that he still hasn't brought any Jelly Roll records. The music itself doesn't matter one bit here. It's the unkept promise.

In New York, Papa has developed what I can only call a compulsive punctiliousness. He's come to construe any random, casually expressed intention as a pledge to be rigorously honored. He's obsessed with observing all amenities, large or small; with being paid back to the penny the pettiest debt owed him by his own family members. (One reason I hate to ask even for a two-bit advance on my pocket money.)

In Vienna he wasn't quite like that. Again I make allowances since I can smell the emotion driving this new finickiness: it's a repressed resentment—a subliminal revenge on the icon he has made of the great U.S.A. Considering himself wanting by American standards, he can outscore America in at least one respect—civility. Let a lady enter the elevator: on all native male heads the fedoras remain stolidly in place—but off comes Papa's with gallant promptitude, with a faint flourish, with a discreet but perceptible bow. The gesture defines his courtliness amid all the coarse elbows rampant in the foster fatherland.

But should I allude ever so gently to those elbows—oh, the instant outburst! Such loyal angry rationalizing! What? I am blaming the country that gave us haven? The energy here, the dynamism? The very force that just brought down Hitler! And if a power like that has some—some rawness here and there, why harp on it?

He can't acknowledge that the "rawness" impacts on him as boorishness. And boorishness will bruise a skin conditioned by European middleclass protocol. With Papa the hurt has been pushed into the unconscious, where it's bound to evoke equally unconscious, indirect counteraction. All elementary Freud.

Now, in the case of Warren's unmannerly forgetting of the Jelly Roll promise, the indirectness of Papa's counteraction is, I'll admit, ingenious.

It's a rebuke delivered with a fine jocularity, part of which is the play-acted slouch.

Also, the jocularity itself is most unusual for him. As I've said, he's become quite a sobersides here, limiting his humor to occasional sharp flashes of wit, always delivered strictly within the family circle, low-voiced as if he were looking over his shoulder. And always in German, presumably because his English is too unsure to be playful in it.

Yet with Warren he makes an exception. With Warren, Papa risks not only playfulness but informality—that is, he sometimes performs for him his "New York slouch" in shirtsleeves. Truly extraordinary. No American who enters the apartment—not even the handyman come to fix a stopped-up sink—has ever seen Papa without a jacket. Warren has.

Why?

Only when Warren finally made good on his Jelly Roll promise did I glimpse the answer. Papa is so at ease with Warren because in Warren he has reclaimed a figure from our original universe, Vienna before the flight. My father has turned him into a new version of Herr Goldner, my former tutor.

Specifics of the Warren-into-Herr-Goldner alchemy in a moment. First let me say that it's nothing very new. In fact, I should have doped out this particular conjuration sooner, so often has Papa waved that wand before. He's long managed to handle the perplexities of his second homeland by transmuting them into reincarnations of persons and patterns of the first.

Example: The day the Koster Co. raised him from worker to assistant foreman, he switched from the *Daily News* to *The New York Times*. Thus he ascended in the news consumers' hierarchy as once structured in Vienna; there a laborer devoured tabloid gossip whereas a manager gained perspectives from a broadsheet such as the *Times*. Papa then evoked from the American paper a Viennese phantom. His first step was to learn how to leaf through the *Times* in the manner of New York middle-class commuters: that is, to fold the paper vertically in half, allowing one to turn pages even when compressed during the rush hour. Papa practices this knack even when uncompressed at home, but he has added a second artfulness; he also doubles back the pages either from the top down or from the bottom up, holding them in place with his little finger. And one evening, with Papa applying himself to this strangely pleated *New York Times,* I realized that there was something about it, namely its size, which suggested another newspaper I'd last seen years ago: Papa had shrunk *The New York Times* by a small but precise margin to the dimensions of the *Neues Wiener Tagblatt* he used to commune with daily in his tall-backed green plush "reading chair" in Vienna. He's tamed the huge American newspaper down to the cozier, more comprehensive identity of his favorite Austrian journal.

Same story with the black ribbon in Papa's lapel. Quite recently, just a few days before throwing the fit, as a matter of fact, Warren asked him about the little black band.

"It is to commemorate the death of our president," Papa said with a slight, proud emphasis on "commemorate"—a vocabulary acquisition from *The New York Times.*

"FDR?" Warren said, "Gosh, he passed away way back in April!"

"My family commemorated Franz Josef more than a year," Papa said.

"Gee, you guys are really feeling people," Warren said, thinking that Franz Josef was just some favorite Mandelbaum uncle, not the Emperor Franz Josef. This he told me later. What became clear to me immediately was that in Roosevelt, Papa mourned a Habsburg.

Papa plays a similar trick with Warren's persona. But as already mentioned, I didn't discover that until the evening Warren marched into our living room, holding aloft a scratched disc with a scuffed blue label reading Dead Men Blues—Jelly Roll Morton.

"Hey, Mr. Morton!" Warren said. "Now you'll hear something!"

But we didn't. We had nothing to hear it with. No record player—a lack to which my father confessed by throwing up his arms high, in cartooned regret, still resolutely, if not quite naturally, droll vis-à-vis Warren. And it wasn't until Warren said, "Okay, I'll bring down my own player soon as it's fixed—you gotta hear this incredibly hep stuff!" . . . not until Warren was gone and Papa turned to Mama, saying, *"In Wien konnten wir Herr Goldner's 'Parzifal' auch nicht spielen."* . . . not until then did I put the pieces together. My father accommodates so well to this odd Warren because he's made him into a continuation of my oddball tutor in

the bygone world across the sea. There Herr Goldner had managed to lo-
cate in a soccer-crazed, homework-hating brat some evidence of intelli-
gence with which to shepherd said brat, me, from grade school to
Realgymnasium, a select prep school. Quite a feat, in view of which Papa
decided to be amused instead of upset by my mentor's antics; like Herr
Goldner's crimson beret worn at so rakish an angle, it convinced our
maid, Leni, that he was a free-love Bolshevik; or whistling the Austrian
national anthem loudly while doing his business in the toilet. Or, more to
the point re Warren, Herr Goldner's bizarre gift on the occasion of Papa's
thirty-ninth birthday, one year before the Germans marched in.

It was a record of the *Parzifal* overture orchestrated by Sigmund
Freud, at least according to its paper cover, which was so wrinkled and
yellowed that Tante Trude, the family's highbrow, swore that Herr Goldner must have picked it up at a secondhand store specializing in musico-
logical spoofs; surely it was a present mockingly over Papa's head; Herr
Goldner, this down-at-the-heels esthete—a two-schilling standing-room
habitué at the State Opera—was making sport of his philistine employer.

Well, Tante Trude or no Tante Trude, Papa stuck to his stance. He
kept on being entertained, not offended, by Herr Goldner, prefiguring
his attitude to Warren. Furthermore, the prosperous pre-exile Mandelbaums never splurged on a cultural extravagance like a gramophone.
Herr Goldner's gift back then was as useless as Warren's now, the second
giver thereby implying an American reappearance of the first. Not to forget that Warren is tall and slightly stooped just like my tutor and only a
little younger than Herr Goldner was in the thirties, when he, just like
Warren now, used to huddle with me over my troubled math homework.

And that's not the end of it either. There may be other, deeper analo-
gies. Uneasy ones for me. I've been brooding over this. I suppose in Vienna I was a rather irregular child, and it took the rather out-of-line Herr
Goldner to redeem me. Currently Warren, with his peculiar Yankee manners, promises to straighten out the still-irregular nineteen-year-old son
who still disquiets Papa today.

Disquiets him more than ever, I guess. I guess Papa is entitled to be
even more alarmed because my present irregularity must perplex him so
much more. In Vienna it was clearly sports mania combined with school

sloth that got smart Fritz such bad marks. Over here Fred's smartness has made a still wider impression—all those Food Trades Vocational High School teachers telling my parents that their kid's too bright to be just a baker: let him study to be a baking scientist. And indeed City College lets me major in biochemistry after a special entrance exam proves that I'm not just a vocational high school primitive.

But what happens? Apart from a couple of incongruous As in English and Phys. Ed., nothing but disappointment. Dreary Cs and Ds in Semi-Micro-Qualitative Analysis, in Molecular Fermentation Dynamics, in Enzymology, in Organic Steam Distillation—in every sensible course leading to a cubicle at the laboratory of the National Biscuit Company from which to launch a soul-stirring career consecrated to the concoction of a yet more cost-effective, overpriced, artificially flavored chocolate wafer providing optimal profitability along with minimal nourishment.

No, that's not how Papa would put it. His weltanschauung is just about the reverse of mine. I simply haven't found a way to make my values fathomable to someone so steeped in businessmindedness like him. Result: he understands very little about his older son. Least of all why here bright Fred's bad grades can't even be explained by his fixation on athletics.

True, Papa sees that I'm still sports-obsessed—off, weekends, to the municipal tennis courts. But each weekday afternoon, after the day's last class until just before dinnertime (often longer, which makes me annoyingly late) don't I spend hours and hours at the 145th Street Public Library Branch, studying and studying and studying? Why with such poor results? Why should such a promising son so mysteriously compound his father's American failure with his own?

A reasonable question. And Papa finally stitched together an answer. An explanation born of solicitude—that aspect I have to appreciate. But the way he came out with it—the resulting scene—mortifying. As jolting as Warren's fit a couple of weeks later.

It's right after dinner. I am washing dishes because it's my turn in the schedule my brother Henry and I have devised for spelling each other on alternate days (*plus ça change,* still doing sink duty à la bakery cellar). Henry, lucky dog, is listening to *The Shadow* on the bedroom radio.

Mama has gone to the Lösers next door to return a borrowed cup of sugar, having been reminded of the debt by her protocol-possessed husband; and that husband, my father, in the living room, bent over the double-pleated financial section of *The New York Times*.

Suddenly, as I'm scouring a skillet, something like a soft cough. I turn around: Papa is back at the kitchen table. Sans *Times*. Staring at me.

"One moment, Freddy."

"Freddy" signals something is up. And he fingers his naturalized upper lip where the alien's mustache used to be. I realize I better let go of the skillet.

"Sit down."

I dry my hands. I sit.

"Freddy. Why don't you do more study work here? Instead of so so much in the public library?"

"Papa," I say, stifling a sigh of impatience, "I've told you. It's much quieter there than at home."

"This is on Amsterdam Avenue?"

"The library?" I say. "Of course. Amsterdam and 145th, on the way home."

"On Amsterdam Avenue," Papa says. "In Harlem."

"Well, sure, the college is in Harlem—"

"Someone in my workplace . . ." Suddenly Papa no longer looks at me but just past me. "A person, he lives in Queens, but he says he goes to Harlem, at night."

"So?"

Papa keeps looking strenuously past me. So this is something very serious, very queasy.

"He goes there for women. They are cheaper there."

It's become so quiet that I can hear *The Shadow* shooting villains in the bedroom.

"Oh for God's sake!" I say. "You don't think that I—"

"You are a young man. I was once young. But if you are working somewhere instead of studying, some job for money, for those women—"

"Papa! I am at the library! Every afternoon—the whole afternoon! Nowhere else!"

"It is not just the bad marks. But you should protect yourself against infection—"

"Papa! I swear! Check me out! I'm at the library!"

"I will buy the rubber protection for you, if you are embarrassed—"

"Listen to me, Papa—I'm at the *library*! Go there any afternoon! See with your own eyes!"

"All right," he says, terminating the conversation because he's heard (like me) the apartment door opening—Mama returning from the Lösers.

"All right," he says again, shoulders heaving with a deep breath. An exhalation of relief. Now he can look straight at me again, persuaded, or nearly so. The specter of syphilis has receded. It no longer hovers between us. But his eyes are still troubled by the mystery of my grades.

"Stop worrying! Will you, Dad, please?"

The "Dad" is to Americanize and thus to please him; to compensate for my abrupt turning away, back to scouring the skillet, so that neither he nor Mama will see the color of my cheeks.

I told the truth about staying in the library but—well, about the sex angle Papa wasn't altogether wrong. This goddamn sudden heat in my face is Mrs. Poynton's fault. I know her name because in the 145th Street branch of the public library that's what the sign says on the information desk. Except that it isn't really a desk, which would be closed in front—it's a table with her legs visible below, clearly visible even to my bespectacled nearsighted eyes; shamelessly, generously, voluptuously visible, often to the top of her wine-colored nylons (since she doesn't bother to pull down her skirt), lavish with lush white hints of inner thigh, triggering a vision of the skirt raised yet further beyond blue garters and snowy skin, legs parted high and far apart and me between them in red-hot utopia, thrusting away toward her helplessly wanton pumping scream of utter lust . . .

Okay, an overheated fantasy. So what if it's doomed to remain one. I refuse to think of it as an embarrassment. Nature, not me, has programmed this surge into male flesh. I'm after its honest discharge in the form of unmitigated, unencumbered coitus with an older woman. Not for me the mush of nice crushes on nicely unawakened girls my own age; not the rigmarole of American romance, purchasing intimacy on the installment plan, dating my way from smooching to necking to petting to heavy petting to wow! *alltheway!!* . . . after the ninth movie-cum-stage-cum-dinner, which I could never afford anyway. No, thank you. No sex through consumerism.

In my thoughts I am analytical and unflustered on the subject. It's my behavior that needs work in this area. I must cure myself of certain inhibitions. Like blushing so ridiculously when the issue is raised—with matching ridiculousness—by Papa. Or the stupidly skittish way I can't seem to help whenever I approach Mrs. Poynton: I walk up to the information desk slowly, glasses pushed hard up against my nose for maximum perception of the thighs beneath. This is to fortify my incentive (without any too obvious tumescence) in working up a move. With a very even tone and a not unmeaningful steady glance straight at her brown mascara'd eyes, I ask if, by any chance, the branch has received that new tennis book by Bobby Riggs called *Court Hustler* (whose release date I've first looked up in *Publishers Weekly*).

Now, all such inquiries of mine, no matter how repetitive and predictable, she humors with a patience that might be loaded with implications. "Well, let's see," she'll say, once more consulting some list on her desk. "No . . . not yet. But why don't you try me again next week?"

And this never with a modest adjustment of her skirt but with a slow lipsticked smile and a stroking away of a black hair curl from her cheek, exposing an earlobe pierced through with a gold ring. A subtle signal of responsiveness? Very conceivably. Yet I can never muster anything more piquant than "Thank you."

After that I wander away, rather far away, beyond the distracting view below the information desk, to the corner of bookshelves in the 200 range of the Dewey Decimal System, holding volumes of cookery science. Here I begin my other library pursuits, equally unconfessable to Papa, though for different reasons. I reach behind Wahl's *Sourdough Techniques* and remove from its hiding place *Das Kapital*; read a chapter; return it to its sanctuary.

Then it's time to apply Marxist thought, but not as sacred dogma à la my bakery boss, Bert. No, I deploy it as a tool flexibly modernized to underpin my final afternoon preoccupation.

I pull out of my satchel a sheaf of papers marked either "Wien"—if it's Monday or Tuesday; or "Frosch"—if it's Wednesday or Thursday. Both are drafts of novels in progress. "Wien" about a youth embroiled in Vienna's pre-Nazi maelstrom. "Frosch" about an emigrant, once a physician in Europe, drawn into the Dionysian turbulence of a bakery cellar where he earns his American law school tuition.

In brief, I've plunged into a venture which, were it known at home, my God, it would raise Mandelbaum/Morton eyebrows sky high in panic. Serious writing in *English* by one of *us*? By Fritz, who's spoken nothing but German for fourteen of his nineteen years? A wild gamble on art by a mad mutant, by the aberrant offspring of a business family struggling its way out of refugee squalor? Why? Why, when my background, my schooling, my job training, should all steer me straight to the National Biscuit Company?

No question, it's an audacity I am committing four times a week in the 145th Street Library branch. A very vulnerable audacity and for that reason all the more thrilling and precious. And the vulnerability is shielded, the thrill enhanced, by total secrecy. Nobody knows what I'm up to. That is, nobody except Warren—of all people, him, through a stupid lapse of mine. But happily even he has only a vague idea.

The Warren thing happened the day we met. We found ourselves walking home from school in the same direction and discovered that both of us lived in the same building, twelve blocks south of City College. I asked him about the tennis racket sticking out of his valise. There was no way of knowing what that simple question would start—the floodgates it would open.

It turned out that he's captain of the varsity team and that said racket of his is a Wimbledon wood-steel-laminated nonwarp model strung with vulcanized polyamide nylon and that the double-stitched sailcloth-quality waterproof canvas racket sheath has a zipper pocket holding four instead of the usual three balls with an unfoldable annex holding two more and that on top of all that, this wondrous thing is a freebie for a college tennis captain, one of several such, each of whose features he's so engrossed in itemizing, it doesn't even occur to him to part ways at the library entrance.

No, he walks right in with me, close by my side, accompanying me right to the food shelves, not noticing, thank God, what's under Mrs. Poynton's table since he's busy describing his freebie sneakers, their air-cushioned soles, orthopedic lacings, elastic heel supports, all with such protracted gusto that I finally have to say, Gee, that's terrific, too bad I've got to settle down to work here now.

"Here?" Warren says, waking up to his surroundings. "You don't use the college library?"

"It's quieter here. See you around the house!"

"But the college library's got more books."

"Well, here I concentrate better."

"But what about all the chem reference stuff?"

Now I make my first mistake. To get rid of him, nothing better occurs to me than the truth.

"I don't need reference stuff. I write here."

"Write?" he says. "Write what?"

"Stories," I say. "And so on. This is my time for it now."

I sit down to suggest my need for creative solitude.

"Write?" he repeats, apparently stunned by the weirdness. "Why?"

"I guess—I think I have a gift. But nice to find out we live in the same house. Let's make a tennis date sometime, okay?"

"Yeah," he says, "But Jesus, you know—gift! I got a gift, but, boy, I stay away from it!"

Him, a gift? After that Babbity sneaker rhapsody? This is so unexpected and presumptuous that I make my second mistake.

"Really," I say. "What gift?"

The question opens the floodgates again.

"Absolute pitch," he says, "like my pop and mom. That's how they met, at Juilliard, you got to have a gift to get in there. And you know what it got them in the end? I mean, apart from the divorce? Artsy-fartsy zilch! Know what Pop was after? Tenor at the Met! Jesus, he ended up in Jersey, Hackensack High, choirmaster! And Mom, she was gonna be Carmen to knock them all dead, except her agents screwed her, every one of them. You ever hear of Arista Records? The worst sweatshop label, trust me. Sound engineer at Arista, that's where Mom's gift got *her.* Absolute pitch! I stay away from it!"

He's carried away so loudly that on the other end of the room Mrs. Poynton rises to her feet and places a red-nailed forefinger against her plush lips.

"Sorry," he whispers. "But the hell with gifts!"

"I'm still a chem major," I whisper back. "Writing is just a hobby."

"Oh, well." He grins, relieved. "My hobby is women. Yeah, let's make a tennis date! So long!"

End of my candor with anybody about my literary intentions. Not the end of Warren and his energetic gregariousness now that he knows we share the same roof. He seems to assume that we are a natural two-some—bespectacled, smallish, wiry me, guardedly quiet with my camouflaged imperatives; and him, this big, massive, talk-happy cliché-handsome, black-tousled hunk of hyper-American vulgarity, a good five pounds overweight, which slows him down as he tries to retrieve my lobs yet gives him an unfair advantage when he hammers in his serves.

"Hot dog!" he crows each time he sinks an ace into my court corner. And when it happens that he wins a match, does he walk normally as we change sides? No, he skips in smug gloating triumph.

Still, the English on his serves is just what's needed to sharpen my returns. I've honed away the fuzziness of my backhand against the edge of his. That plus my superior speed plus the mounting crispness of my strokes have begun to turn the tide in our games, though you'll never catch *me* skipping after a win. All in all, I'm glad I've switched Tuesday and Friday afternoons to tennis with him, making up for the loss in library time with a long session in the 145th Street branch on Saturday. A much more focused session, since on that day there are just some red beard's boring trousered legs under the information desk.

All in all it amounts to a net gain in literary concentration as well as backhand technique. Not to speak of the benefits of our posttennis huddles, when I sanitize his grammar and he eases my math pains. In that sense I do value him as partner.

He's also grown popular with my whole family (no wonder they'd all share in the shock of his fit to come). Papa, of course, beams at him as Herr Goldner redux. My brother, Henry, overflows with fourteen-year-old joy whenever Warren brings him Pepsi-stained baseball cards left over from his, Warren's, childhood.

But it's Mama who's become fondest of him. Excessively so. Ours is a family of nonsmokers, but within a week of Warren's first appearance she bought, at Woolworth, a star-shaped plastic ashtray. This she placed on our work desk for him together with a small stack of Doublemint gum and a Pepsi-Cola bottle in a bowl of ice cubes since Americans like their drinks chilled. All offerings of her gratitude whose nature she's spelled out to him over and over again: how wonderful that thanks to him I am no longer such a loner. My brother, Henry's, many roller-skating buddies swarm and clatter through the house (a legitimate reason for my library sojourns) but until him, Warren, she's never seen *me* bring home a friend, let alone such a nice, good-looking, well-turned-out young man with nice dressing habits. As if Warren had saved me from ending up as a bedraggled pathological hermit. And as she effuses away to him, she keeps wiping her hand against her apron, disturbingly reminiscent of our maid, Leni, who was the apron-wearing one in our Vienna household and who wiped *her* hands against it when thanking my mother for a big Christmas gift or whatever.

And Mama, wiping like that, often effuses on yet further about a fine friendship like that, two smart young men, how this could develop beyond sports and school work to other important things in life . . . and at this point, before running back to the kitchen, she'll trail off into a mysterious smile.

It's a mystery I've been very content to leave obscure. Yet it becomes clear—all too clear—just a couple of hours before Warren throws his fit.

Actually, the chain of events producing that fit starts with Mama. As the two of us walk in that day, she hands Warren a white metal cylinder she found earlier standing on our doormat. The cylinder lid has a yellow sticker with four words in block letters: FOR WARREN FROM MOM.

"Oh, right," Warren says. "My dinner."

"Dinner?" Mama says, recoiling. "Warren, this is your dinner?"

"Yeah, lamb stew or something," Warren says, putting the cylinder under his arm, on top of the Wimbledon racket.

"In this!" Mama says. "*Ach,* Warren! Your dinner in a thermos bottle!"

"Well, Mom's got to do a night recording session—"

"Excuse me," Mama says, "everybody in this country is so busy, busy working, so breakfast coffee in the thermos, this I understand. Even lunch sometimes if necessary. But dinner, this is the big meal here—in a bottle!"

"Well, I've got crackers to go with it upstairs—"

"Excuse me!" Mama not only interrupts him again but blocks his way and mine into my room. Instead of wiping her hands on the apron, she jams them fisted against her waist, arms akimbo.

"Warren! Tonight you will have a true dinner with us! Fresh cooked!"

"Goodness me, ma'm," Warren says.

"Nothing against your fine mother working so hard. But something warmed up with crackers—no, you will eat true food with us!"

"Ma'm, I don't want you to take extra trouble—"

"No trouble! Perfect tonight. Franzl—Mister Morton—he telephoned this morning, he will be late because of inventory matters, so I have time to cook Paprika Chicken!"

"Ma'm, really—"

"No, no—no, really! And at the market today, they only have big chickens, so there is a lot! Anything you want, white or black flesh—"

"She means dark or white meat," I clarify, wincing.

"And egg noodles and gravy from my mother's recipes, even if you cannot get the real sweet onions here, but I have a trick to make up for it and cucumber salad and first liver dumpling soup, but the dessert I will not even tell—it is a surprise!"

"Ma'm, this is too much—"

"No, just right—you will see! And *this*"—her finger stabs at the thermos under his arm—"you keep this! For quick lunch tomorrow!"

"Ma'm," Warren says, "I don't know how to thank you—"

"No, I don't hear thanks. But then, later, after dessert—"

"Mother," I say. "Please. That's plenty."

"I don't mean food," she says, much slower, very meaningfully. "You can guess? It is Friday."

Suddenly she smiles the mysterious slight smile she puts on when hinting what two nice young men could do together.

"Friday night!" she says, beaming at me with mystic glee. "Remember, Fred, I know about Friday night? I found out at Parents' Day at City College? The Friday-night dances! At the gymnasium! That's where you two nice young men should go together!"

Off she runs to the kitchen with a titter positively teenage.

I'm left alone with Warren, his thermos bottle, and my embarrassment. Of course I know she knows about the Friday-night dances at the gym. There is no escaping her knowledge. She brings up those dances, nudgingly, just about every Friday night. And if truth be told, on one particular Friday night, I mentioned casually at home that I'd noticed this new Ping-Pong place which had opened on 157th Street which I might as well check out. Since one doesn't dress up for Ping-Pong, I secreted my blue-and-white polka-dotted tie into my jacket pocket. Halfway to the college, just past the library on 144th Street, I found a plate-glass window with my reflection and put on the tie with a dashing big knot. But by the time I reached 140th Street my glasses became thicker and heavier on my nose, the tie constricted around my neck, and the prospect of American courtship games became too strangling. Another block, and I ripped off the tie, invoked Mrs. Poynton's thighs, and declared them superior to anything obtainable at the gym. I won a lot of Ping-Pong games at the new place that night.

Naturally, none of this is any of Warren's business as we settle down in my room, after Mama's dinner invitation.

"Your mom's a sweet lady," he says. "But that gym dance—Jesus!"

"Forget it!" I say.

"Yeah, that dance is a joke," he says. "Nothing but Hunter girls. Bronx stuff. Those kids are from hunger."

He puts down the thermos, takes out his cigarettes, eases himself into the chair. With worldly, sophisticated deftness he taps a Camel out of the pack; lights up; compresses eyes against match fumes, leans back, puffs, watches his perfect smoke rings float away. Repose—terse, knowing repose—comes over him when discussing women.

"Up in Boston," he says softly, cunningly, "Tennis dances, Harvard or MIT, graduate level, that's for me. Heiresses, there's your ticket." He watches another smoke ring dissolve. "Country club socials. Class way to get my patent funding. Some loaded gal with great ankles. I tell you about my master's thesis? Basis for my patent: fractionating hydrocarbons by differential pressure. Revolution in cracking the petroleum molecule. I'm gonna turn the oil game upside down. Just takes some million-dollar baby to stake me. Gonna land me one up there, at some tennis gala. And then, watch out, Texaco! Move over, Shell!"

Suddenly, tapping ashes into the star-shaped ashtray and perhaps reminded by it of its donor, Mama—he sits up.

"So how are we gonna get around the gym dance thing with your mom?"

I've already pondered that while he was rambling on.

"Just tell her you've already arranged a Ping-Pong date for us later tonight," I say. "A foursome with girls. She'll like that."

"Great!" he says.

So that difficulty seems solved. No hint of a fit or any other complication ahead. Papa, true to his telephoned warning, is working late. Yet this, far from a problem, proves pleasant all around, at first. For one thing, Warren has time to complete all three multiplicative operations of my Vector Analysis homework assignment. And when Papa does arrive, the door shuts behind him with a vibrant thud. Only if it's late on Friday, after 8 PM, does he let the door sing out like that. It voices the glad fact that the time is now safely past the end of Sabbath services at Schulchan Sholem around the corner. Tonight my father's job has once more detained him long enough to make feasible a privilege he could never, in all good conscience, claim in Vienna. There, being boss, he controlled his working hours. Here, however, when Mr. Koster decrees that his assistant foreman better finish inventory even after all the others have left—what choice does Papa have? Not his fault that he can't reach the synagogue on time. And so he is happily reduced to acting as his own cantor at home.

Of course there's still the matter of the *minyan,* namely the minimum of ten congregants required for Sabbath prayers. Leave it to my father to finesse that. Again he uses his flair for generating in New York today phenomena of Vienna past. On Friday night he can re-create through my brother, Henry, and myself the full liturgical ensemble of the Huber Temple, which was once our stately house of worship.

Henry's voice is still child high; he doubles for the Huber Temple's boys' choir. My baritone represents the adult choral group. Papa has never made these appointments official. But they are implicit in his gestures. He will signal me to join his prayer song at a certain point by nodding slowly in my direction the way Oberkantor Kogan used to nod slowly at the choral group. When inviting Henry in, Papa will point his little finger at my brother just as the Oberkantor once pointed at the boys' choir. Never mind that there are just two of us, both amateur vocalists. Papa seems comfortable with the notion that the Almighty, aware of emigrant straits, will understand.

And today, when Mama tells him of our unexpected dinner guest, Papa is also comfortable with Warren's non-Jewish presence at our Sabbath Eve. Not merely because with Warren he's come to feel comfortable, period. But tonight he reinvents in Warren not only Herr Goldner but Herr Alois, the Christian sexton who used to switch off the temple lights after services had ended. While worship was in progress Herr Alois used to sit in the checkroom reading the *Kronen Zeitung* soccer pages. Here the equivalent is the World Series coverage by *The New York Times*. Papa hands the paper, unpleated, to Warren in my room.

Mama bustles up to Warren, proffering a tray of crackers garnished with a savory substance just borrowed from Mrs. Löser, whose cuisine is much more New World than hers. The substance is the American delicacy of peanut butter, which—Mama hopes—will keep Warren from resorting to the thermos bottle until after prayers, when dinner will be served.

And so all appears deceptively well: Mama's muted Paprika Chicken puttering in the kitchen; Warren in my room, entertained by hors d'oeuvres and home runs; Papa in the living room with his two sons honoring the Sabbath with our devotions.

I participate uneasily. Not because of any foreknowledge of the fit just ahead. No, simply because my feelings about prayers are so mixed. After all, I am an agnostic—another subject undiscussable with Papa. My interest in the Sabbath is purely historical, but that doesn't make it a superficial interest. I will not just simply turn my back on a belief system that sustained my father against those boots and whips at Dachau. My new name might hide my Jewish identity—I myself won't deny it. On the contrary, to the degree that I am skeptical about the religious dimension of this identity, to the same degree I am curious about its cultural roots. To doubt effectively I better be knowledgeable about the object of my doubt.

Result: I've sacrificed some of my Karl Marx time at the library to the *Encyclopedia Judaica,* specifically to the entry on the history of the Sabbath service. And so I know that since the sixteenth century the core liturgy has consisted of six psalms culminating in a cabalist hymn that's downright erotic in mood: it serenades the Sabbath as a bride to be wooed and embraced in sacred ecstasy. Steamy stuff, which always tempts me to ask Papa how aware he is of the gist of those Hebrew phrases he is so fervently warbling.

To Papa, though, the meaning of the ritual seems to be secondary to its theatrics. He stars in the production, one son to his left, one to his right, both just slightly behind him, and three of us decked out in skullcaps, flowing fringed prayer shawls, and opened prayer books.

My brother mouths the words obediently while his mind may or may not be with *The Green Lantern* or whatever other radio serial he might be missing at this hour. As for me, well, Papa is always so caught up in his aria, he seldom realizes that little more than a hum leaves my lips. This, out of a certain resentment. "The sound of the Lord," Papa sings out Psalm 29. "The Lord echoes across many waters, the God of glory thundereth . . ." But the real glory here appears to be Papa's in the fulfillment of his cantorial dreams. And not just his cantorial ones: through bypassing the communality of the synagogue; through engaging God alone (his sons being mere extensions of himself); through treating faith as his own strictly private enterprise . . . isn't he practicing under his yarmulke an intemperate Yankee individualism? An antisocial aggrandizement? Isn't there a capitalist ideal involved here which is beyond his reach in his Koster Co. smock but which he attains in a prayer shawl? And isn't that subverting piety? Reducing it to an ego trip?

I wonder. I really do wonder.

And yet, and yet.

There's something else. On all such Friday evenings there comes a point which shakes my reservations. It's the moment Papa changes—literally, physically—the direction of his prayer when he starts chanting Psalm 30. Until then he's been facing the coffee table, as he should, because that way is east and therefore Jerusalem. But as he reaches Psalm 30 he shifts position slightly northward. Instead of rocking back and forth, hunched, he straightens up, lifts his face toward a bottle on a small black wooden shelf set high into the living room corner. It's a ledge installed by some previous tenant and left empty by us until May 1 of this year. Every time Papa prays toward that bottle, May 1, 1945, jumps out of it like a djinn together with all those giant black headlines roaring from the newsstands. On that day Papa had brought home the bottle, obviously some expensive French rosé—its label so elegant with calligraphy. Our goblets worthy of such vintage had been left behind in Vienna. We must make do with water glasses. Mama had them ready: a small one for my brother, Henry; three bigger ones for the rest of us. Papa lifted his.

"We are rid of the beast," he said. "Today Hitler is dead. We are alive. We drink to God in thanks."

We drank the thrilling tart liquid.

"And the rest of the bottle," Papa said, "we will drink in thanks to God when we hear that Grandma Riddah is safe."

He then took out of his jacket pocket the postcard he always carries and laid it next to the bottle. It's a blotched wrinkled card protected by a plastic Baggie become clouded with age but transparent enough to let glimmer through five words scribbled at disjointed angles to each other. *"I am well. Love. Riddah."* The card, having traveled long and hard via Switzerland, Spain, and Portugal and forwarded to us by the Red Cross, is postmarked Theresienstadt. The last time I saw it below eye level was on May 1, when Papa put it on the kitchen table, by the wine bottle, and the four of us stood around it, glasses in our hands.

We drank up. Papa took bottle and card, walked to the living room with us behind him. He rose on tiptoe, reached high, placed the bottle, with the card leaning against it, on the corner shelf.

Throughout all the days, weeks, months since then the card has remained up there, leaning against the bottle that's still half undrunk. Every so often Mama climbs the stepladder to wipe away the dust which seems to gather extra fast on those two objects like some sacerdotal shroud. And Friday after Friday, with invariable punctuality, the little shrine pulls Papa around and up when he launches into Psalm 30.

This Friday, too, he turns like that, my brother and I repeating the motion behind him. This Friday, too, the three of us raise our faces. This Friday, too, we keep them raised until the psalm's end: "Thou has changed my mourning into dancing, hast removed my sackcloth and girded me in gladness . . ." And with the psalm nearly sung, this Friday, too, Papa is about to shift position back, eastward, in the direction of Jerusalem, to end in the joyous "Come, oh come, my friend, come meet the lovely Sabbath, come and enfold the beautiful bride!"

But not this Friday.

Today something intervenes.

A strange, low, growly sound. It issues from the door which, I realize now, isn't quite closed, the door to the room where Warren is relaxing with the *Times'* coverage of the World Series and whence other strange sounds now dart, something like choppy aborted clearings of the throat. They stop, and Papa, his chant interrupted in surprise, is about to resume. But the sounds resume as well—they are deeper and breathier now, resembling severely pressed-out grunts. Papa does go on to finish the psalm, only the grunts intensify, become choking groans. My brother and I exchange glances. Papa continues for another moment, stops. He turns around, nods me to my room.

In a flash I am there.

It's Warren. Behind my homework desk he sits crouched, doubled over; his hands clutch his belly, his mouth is oddly distended, *Times* pages are scattered on the floor.

"Warren! What in the—"

No chance to finish the sentence. He's bounded out of the chair. He runs—still doubled over, still clutching himself, still groaning—he runs through the living room, past Papa, past Henry, past kitchen, across the hall. He rattles the apartment door wildly because in his mad haste he's turned the knob the wrong way, turns it right, stomps out, door left gaping wide open.

Of course we rush after him. But Mama, closer to the door in the kitchen, has already preceded us into the corridor. Breathless, bewildered, we meet her by the elevator.

"He has run up the stairs!" she says. "To his apartment! He must be sick!"

"He didn't explain?" Papa says. "Not one word?"

"It is the peanut butter," Mama says. "I did the canapés wrong—"

"We should check on him," Papa says.

"We must call Dr. Raubitschek," Mama says.

"Fred, you check on him!"

Prayer shawl floating behind me, I take three steps at a time on the two flights that separate our apartments. I pound against the door of 6A; keep pounding at least for a minute before it opens.

The hall light is turned off. It takes me a moment to make out Warren, standing there, stands straight now, though one hand is still pressed against his heaving belly.

"My God, are you all right?"

"Monotones . . ." he breathes.

"What?"

"You're all such monotones . . ."

"You're not sick?"

He shakes his head, coughing, through his mouth, which is oddly distended again.

"Bunch of dead-serious monotones . . ."

He is covering his mouth, but not before I see that it's chuckles he is coughing away.

"You've been laughing!"

"I didn't want to! Not at guys praying—praying their heart out!"

"Is that why you ran off?"

"I couldn't choke it back anymore."

I was unamused.

"My mother thinks it's her canapés," I say. "She's calling a doctor."

"Oh, Jesus."

He closes his eyes, blows up his cheek into a grotesque disconcertment quite unlike him. His bloated face loses all its handsomeness. Somehow this sight is mollifying.

"Wait a minute," I say. "Let's think. I have an idea. We'll say it was a sudden allergy attack. That's what it was. I'll tell my parents you have hay fever."

"Yeah! But—they'll buy it?"

"Why not? The radio said there's still a high pollen count."

"Yeah! Tell 'em I'll be right down—but not if you guys are praying! I'll just break up again! I can't go in if I hear you praying!"

Nobody is praying when I return to the apartment. No more prayer shawls, so I take off mine, too. They are all gathered around the telephone, where my mother is being very urgent with Dr. Raubitschek's answering service.

"Mama, cancel the message," I say. "It was just a hay fever attack."

"Hay fever?" Papa says. "He needs medicine?"

"He's already taken it, he's all right again. He'll be down in a minute."

"He is able to eat?" Mama says.

"Sure. These attacks pass fast."

They buy it, not knowing any better. We'd never heard of hay fever before coming to the U.S.A., not one of us has suffered from it yet, and just this certifies it as an American disease, authenticating the fit.

Warren duly reappears, flaunting a large white handkerchief with which to minister industriously to his convalescent nose. He has also put on a dark jacket, a white shirt, and a blue silk tie, perhaps to compensate for the disruption with extra decorum. Still, something remains wrong.

The evening can't quite get back to an even keel. Of course we all try to proceed as if nothing special has happened. Mama ushers Warren to the one chair at the kitchen table that's an armchair. She runs to serve the liver dumpling soup and, as soon as we've started spooning, runs off, returns with unnatural speed, still buttoning the top button of her ankle-length pearl gray hostess gown. It's her first American luxury, bought only this year at Macy's Washington's Birthday sale; she trips repeatedly over its unwonted length as she serves the Paprika Chicken (leaving against universal protests her own soup uneaten). Papa, in an attempt to make our guest feel at home, begins to use knife and fork the American way; methodically, showily, he cuts up part of his drumstick with both utensils, then shifts his fork from his left to right hand to spear the pieces, always dropping knife against plate with a clink that curls my toes. My brother, Henry, gags on a noodle. And out of the blue Warren launches his attack on the music world.

Nobody has so much as mentioned music, but he hurls a tirade against the entire field. Instead of chattering on in his customary cheery way, he talks fast and driven about the terrible racket the music business has degenerated into in all branches, like the record companies, the slave-driving cheats they all are, hounding even Jelly Roll Morton to a bad end, the thieving that's routine to Broadway musical producers, the classical field no better with those book-doctoring impresarios, and the Met run into the ground by egomaniacs . . .

My parents display a polite sharing of his rage. They cluck tongues and shake heads, but basically they sit there, stunned. I begin to suspect that Warren might be ranting like that out of a guilty conscience. Maybe the point he's conveying—to me—is that with all of music being so rotten, tone deafness, even if comical, doesn't matter . . .

Is he really saying that? And how much longer would he go on raving and raving—if Mama didn't suddenly sniff the air; jump to her feet; trip over the long hostess gown again; recover; yet reach the oven too late.

"The *Vanillakipfel!*" she says, aghast. "The dessert!"

"Jesus," Warren says, jarred out of his polemics. "I've been carrying on."

"I put the flame too high!" Mama wails softly.

"My fault," Warren says, "jawing like that."

"The burn smell! It will make your allergy come back?"

"No, no, Ma'm, I'm fine." But in his dismay he's blown up his cheeks again.

"And there is not even enough batter for another portion!"

"Ma'm, I swear, I've got no room left anyway from all your delicious food." Suddenly he takes a deep breath. "And see, I've got an idea. If we skip dessert—Fred and me—we can still make it to the dance."

"The Friday-night gymnasium dance!?" Mama instantly brightens. Not me.

"Yeah, why not?" Warren says.

"Oh, Warren! That is wonderful!"

"I think it's too late now," I say. "It's almost ten."

"But you can leave right away," Mama says. "This moment."

"Fred has to wash the dishes today," my brother, Henry, pipes up. "It's his turn."

Mama doesn't even hear him. She's run to my room, returns in seconds with my blazer and that impossibly yellow birthday-present tie I couldn't exchange.

"Mother, I can't go," I say. "It's my turn to do the dishes."

"I will wash them for you!"

"But the dance is over at eleven."

"So we'll take a taxi," Warren says.

"You must inform me of the fare," Papa says, not to be left out. "I will refund you."

By then Mama has already put the yellow tie around my neck.

Out on the street I try to argue that we should go to the Ping-Pong parlor for a few games or see a movie—my parents will never know the difference. But Warren is too busy hailing a taxi to pay any particular attention. In the taxi he still won't listen, demanding that I straighten his tie, then insisting that I shut up and hold still while he reties the knot of mine.

By the time he is finished, we are there. So fast is the ride with the night traffic sparse in the streets. We've stopped in the lamplit middle of the City College campus.

The glowing windows of the gym send through the dark soft moanings of a swing band's trombones. The skin contracts down my spine. My spectacles seem to thicken on my nose. The yellowness of my tie intensifies.

"I'm not going in there."

"What's the matter?" Warren says.

"You yourself said this dance is a joke."

"So we'll go for laughs."

"You're just doing this because *you* laughed!"

"I promised your mom. Keep the change, buddy."

He gets out on his side of the cab, opens the door on my side three seconds later.

"Come on."

I sit.

"You scared or something?"

"Are you kidding?"

"So?"

"I forgot my sunglasses," I improvise wildly.

"Excuses!"

"No, they're prescription sunglasses. Against the glare of the gym lights. I can't go in with the ones I've got on."

"So let's take them off."

He has the nerve to reach into the cab and take them off me. He stuffs them into my jacket pocket.

"Folks," the cabbie says. "I can't stand here forever."

I have to get out.

"Hey!" Warren says. "No-specs Fred! Look at you—Humphrey Bogart!"

"I can't see without them," I say. "I'll pick out a dog."

"Never fear, Warren's here. I'll steer you to a beauty."

The campus looks different, dangerous, at night . . . hazy without my glasses, transformed by those trombones. We crunch along dim gravel between shrubbery I don't recognize. He guides me lightly by the elbow, past a puddle, humming to the music which swells as we come nearer. I begin to suspect that hum of his. Is there amusement in it? . . . Certainly there is amusement in it, just as there's amused condescension in the way he guides me—probably also in his Humphrey Bogart compliment. He's having his superior fun with me and my nearsighted shyness, just as he's had his fun with my parents. We're all his laughingstock, we refugees with our Fourth Reich ambitions in America, wanting to be golden-throated cantors or great Yank millionaires or incandescent love-makers to librarians or writers in English overcoming so much German in the brain, or, for that matter, monotones wailing at God to retrieve Grandma Riddah from her Auschwitz ashes . . .

I want to seek haven in the nice safe Ping-Pong parlor. I decide to break away from him.

Too late. The gym entrance looms just yards ahead. The brightness of its foyer blinds. Feminine titter alarms me. My uncertain vision surmises skirted shapes huddling in hilarity by the checkroom counter. I can't— not in plain sight of those girls—I can't suddenly turn around and run away from the dance.

Prodded by Warren behind me, I must climb up the stairs. They are so crowded with people coming down, I take hope: this hour nobody will be left on the gym floor.

Wrong. When I enter there's the murmur and the milling of a twilit crowd. Most overhead lights familiar to me from Phys. Ed. class are dark. The wall lamps between the exercise ladders give enough light to bathe the air in dusk. A dozen pale indoor moons have risen. I squint my naked eyes—the moons are white balloons trembling against the ceiling.

Warren taps me on the shoulder. His finger points. At what? A slim-frocked silhouette? A slight smile floating in a cloud of hair?

Without warning, "Stardust" starts to undulate from the loudspeaker with a hundred desirous violins. Warren, damn him, deserts me. Suddenly cheek to cheek with someone, he melts away into the violins.

Sometimes I wonder why I spend the lonely night dreaming of a song . . .

And together with those sinuous strings something wells up all around me; something brewed of magic murk and my astigmatism and the scent of perfume spiced with gym sweat, something like Fred Astaire's wondrous, fabulous never-never-Manhattan that once flickered four thousand miles away on a dubbed movie screen in my childhood city. *The melody haunts my memory . . .* The melody tides me, goose pimples and all, toward the slim frock and the cloud of hair.

Inhale. Exhale.

Do it.

Fred, do it.

"May I have this dance?"

1949

Rendezvous at Salt Lake City

Just today, the day of her arrival, has to bring the first real downpour of the summer session. And this isn't just some moist little tantrum either. Drops drum down with a methodic, malign relentlessness that intends to last for many hours. Which naturally leads to thoughts about her plane: will she land safely, and on time? And when she does, she won't even find the jagged Rocky Mountain melodrama promised by my letters and picture postcards. The clouds hanging down to the horizon are as humdrum gray as any over the Bronx.

The weather is the major surprise this morning. But as I walk out of the faculty residence, across the swimming flagstones, there is also the honk. More of a half honk, really, a stifled timid car horn mutter that unmistakably announces Eugene.

And sure enough, it's my graduate assistant twisting himself out of his dented Volkswagen.

"Oh, uh . . . Fred!"

That "Oh, uh . . ." of his represses the "Mr. Morton" I've asked him to kindly cut out. But it's an "Oh, uh . . ." charged with more respectful hesitation than any formal address. The very sound seems to sprout a venerable academician's beard on my twenty-four-year-old chin. Sometimes Eugene can make me feel like a damn turncoat. For too many years, in New York no less than in Vienna, I was such a stalwartly rotten student, at war with school. All of a sudden I'm teach, on a college campus yet, with an assistant—superteach! To defuse this treasonous dignity foisted on me by that assistant, my response is pointedly juvenile.

"What the heck are you doing here, Eugene?"

"Well, I've brought the English II compositions."

"Weren't you going to give them to me at Smith Hall?"

"Well, see, it's raining. I thought I'd drive you over."

Smith Hall, where I conduct my creative writing class (so-called), is a bare two hundred yards away. Nonetheless there is Eugene, one hand keeping the car door wide open, the other holding an umbrella over me. God forbid that my head, protected anyway by its thick thatch, should suffer a single droplet when his already half-bald pate is dripping. But maybe it's just the difference in hairlines that justifies such homage. Me, with my almost adolescent pompadour, I'm already a published novelist; whereas he, with his skimpy widow's peak, still toils at his M.A. dissertation on the theological roots of T. S. Eliot's censure of John Milton. The contrast makes "Oh, uh . . . Fred" an especially brilliant youth deserving special deference.

Silent self-satire has become a habit of mine here. I cultivate it to fight off the ego but also to cope with the sheer craziness of the situation: finding myself suddenly marooned on some doubtful altitude for which I'm unprepared, whose rarefied air I still have to learn how to breathe. Of course Eugene would never suspect that the Brilliant Youth could ever suffer even a moment's doubt. For him I'm riding a smooth crest of glory to which he's been hired to minister. Sometimes I catch a quick sharp sideways glint from his watery blue eyes—a dart of curiosity, as now during his umbrella-holding homage: where do I get off commanding such precocious, unmitigated esteem?

Actually, old Eugene does some mitigating himself. Often he presents his services to me not as subservience but as compensation for some damage he's done. Right now, during our ludicrously short ride to Smith Hall, he points to the rubber-banded bundle of English II compositions in the glove compartment. "Sorry," he murmurs.

Another "Sorry" for another wrong to be righted by some extra stint on my behalf. Eugene, in fact, commits quite a few boo-boos (out of atonement-proneness?), such as photocopying the wrong story from *Dubliners* for my creative writing course. Or his current "Sorry" re the glove compartment bundle: giving my English II class the wrong deadline. This he did last week subbing for me while I played Brilliant-Youth-in-Residence at the Utah University Writers' Conference; he told the class that the next essay was due not Monday, as I'd instructed him, but only today, Wednesday. And that flub happens not to be minor; it affects my reception of her who'll be stepping off the plane this afternoon. Much of that afternoon will have to be given over to the damn glove compartment bundle since I must include my English II grades in the class profiles Dean Neff expects tomorrow. Bad enough her first day here will be rained out. Worse, her poet-swain will have to stoop donnishly for hours over a heap of sophomore scribblings.

Now, Eugene probably guesses how I hate being a donnish stooper in her sight. Constantly, if ambivalently, serviceable, he's ferreted out for me the one un-Rotarian hotel in Salt Lake City with bebop rather than Muzak coming out of the lobby loudspeakers—in other words, lodging congenial to someone like her. So he must have an inkling of the character of my "special visitor" (his parlance) and perhaps surmises how his English II goof might spoil plans I made for her and me today. Hence: more guilt to be expiated by more serviceability.

As we stop before Smith Hall, he grabs the English II bundle before I can reach for them, runs around the Volkswagen to open my door.

"Oh, uh . . . after your class," he says, shepherding me under his umbrella across the sidewalk, "no problem driving you to the reception."

"For God's sake!" I say. "Those few steps?" (The dean's reception marking the end of the writers' conference is just around the corner.) "You don't have to wait around!"

"Well, it's pouring," he says. "I've got my dissertation work with me. And no problem driving you to the airport afterward."

"Eugene, I already have a ride!"

"No, really, I live near the airport anyway, no problem."

Thrusts the English II bundle at me, ducks away.

Right from the start he's been so keen on chauffeuring me about, especially on nonuniversity business. And it's when he's driving me on personal errands that I've noticed how closely he's watching all my moves, his lower lip hanging a bit open, damply. As if salivating with avid curiosity. Hoping that I'd give away in private life the trick of being a Brilliant Youth? Sniffing for some underhand knack of mine which he could then put to use? Or am I just being shamefully suspicious? Paranoid on an edgy morning?

At any rate no such Eugenesque avidity in the room I'm now entering. In a way, that's odd. After all, this is Creative Writing, where the students are licensed to suck talent out of the instructor. But then, nobody here is a striver from Chicago like Eugene, hell bent on Pulitzer laurels before forty. No, these are all down-to-earth locals from the Utah Nursing College who've opted for a writing course simply because it's a virtually un-flunkable elective.

Still, at my entrance they hush up, straighten up from mutually inclined shmoozing angles. This always surprises the New Yorker in me, on top of the surprise that I should have an inner New Yorker in the first place. Me, the chronic gringo, perennially at odds with the new land, who's rooted himself doubly deep in its language perhaps because he can't be comfortable with its culture. Well, whaddayahknow? I seem to have been properly coarsened after all by the streets and schools of Manhattan, by raw bakery cellars, by the roughhouse at Food Trades Vocational, by all those seething elbows in the City College pressure cooker. And so I find myself having to adjust when facing Mormon discipline— the blandness of it.

With my nurses, though, it's discipline with a twist. At my entrance they sit up a bit too cartoonishly at attention, too bolt upright. Having reached the podium, I sink into my chair with octogenarian gravitas before I acknowledge their acknowledgment of me with an impossibly slow, solemn nod.

It's a game we developed soon after I started teaching here two weeks ago. It helps me master the absurdity of the encounter by having fun with it. Not only is the only male in the room the professor; but the professor is practically the same age as the students. (In a letter to her who is arriving today, I confessed that I find this anomaly tangy. Her answer, a characteristic "Just teach the bloody class—don't date it!")

"All right," I say now. "At ease. Permission to relax. Lean back, young ladies."

They obey, again with humorous exaggeration. They slump. They let arms hang down. They stretch out legs, even loosening them carelessly. And what makes it all so lighthearted is that there's hardly any sexual tension. These are all large-boned Scandinavian blondes. They could be Vikings in drag with their big-sleeved athletic blouses, their long New Look skirts. The only one coming even close to being my type is Miss Handson up front, the only one with a higher hemline, presently displaying the only interesting un-Valkyrien pair of knees in the lot. She is also best at maintaining the playful tone of the hour.

"Just how relaxed do you want us to be, Mr. Morton?" she asks, inclining her head sideways in roguish interrogation.

I incline mine right back. "Not to the point of sleep, please."

"No dreaming allowed?"

Today she's pushing things a bit. But she also gives me a great idea.

"Why, Miss Handson," I say. "You are psychic. Today we'll do a dream exercise. Let's take out our notepads."

They sit up again, puzzled this time, including Miss Handson, who smoothes her skirt down. They root about in their valises for the notepads.

"Weren't we going to discuss narrative strategy in *Dubliners*?" Miss Handson wants to know with a theatrical little pout.

"Next time," I say. "Today write down any part of any dream you remember."

"Any dream?" Miss Handson asks, emphasizing *any* with a certain pseudoshocked pseudoastonishment that ripples a titter through the class.

"Any," I say. "Be brave. But don't write the dream down to the end. Invent an alternate end that's still in the mood of the earlier part."

"Gee, Mr. Morton," Miss Handson says. "I'll have to invade my privacy."

"Gee, Miss Handson," I say. "That's Creative Writing for you."

Outright laughter. They always set me up for a nice punch line. And now that we've had our sport, we can all buckle down to work. They knit their blond brows over their notepads. And me, having postponed the

Dubliners class discussion till next time, I can use the hour to grade English II *before,* not after, her arrival.

But even as I wield the red-ink professorial pen, her damn photograph begins to act up again. It's wedged into the innermost fold of my wallet, which I keep buttoned away in my back pants pocket. In vain. Her image passes through leather and cloth. This time it appears to imprint itself as a silhouette, a sort of watermark, on whatever English II sheet I happen to be correcting. Glimmering through lines of script, there she is behind the desk of her joke job—associate editor of *Boys' Life,* the Boy Scout magazine. She's smiling her tiny-nostriled fine-cheeked smile inside a glistening dark storm cloud of hair. A she-cherub's sweetness spiced with an Amazon's mane. In the photo this mane is diabolically positioned so that the Boy Scout motto on the wall behind her is blotted out in the middle. BE PREPARED reads BE RED.

Typical her. Typical of her phantom photo to waylay me unpredictably. Usually it fades after a minute. Today, perhaps because I'll see her in the flesh so soon, it lingers. More than lingers—moves; tosses the aureole of ringlets; curves lips down at the both ends. But I don't let her tart smile distract me, I align it with my own. Together we grin at English II's monolithic wholesomeness. Composition after composition as squeaky clean as Salt Lake City's streets; sanitized, all the messy ambiguities lurking in the theme I assigned: "Lost and Found—any experience evoked by the phrase." Hints of voids intuited or purposes retrieved? Nah. Just plodding tales about the favorite hymnal with the blue silk bookmark left on the church pew or spotting on a bus seat those kiddie skates with silver pom-poms. And the hidebound diction. Not that we— she of the watermark mane and I—expect anything like her firebrand prose when she was polemicist in chief of the *Hunter College Bulletin.* No, we're merely amused together how these essays fence in every clause with commas, needed or not. Heavens, no untidy spilling over! As for the handwriting—plain, orderly, nary a blotch or unnecessary curlicue, lines tightly formatted as if typed.

Suddenly the hair cloud shifts a bit. The grin at its center aims at *me.* Damn it, it's the same grin that issued from her letter week before last— "You little Teuton you, typing your effusions in neat little paragraphs, so that it comes out like 'Please consider this missive as my application to be the continued object of your affection'. . . ."

Which is a wicked, vile allusion to what I should have never shown her earlier this year, namely a sample of my letters to the English Department heads of five far western universities (which in the end got me the Utah job) starting with "Please consider this an application for a Summer Session position" and ending, similarly paragraphed, with quotes such as "extraordinary literary debut" documented by photocopies of my reviews. Wicked and vile of her to mock me with that when she knows damn well that my application style was simply howling with the wolves, academizing with academe; a prank, so to speak, to snow the panjandrums of pedagoguedom, fool them into letting me, a foreigner who's pirated the mainland language, teach it back to its native owners, on the university level yet. She knows all my deep-down impieties because she's the only person to whom I've really opened up. For the same reason she also knows that I chose to apply only to universities beyond Chicago for a very unacademic purpose: having tackled Vienna in my first novel, New York in my second, I intend to take on "America" next. And to see through "America" incisively, I must see more of it, in particular the rootin' tootin' shootin' mythopoeic Far West. This I explained to her in detail as my motive for putting some two thousand temporary miles between us.

And didn't she accept that? Did she raise any kind real objection? Then what's with her watermark grin now? Why not wipe that cynical curl off those lovely lips? Because she needs the curl—needs it for her derisive Noo Yawk "Yeah?" "Yeah?" the curl says, "aren't we oh-boy proud of those two thousand adventurous miles west? Proud of proving your manhood by missing me more than missing your parents across that distance? What the hell are those two thousand miles compared to my nine subway stops? Those we traveled together on the Lenox Avenue line, both lugging my clothes cartons from the Poppa/Momma Bronx to my half basement on East Fifteenth Street? Compared to that your two thousand miles west are zero, zilch, bubkes, because you're going to cancel every inch of them by traveling back east again after the summer, right back into your *Papa-und-Mutti-Heimat*-nest in the

Fourth Reich in Washington Heights. Right or wrong? *Ja oder nein?"*

She hasn't actually pronounced all this out loud, in so many words. So far. Just sneaked hints into some of her mordant asides. But now her grin—the grin of the watermark—predicts that she might come right out with it presently, during her visit. And if she does? Then the thing will be to summon the guts, the moxie as they say around here, to spell out to her the reason why I can't join her just yet on East Fifteenth Street. And there's a lot more to that reason than moments like last Friday night when, walking toward the white-bread courtesies of the Faculty Club dinner, I heard sounding suddenly, softly, in the Rockies' giant sunset, Papa's prayer wail so far away in New York together with the rustle of my mother setting up the Sabbath candles in the kitchen. Such moments happen; they're twinges, fading fast. It's not mere sentimentality that keeps me from moving in with her just yet. It's just that I could use a reprieve, or, better said, a grace period, a chance to catch my breath after too many abrupt metamorphoses in too few years: rich brat in Vienna to Eighth Avenue baker boy to chafing City College chem major to published novelist at an improbable age. I mean, the very year of my graduation my first book erupts in my second language—in itself proof how drastically, irreparably I've catapulted out of the homeland for good? After that, please, a little more time before leaving my family home for good; more practice in ridding myself of the sense of exile-within-exile. Won't she understand that?

Riiiiiiing!!! . . . goes the hour bell. Snaps me out of being the nervous lover—too nervous to continue grading compositions. Snaps me back into playing the Brilliant Youth.

"Thank you," I say to my nurses as they file out and deposit on my desk their efforts of today. "Thank you for your amended dreams."

"Off with you!" I say four minutes later to Eugene as he drives me around one wet little corner to the dean's reception. "I told you, I already have a ride to the airport later! Now go on home! Vamoose! Scat! Git!"

"So kind of you," I say, five minutes later, performing next to Dean Neff on the writers' conference farewell reception line. "So kind of you," I say to yet another car dealer's cultural wife in response to her right deep appreciation of my insights into Frans Kafka and Arthur Snitzler (*sic, sic*).

"My pleasure to inscribe it to him, too," I say for the nth time, now seated behind my book-signing stand. "What is your cousin's name?"

And just when it seems that I've finished my reception act, already heading for the exit, I'm stopped by one more matron in emancipated slacks, this one with a western twang so extreme I have to say "Beg pardon?" twice. Deciphered, her question turns out to concern Franz Werfel's early revolutionary poetry, about which she's amazingly—and inconveniently—well informed. I have to resort to elaborate digressions involving the tonality of Prague literary German to obscure my ignorance.

At last, the last one out, I run through the soaking parking lot in search of the long yellow trailer Wallace Stegner promised would be there.

And there it is indeed. Inside—my first time in such a gypsy vehicle—inside there's much surprisingly homey orange upholstery plus a domestic smell coming from the kitchen corner. Stegner is bending over the gas stove while Nabokov hefts a wine bottle with the bandaged hand I've noticed at the reception. I'd not expected him, and somehow the presence of both stars of the writers' conference makes me feel like an apprentice intruding on two masters. Stegner's masterfulness, however, is modified by the fact that he's slicing potatoes into what smells like chicken stew.

"Here you are," he says to me. "Finally made your escape?"

"Skin of my teeth," I sigh, now enacting the jaded fellow luminary, beset like my two peers by the common herd.

"When did you say your girl is landing?" Stegner asks, presently slicing carrots. "Half past two?"

"Two o'clock, to be exact."

"Because Bill," Stegner says, "my friend Bill's changed his flight from L.A., so he won't get here till a quarter to four. You two mind waiting at the airport before driving back? We'll have a chicken picnic. Late Bill gets the leftovers."

"That's fine," I say. "Thank you."

It should be fine with her because she wrote me how much she liked Stegner's "Big Rock Candy Mountain." A picnic with the author might make up for all the English II compositions still ungraded—the donnish stooping I'll have to do after all.

"This dean's bacchanal we just experienced," Nabokov says; to my surprise he says it in my direction, having mostly ignored me during the conference. "One frisson after another, from the no-alcohol punch to the no-cleavage décolletage of the barmaid. Did you notice?"

"Yes," I say, though I didn't.

He lifts the bottle toward me. "Some middling Riesling?"

"Not right now, thanks."

I'm uncomfortable admitting to these sophisticates that I share icky abstinence with the Mormon locals. But much worse than uncomfortable is what hits me belatedly, abruptly—the effect of Stegner's "chicken picnic" on her who'll be walking off the plane so soon. All her accounts of being force-fed chicken breasts throughout childhood and beyond! One of the things that drove her out of the parental apartment was the chronic smell of boiled chicken.

I stand in the Stegner trailer recalling that, smelling boiling chicken, petrified.

"Someday I'll get up the nerve for *that*," Stegner says with a nod at the bandage Nabokov is unwinding from his finger.

"To be worn at a book signing with an expression of manfully contained pain," Nabokov says, wiggling a now naked and unscathed thumb. "Then they won't dare ask for one word of inscription beyond your signature. They'll stutter their gratitude for just scrawling your initials."

I can't let her deplane into this chicken smell. She might even have an allergy. I remember her hair cloud shaking with sneezes for minutes on end after fleeing the fumes of her mother's chicken soup.

"Mr. Stegner," I say, "my girl would love a picnic with you. But I just remembered, she had to get up at dawn today to make her plane. The poor thing will collapse if I don't get her to my hotel right away. So thank you, but we'll just take a taxi."

"*Taxi?*" Nabokov says. "In this town? I took one to what passes for a Natural History Museum here. The brigand charged me half my conference fee."

"There's probably a special airport fare," I say.

"Yes, higher," Nabokov says. He points the bottle at me again. "You're a crypto-teetotaler. How so? Your dust jacket claims you're Austrian."

Just now he decides to pay attention to me, when I have no time for magisterial banter.

"I guess I wasn't brought up right," I say, walking to the door.

"Your accent has badly atrophied," he says behind my back. "Prove your provenance, Friedrich. Speak some charming German."

"Well, right now I have to get to the airport."

"We'll drive you there."

This stops me midway and turns me around.

"In exchange you brush up Madame's German on the road."

"I beg your pardon?"

"Mrs. Nabokov's German mustn't get rusty. She checks my translations."

"My God," I say, "to drive me out there now, in the rain—"

"There'll be more rain in Wyoming where we'll head next, and I hear mud boots are priced best at the airport shop. Two birds, one stone."

"Wonderful!" I say. "My visitor, she's read your stories in *The New Yorker*—she'll be delighted."

"Why, that makes her an angel. In that case, German lessons only to the airport. Not fro. Fro you may dally with your angel. We won't leer from the front seats. *D'accord?*"

"*Oui!*" I say. "*Très bien! Danke schön!*"

It turns out there's little chance for German practice on the way. Up front in the Oldsmobile, Madame Nabokov squirms behind the wheel, all dainty silver-coiffed bone china, entirely consumed by driving, too busy peering through the flooded windshield when she's not fretting over a map. And he, in the backseat with me, ruddy bulky him, he is rooting through the welter at our feet, socks, sweaters, galoshes, God knows what else. He reaches deep down, pulls out a half boot.

"Your novel," he says, staring at the worn black boot leather as if its cracks reminded him of my book, "I imagine its milieu is *Mitteleuropa*?"

"Yes," I say. "Vienna."

"Do you give that city what it deserves?"

"Well," I say, "the story has moral dimensions, yes. I deal with the years leading up to Hitler."

"Ah, but *Alt-Wien* also spawned Freud. A much more subtle shaman. Freud needs defrocking. Do that in your next book."

It's a bit much. With all due respect and gratitude for the ride, he has no business instructing me what to write next when he's never read a word of mine in the first place. Whereas I have read a couple of his stories and would have told him, had he given me the time of day at the conference, how I respected him as a fellow literary émigré senior to me not only in years but in polish and even in my special pride, range of lexis, although his style tends to be overly Latinate—an opinion I'd never voice to his face, in contrast to his rude, lordly orders to me concerning the theme of my next book.

Which I can't let pass in silence.

"My next book is finished and coming out this fall," I say. "It's a novel set in a New York bakery cellar."

"Ah," he says, tugging at the laces of the boot in his lap. "Well, as long as you don't pull another Gorky."

Gorky?

"Did you say Gorky?"

"Red Max did heavy lifting with flour bags," Nabokov says, engrossed in yanking the lace out of the boot. "Or so he claimed."

"Maxim Gorky was a baker?"

"Before he turned literary whore. Fat Bolshevik royalties per trick, you know. A poor example to follow."

"My new book," I say, "doesn't follow anybody's example."

He doesn't even seem to be listening.

"Enough exalting the proletariat," he says, preoccupied by the resistant bootlace. "We have too many post-Depression hymns to the unwashed."

"That's not how my book strikes early readers," I say, loudly. "At least not from the first advance quote just in." Pause. "From Thomas Mann."

This is my precious hoarded secret, known so far only to Crown Publishers and to my hair-cloud girl. But I am losing it at him. Car host or not, he's simply too insufferable.

And my missile hits home. He does look up from the boot lace—stares at me, imperious dark eyebrows raised askew.

"Mann!" he says. "How did you fall into such hands?"

"My editor sent him galleys."

"Our Herr Doktor Mann," Nabokov says, "is a plaster saint."

That leaves me speechless for a moment. And as if also struck dumb by such nastiness, the rain drumming on the car roof stops.

"I'm sorry you feel that way," I say.

Up front in the car, the click-click of the windshield wiper has stopped as well. The double silence is doubly unpleasant. Even Nabokov seems to sense that.

"Of course," he says. "Sometimes good books are liked by plaster saints. Let's not worry about it."

"I don't," I say, crisply.

But suddenly *he* seems to do just that. He drops the boot into his lap; fidgets in a way quite unlike him; rotates the car door crank to pull the window down; sticks out his jowly head; then resumes pulling at the boot lace with greater, tenser force.

"These laces," he says with much heavier, more guttural Slavic consonants, "I bought them in France. They never slip, never tear. But absolutely unobtainable here. Nowhere!"

"Really," I say, confused by the sudden shift in tone and subject.

"So these laces must fit the new boots I buy. I must make sure!"

He frowns at the sun rays now slanting into the car. Abruptly he speaks rapid Russian to his wife at the wheel. She turns around for a moment, looking at me as well as him. Has he asked her to help us out of the unpleasantness? The small talk he's swerved into hasn't cleared the air. His left hand dives into his back pants pocket, emerges with a crumpled bit of green, a veritable spitball of a dollar bill, which he drops into the half-unlaced boot on his lap. He mutters more rapid Russian at his wife. And—amazing—she throws over her shoulder a slim brown leather handbag. He catches it, struggles with the clasp, opens, takes from a purse two neatly folded dollar bills, drops them on top of the spitball in the boot.

"Did you notice?" he says, eyes blinking at me, "the meadow?"

"The meadow?"

"The meadow we passed a minute ago. They are already out. I think I have seen some *melissa* annettas."

As if desperate to make himself clear, he kicks at a pole sticking out from the jumble underfoot. Another kick, and from under a rag the other end of the pole juts out, with a net attached. A butterfly net.

"You mean," I say, "butterflies?"

He nods with a grateful smile even more uncharacteristic of him than his fidgeting.

"The catching is best right after rain. Their wings are sodden. So, if you will take a taxi after all . . ."

His hand dips into the boot, comes out toward me. He is offering all three dollar bills, spitball and neatly folded ones.

"For the fare. Please."

Astounded, I can only shake my head.

"Please! The least I can do. You can call a cab from there."

And, really, there is a phone booth by the Texaco sign. I hadn't even noticed that Madame had stopped the car at a filling station.

Waiting and standing, standing and waiting at the service station, I want to kick myself. What kind of absurd gallantry was that? Not accepting the Nabokov money just because Mrs. N. had chipped in? At least I should have first checked my cash situation! The dollar-ten in my pocket will never cover cab fare to the airport *and* back to town. And borrowing from my visitor—assuming she'll have anything to loan—what a way to greet her! So my single dime must be used to phone Eugene, to whose Volkswagen I must resort after all, an embarrassment in itself. But also a frustration that grows with every minute the son of a bitch keeps me waiting. Waiting while her plane prepares to descend.

Waiting at this service station here that seems so totally detached from the scenery all around. Waiting, exposed to a dissonance of smells: noxious burps from exhaust pipes between whiffs of wilderness, green, pungent, effervescent, a heady distraction from my wristwatch. For the first time I smell the Rockies freshly washed after a downpour. And I see them through the clear-scoured air as if for the first time: so unlike my childhood Alps, the Wasatch range towers unprettified, undotted by chalets, unpatched by hay fields. Nothing but sheer mountain, absolute out-and-out peremptory mountain, continuously and pungently wooded . . . steep aromatic jungles from which flare those crags miles high, monumental in their granite nakedness and with a savage exhalation of their own.

To all this the fill-her-up cowboys here pay no mind. Too busy kicking tires and chewing gum while the grease monkey checks out the carburetor. Away they zoom through their Texaco-Pepsi-Woolworth world, sealed off from leaf and boulder by some glass wall. The majestic contours on the horizon don't concern them. Beating the speed limit does. The highway is their true fatherland.

But having lost mine, ex-Austrian and very imperfectly Americanized, I am susceptible to a terrain so magnetically exotic yet still so undiscovered by its inhabitants. It pulls, it prickles when I'm already nervous, clock-wracked, cursing Eugene for still not showing up, less than twenty minutes before her landing time. It stings my skin, this landscape tingingly reborn through rain. It presses against me like some panoramic virgin, a barbarous beauty whose raw perfumes challenge me—to what? Deflower, decipher, debunk it? Or debunk my own excitement over it? Is Nabokov trapping its meaning right now with his butterfly net?

I can't figure it out. All I can do is wonder what's keeping cursed Eugene when her plane is due in quarter of an hour. And suddenly the merciless minute hand of my wrist points clear across the continent to way downtown in New York, some spring night in Manhattan earlier this year, right off the waterfront; me, also waiting in connection with her, also to a counterpoint of scents—acrid steam from the Chinese laundry on the street corner where we were supposed to meet and the salty-sweet emanation from the harbor's fouled brine. And, rising out of the dark billows, the statue brandishing her torch, titanic, marmoreal, like the Rockies now. Like the Rockies now, she clicked that night for the first time into hard-edged focus. I realized that she was angled away from me. As if I'd already lost my chance to be a gladiator in her arena . . . no wonder Kafka saw her holding high not a light but a sword. As if I'd fallen short of her adamantine expectation, heightened as it was by those acolytes of her imperative, those skyscraping exclamation marks thundering Power! Wealth! Supremacy! . . . I wasn't up to the size of her challenge—no more than I'm to that of the Rockies now. This formidable dare she was flinging at flotsam like me to come and get it, unhuddle from the dingy needy masses, throw off gooey bonds, shake loose, stand free, stand alone and apart, stand out, shoot it out, let the slobs rot in the dust, lay hold of your hunk of America, your great big gob of anything-goes, loot, fame, glamour, glory, Cadillacs, spotlights, Fred Astaire champagne, and Nobel Prizes. . . . That night I wasn't immune to the voltage of her hype, and I wasn't up to it either. Nor did I have Nabokov's seasoned irony as armor. Nor did it help that at least I'd done better than those Chinese laundresses sweating their lives away. No help at all. My failure was all the more insidious because I'd failed just outside the border of success.

Yes, failed. That's why I was standing there that night over half an hour early, before 9 PM though we weren't supposed to meet until half past. The jam sessions at the Jazz Cave, she'd told me, didn't heat up until ten. So why in hell was I so early? Basically because my damn novel had sold a miserable two thousand copies, not even quite, and *The New York Times* had deigned to take notice of it only on page 42 of the Book Review, where the words "extraordinary literary debut" blurred away into the litter of little university press ads. Had I sold ninety thousand and glistened on the front page, my dinner host earlier that night, Mr. Edward Dodd Jr. of Dodd, Mead Publishers, would not have said, Yale-brisk, "Sorry, must push off," the moment he was done with his sirloin. Even if the Thomas Mann quote had been in by then, it still wouldn't have saved me from the bum's rush. I did try to salvage some dignity with an offhand "Yeah, high time for me, too," and, while the Yalie back was turned (waving to some fat fellow nabob a few tables away), I reached for the velvety blue matchbox with fretted club lettering, palmed it in revenge—me, the alleged Brilliant Youth, beset by odors from the Chinese laundry and the brine bilge lapping the colossus while I waited for her.

Of course finding me waiting pleased her that night—I being usually the late one (and bound to be so again at the airport with the unspeakable Eugene still not in sight). What did not please her, what I had to account for, was my tie-and-jacket. *The Union League Club?* she said, curved my pinkie nicely at tea? I told her we never got to tea, Mr. Big Junior had to push off. Hm, she said, an extenuating circumstance—anybody hanging around the Union League was not fit to enter the Jazz Cave unless that person had been kicked out of the club. Had I been practically kicked out? Could I swear to that? I swore that I had been practically kicked out. All right, then, she said, but first she had to make me decent.

She pulled off my tie; raised her mane above her head; with amazing female dexterity she wound the tie several times around the mane before letting it drop; turned around to let me see: she now had a wonderfully riotous pigtail tied by a gypsy ribbon.

"Let's go," she said.

We went, me tieless, my hand crushing the matchbox in my pocket. Somehow we had told the siren in the harbor to bug off.

Bug off! is what she might well tell me now—I am braced—for arriving late at the airport. Eugene, believe it or not, doesn't screech up to the service station until ten to two, and then with an infuriating explanation: he had to give the car a good wiping, the rain always mottled the varnish rather badly.

"I appreciate that," I say through clenched teeth, "but let's get going."

"We'll be there in seven minutes," he says, screeching through puddles. And I would have let it go at that if the dense dawdling traffic hadn't stretched those minutes excruciatingly, and if furthermore I hadn't noticed that the freshly wiped polish of the car highlighted the ugly dent in the left fender, and that dainty Eugene had a red ketchup stain on his white shirt (my phone call must have caught him during one of his inevitable hamburger lunches), and if, finally, Eugene—already in sight of the airport but aware of the grimness of my silence—hadn't said by way of added apology, "Oh, uh, see, I wanted to make the car more presentable for a New York lady—"

"New York lady!" I burst out at him, "She's from the Bronx! We met at a City College dance—a subway ball, we called it! Who cares about a presentable car!"

He winces, wordless. But no time or patience to feel sorry. The airport bustle is upon us. He parks, still wincing.

I charge into the arrival lounge. Sure enough, the plane directory says Flight 27 from New York has landed and debarked. So she must be here. Yet she is not. Nowhere in the crowd milling along the luggage belt.

"Fred!"

Her voice. It's her. But how can it be her? No hair cloud? Gone, all that untamed magnificence? The silken wealth through which my fingers loved to luxuriate? Gone! Cut away into short curls not at all redeemed by the new bangs down her forehead.

Flabbergasting. I am transfixed, can't move. She has to run up to me for the kiss.

"My God!" I say. "What happened?"

"Same old thing," she says smiling, though without the mane it's not even her smile. "I get there first, and you come along in your good time."

"I mean, what happened to your hair?"

"I had it cut, obviously."

"My God."

"My God what?"

"I—I just didn't know that you were the beauty parlor type."

"I had it done in a tiny joint in the East Village! It's a Sicilian cut." She disengages herself. "What's the matter with you?"

What's the matter with *her*? That cut is an amputation, a slicing away on what my lips and hands loved to feast. And that's not the only thing. That coiffure represents an *embourgeoisement,* a betrayal of our rebel faith by her—her whom I've always admired for being the true practicing bohemian between us two. Till this moment, when I'm too hot to articulate my shock.

"I have to catch my breath," I say.

"Me, too, at such a welcome. Look at your face!"

"I think I'm entitled to be surprised—"

"At this beauty parlor vulgarity? Is that what you mean?"

"Well, it's quite a shift in taste—"

"Which you find unbearably offensive?"

A rubbing sound next to me. Eugene has discovered the ketchup stain on his shirt and is rubbing away at it like mad with his handkerchief. Obviously an attempt to absent himself from a most painful scene.

"Oh, this is Eugene Welka," I say. "And this is Marcia Cohen."

"Hello," she says, turning away, toward the luggage belt. "Well, there's my blue suitcase coming," she says. "Not a moment too soon. I'll take it right back to New York with me now. Nice to have met you, Mr. Welka."

"Now, wait!" I say.

"Wait for what?"

"You never mentioned this—in none of your letters. Not one word about this hair thing!"

"I had it done just the day before yesterday! I should have sent you a cable?"

"You could have mentioned somewhere in all the stuff you wrote me, you could have mentioned your intention—"

"I have to ask permission?"

"Well, some sort of notice—"

"I see. You have a veto right!"

"You don't understand—"

"Oh, yes I do! All too well!"

We stare at each other.

"Excuse me—excuse me, please!"

Eugene, ever serviceable, reaches for her blue suitcase as it glides by, can't get a good grip right away since the stain-rubbing handkerchief is still in his hand, does manage to lift the thing off the moving belt but in the effort stumbles against us so that I'm thrown against her.

Her slim back under the blouse feels as soft as ever. Her eyes, even without the mane, still have that lovely chocolate glow, especially now that they are brimming.

"I'm sorry . . ." I whisper.

"Oh, my Fritzl." Her lips move against my chest. "You're such an idiot."

May 1955

Best Man on the Baltic

Four in the afternoon, and the scenery cascading past the train window is quieting down. Dolomites and Swiss Alps have long subsided. Stuttgart with its patches of weathered bomb ruins has passed. Come and gone, the picturesque hills around Frankfurt, dollhouse window boxes dripping with flowers. Now there's just the blandness of Thuringia's neatly farmed low knolls flattening into the north German plain.

All quite orderly, unremarkable, placid, undiverting. No longer an excuse to ignore the notepad waiting for me on the compartment table. Not just waiting—waiting urgently as the Italo-Scandinavian Express rushes me, God knows how many miles per hour, toward tomorrow's Olympian encounter. Time to sketch out gambits and topics for a productive dialogue.

The scenery may no longer be a factor, but there's still the other distraction. The thing right next to my notepad: an oblong leaflet with the reverse schedule of this express; namely, the timetable of stops not going north, my current direction, but south, from Hamburg to Palermo. Instead of writing notes on my pad, I am staring at the thing.

If I had thrown it away before Stuttgart, I might already be at work now. But in Stuttgart Herr Vis-à-Vis entered the compartment to occupy the window seat opposite mine. Right away he suggested (as some blond Germans do) an *Obersturmbannführer* still at large. This one, though, is camouflaged by American accoutrements: tie of a somewhat flamboyant green; huge Hollywood sunglasses; jazzily tapered trousers. These trousers he subjects to a fastidious adjustment whenever he folds one knee tightly over the other. He pulls up the upper trouser leg just a bit so that its crease will not be tautened away, then lifts that leg, also just a bit, so that he can smooth the *lower* trouser leg to avoid wrinkling. God forbid.

His manners are conspicuously correct. He displayed them first in terms of cigarette etiquette. Stupid me forgot to ask the Times Rome Bureau (it arranged my transportation) for a *Nicht-Raucher*. Naturally I end up in a smoker car. Nevertheless Herr Vis-à-Vis hesitates after he's taken out his pack of Camels (another American accoutrement); he leans forward with a crisp, polite *"Erlaubt?"*; collects my *"Ja, bitte"*; gives an elegantly grateful little bow supplemented by a heel click (not easy when you're seated); lights up; and times his puffs so neatly that almost immediately after he's stubbed out, the train's stooped babushka'd Balkan slavey shuffles in, empties ashtray, wipes it clean. Voilà! Herr Vis-à-Vis as good as never blemished the gleam of the little glass bowl.

And the mineral water business. He buys one from the passing vendor, who places the bottle in the middle of the table between us. Instantly Herr Vis-à-Vis slides the bottle deep into his territory, with a mumbled "Pardon" for the border violation.

In sum, stringent propriety reigns in the compartment. This precludes any disorderliness on my part, such as opening the window and throwing out the Palermo train schedule. I could tear it into little pieces, but that would look like a tantrum to Herr Vis-à-Vis; to this very methodical sipper of mineral water whose sunglassed glance rests on me for never longer than three seconds while he puts lips to straw, then addresses himself for at least two minutes to the landscape in the window before turning back for another straw suck combined with the next three-second gander at me. Clockwork Teuton. The hell with him.

Another way would be to gradually crumple the Palermo schedule and casually drop it into the wastebasket. However, the basket—polished aluminum inside its wickerwork shell—is so shiny clean that even my squeamish fingers would have no problem reaching in, retrieving the crumple, and uncrumpling it again. So the Palermo schedule stays on the table, upstaging the notepad, which remains blank. Any impulse to get rid of that schedule founders on negatives, of which some may be ludicrous or neurotic or both. I simply must motivate myself more firmly with solid reasons for the riddance.

Okay: This schedule is there as the result of an imposition on which she has no right to insist. She started the problem with the letter she sent me care of the American consulate in Tunis. Of course back then, two weeks ago, no inkling that Palermo would ever constitute an imposition. Palermo was simply the destination of the ship I'd take the next day. The idea was to unwind in Sicily after North Africa; that is, after a mesmerizing but strenuous trek through Morocco and Algiers into Tunis, flooding my diary with raw impressions to be filtered one day through the typewriter. Palermo was to be a siesta until she walked off the gangplank of the S.S. *Andrea Doria* into my arms. Together we'd then journey toward our nicely orchestrated gigs; hers, "Salzburg Restaurants" for *Gourmet*; mine, "The Salzburg Festival Backstage" for *Holiday* magazine.

No imposition as yet. But in Tunis, this letter of hers ended with words which would give force to the imposition to come. Words still swirling through my Hamburg-bound train compartment right now.

> *It's been so long since you left New York back in April that I've begun to look with favor upon strangers—our compact, remember? So I can't wait to look upon you dockside, Palermo.*
>
> > *Cliché, and Immer noch Deine—Marcia.*

In our code "Cliché" means "I love you." But "Immer noch Deine" is a phrase she's picked up mysteriously somewhere, perhaps from some other German-language suitor? Some stranger looked upon favorably? In that case, all the more interesting that she would qualify "Immer Deine," a lover's sign-off, with "noch," changing the phrase from "Always yours" to "Always yours, still." Implying what? "Always yours, so far"? Suggesting an "always" subject to cancellation?

I just kept standing there, by the Tunis consulate's Service Desk, holding her letter. Finally I turned to my other mail, first to the red dépêche envelope on top. A cable from Francis Brown, editor of *The New York Times Book Review*. Would I interview Thomas Mann on the occasion of his eightieth birthday, 2,500 words, with a May 25 deadline?

Would I!

Wow. The *Times* message was a kick. But it was clouded by that damn ambiguity of her "always." An ambiguity, though, which still did not amount to an imposition.

Not until I got to Palermo did the imposition begin to materialize. True, it was helped along by the elusiveness of my interviewee. Phone calls to Mann's home at Lake Zurich produce only endless rings and irritated long-distance operators. My telegram to him also goes unanswered. The *Book Review* does respond promptly to my SOS, saying that the *Times* Rome Bureau has been instructed to assist in tracking down my Nobelist prey; followed by a second cable containing Mann's minibio in the form of his *Who's Who* entry "as background information." As if I needed a quick course in Thomas Mann basics. As if the *Book Review* were unaware of my previous writings on Mann's life and oeuvre, like my recent essay in *The Nation*, centering on a visit to Mann's house—not to speak of Mann's glowing praise for my last two novels. As if I'd been offered the interview for no very good reason.

But outannoying all this is her cable handed me by the concierge of the Hotel Palermo. It's this message that crystallized the imposition. It accounts for the perverse presence of the Hamburg-to-Palermo train schedule in my Palermo-to-Hamburg train. This message sticks in the memory as a small masterpiece of innuendo.

CONGRATS ON SUBLIME TIMES MANDATE PUN INTENDED NO CON-
GRATS FROM MAMA MORTON WHOM PHONED PER REQUEST MAMA
NOT THRILLED FOR BOY THAT HE INTERVIEW MANN MAMA THRILLED
FOR MANN THAT HE INTERVIEWED BY BOY TILL PALERMO IMMER
NOCH DEINE

MARCIA

Brava. Brilliant Mama's boy baiting. But nicer would have been a message saying, Forget going all the way down the Italian boot again now that you'll have to go all the way up for that sudden tight demanding deadline. Forget Palermo! Meet you in Zurich!

Of course she might consider this feeding the Mama's boy in me. Letting me welch on still another obligation to a relationship over ten years old. Except that Palermo never figured as an obligation but simply as a convenient meeting point that she has now pressed into an obligation entailing considerable strenuousness. She composed that cable fully aware that right after my Thomas Mann labors I'd have to tackle another rather formidable mission: the Salzburg Festival piece, due on July 1 as a nuanced seven-thousand-word parsing of the aesthetics-cum-politics of that highbrow jamboree, based on substantial pre-Fest interviews, research, etc. The travail involved appears to have escaped her. Ergo, it will have to be spelled out. Ergo, I will do so in a cable tomorrow suggesting, reasonably, that we meet in Salzburg itself, saving me the trip all the way to Palermo. Ergo, I should tear up the back-to-Palermo schedule.

Aiding my intention now is, of all people, the dining car steward of the express. He struts past, a *Kommandant* in black tie, summoning passengers with a stentorian baritone with bilingual imperiousness. *"Erstes Abendessen! First dinner sitting . . . Erstes Abendessen! First dinner sitting!"*

Promptly Herr Vis-à-Vis screws the lid back on his half-drunk mineral water bottle, uncrosses his legs. As soon as he leaves for his *Abendessen* I'll do my tearing up in private, proceed to formulate my Mann questions on the notepad, following which (consonant with my reward system—food only after work) the second dinner sitting should be very enjoyable.

No such luck.

Herr Vis-à-Vis remains vis-à-vis, right in his seat. From his left jacket pocket he produces a well-ironed plaid handkerchief; from his right pocket, a phallic shape wrapped in silver foil. Delicately he peels back a bit of foil; reveals a slim wurst slenderly veined with fat; takes a petite bite; chews with small discreet jaw movements; dabs mouth with well-ironed plaid handkerchief; and, after each swallow, casts a quick glance at me as if to ascertain that the daintiness of it all is appreciated.

It is not. Once more the bastard has made me feel uncomfortable about a gross act like ripping up a train schedule. But why rip in his sight? Here's an idea that should have occurred to me earlier. There are secluded venues on board.

Well, it turns out that both W.C.s, on opposite ends of the car, are locked with red *Besetzt* signs. They stay *Besetzt,* no matter how often I commute between them.

Back to the compartment, where Herr Vis-à-Vis has progressed to dessert. He holds a chocolate bar wrapped in a paper napkin so white that it seems to light up the dusk of Niedersachsen, through which our train is clattering. I resume my seat. Herr Vis-à-Vis is nibbling on the chocolate bar as daintily as he did on the wurst, interspersing tiny nips with brief glances in my direction, glances impeccably incidental, the very opposite of crude gapes. Yet they now also appear to take in the still intact Palermo schedule on the table.

This stimulates an angry question. Why did I bother with that schedule in the first place? After all I picked it up at the *Informazione* of Palermo's Central Railroad Station, precisely the place that supplied an added reason *not* to return to Palermo. It was at the station's post-and-telephone office that I did all my frenzied long-distance phoning (charged to the *Times* Rome Bureau) not just to Mann's house in Zurich but to his publishers, Knopf in New York, S. Fischer in Frankfurt, to Mann's daughter Elisabeth Mann-Borghese, in Fiesole, who was always out the first few times I called her. When I finally got her in, pay dirt: she had the itinerary of Papa's East German lecture tour. I reached him in Weimar, cried *Bitte schön! New York Times! Deadline!,* nailed down a date for tomorrow, May 18, in Travemünde. And Travemünde is the rub—the clincher that makes tearing up the Palermo schedule a perfectly logical act. Travemünde happens to be on the Baltic coast, way up north near the Danish border, much further distant from Sicily than Mann's home at Lake Zurich, hence requiring much more traveling back and forth, were I really to meet her in Palermo.

In other words, were I to give in to what I'm certain now is the demand implicit in her Palermo expectation: Stop using "sublime mandates" as excuses! Stop welching on our understanding! Stop being doubly spoiled by Mama and success! Stop regressing into the parental nest on 151st Street between your fancy acts abroad! What are you, some kind of veteran wunderkind? It won't wash anymore, this stance of the inspired innocent who must be sheltered from the rigors of maturity and commitment! How long are you going to hide in your glorified kindergarten where you neither drink nor smoke nor drive nor even open a checking account nor establish a pad of your own nor share a joint nor picket the Pentagon nor acknowledge any responsibility that defines coming of age, be it rebellious or Babbity or marital or whatever! Get serious—and that includes us! Stick to your promise of Palermo! Stop the kid stuff or I'll stop being *Immer noch Deine!*

Those are her arguments, spoken or unspoken, and they are as ingenious as they are unjust. God damn it, I find myself rehearsing them instead of jotting down questions for tomorrow. My delinquency intensifies with every mile-devouring whistle of the locomotive. And the blank white void of the notepad confronts me very brightly now, thanks to Herr Vis-à-Vis. A few minutes ago, after he finished his wurst in the dusk, he rose to his feet, heels together, pointed to the overhead lamp with a basso *"Erlaubt?"*; acknowledged my nod with a bow; turned on the light switch; sat down, adjusting trouser legs minutely; unfolded the *Frankfurter Allgemeine Zeitung;* vanished behind the headline *"Adenauer Angriff im Bundestag."* But every three minutes sharp, he lowers the paper to turn pages and get in his inevitable ogle at me, never more than a punctiliously casual second long.

Meanwhile the electric glare seems to have stirred the Palermo train schedule alive. Its smudged lettering vibrates with the increased speed of the train. It positively sizzles with her injustice. Would a heedless kiddie of a lover spend more than two years—longer than some marriages last—on *Asphalt and Desire*—my novel about a brilliant aspiring pungent young woman—*her*—who takes on the Manhattan wilderness? A book admired publicly by an Aldous Huxley and a Thomas Mann, not to speak of the Book-of-the-Month Club, which made it an A book, just short of a Main Selection? That I devoted all of *Asphalt and Desire* to Marcia, dedicated it to Marcia—isn't that serious enough? No, not for Marcia it isn't, not as long as I betray a shred of boyishness.

Whereas I, by contrast, I adore her mixture of keen ambitious blue-stocking and enchanting child. The quicksilver moods turning her from seductive, ravishing, silken-thighed to puppy-pouncing to dagger-tongued. Year after year my infatuation deepens into helpless love. I adore the coltish little leaps that are her running, how she bends her exquisite little nostrils away, into a grotesque angle, so I won't be bothered by the exhalation of her cigarette smoke. At the bon voyage party she put together for me just before this trip, I loved the way she came out of her kitchen, her lips smiling because she knew she was bringing me a surprise treat while her long-lashed lids were compressed shut, her eyebrows drawn down into a baby grimace because she couldn't bear to look, let alone smell, the Camembert oozing so rankly.

And last year in Merano, joining my talk with Ezra Pound, she suddenly zinged that Mussolinist with the most polished barbs, only to tumble an hour later down an orchard fence because she became so Bronx-excited over plucking a peach fresh off a tree. I don't know which I adored more.

I even adore her idiosyncratic short-temperedness. She makes such a wondrously sore loser. Flubs a tennis return, throws the racket down with both hands in a tot's tantrum, then straightens up to look down her Hedy Lamarr nose at me with Dorothy Parker gall: "Proud of his tony forehand, is he, our muscle-happy baker boy?"

This duality of hers I find no less enchanting during our "night school" sessions in her Washington Place apartment; when, with her absolute verbal pitch, she de-purples and disciplines my prose before typing it up for whatever editor; when she has me decipher Rimbaud and Verlaine (she had six years of French, I none at Food Trades Vocational High, none as CCNY chem major); when, during her complex tutorials the kitten tongue licks out to moisten the cherub lips. Who cares at such moments who the child is and who the adult?

Well, she does. She frets, she's furious almost each time I kiss her cheek instead of her mouth. I'm still infantilizing her! After eleven years! Refusing to act grown up and treat as her as a grown-up twenty-seven-year-old woman! An accusation that's begun to sound more and more like a complaint that I refuse to make an honest woman out of her. Of course she'd never stoop to the phrase. Yet the symbolic resonance of

"Palermo" is such that meeting her there would presumably be a nice step toward that nice burgerish estate.

Isn't that what the "Palermo" issue is all about?

Well, sitting in the harsh electric light of my Hamburg-bound compartment, I'm starting to wonder about something. I wonder whether I shouldn't calm some of her worries over my inability to grow up. Perhaps I should assure her that I have no trouble acting adult when it's *my* turn to look with favor upon strangers. That happens, per our contract, only when I'm not in New York, traveling alone. But when it happens, it happens in quite a grown-up way. Perhaps I should get a sworn deposition from Edwina—or was it Angelina?—anyway, that Irish architectrix, a deposition certifying my mature deportment during a tango on the dance floor of a Tangier nightspot just a few weeks ago; my adult foresightedness with which I realized that our cheek-to-cheek might dislodge her tiny pearl earrings; my adult prudence with which I prevented them from dropping on the floor by nibbling them conscientiously off her ears in order to suck them for safekeeping into my mouth; my very adult sense of equity with which I then had her reclaim her rightful property with her tongue.

Your classic Mama's boy doesn't engineer such interludes. But, licensed by our compact though they might be, I could never mention them to her. Nor should I dwell on them now even if they provide a certain vengeful pleasure. Better to keep my mind on what I've still failed to do for tomorrow. That notepad remains stark blank. Next to it, on the table, the back-to-Palermo schedule simmers and trembles though the train has slowed into a smoother ride. We are pulling into Hanover, last stop before Hamburg. Early tomorrow morning a short rail trip will take me from there to Travemünde, to the interview for which I have yet to jot down a single solitary goddamn question.

By now the blankness of the notepad has become intolerable. Since I can't bear to look at it, I turn it upside down. Underneath, unfortunately, lies that irritating *Times Book Review* cable with the Mann minibio. To goad my truant mind I force myself to read those data. Nothing new or helpful whatsoever—until a number flares out. 1905. Thomas Mann married Katherine Pringsheim in 1905. He was thirty then. Exactly my age now.

The bio drops from my hand on top of the Palermo schedule. Both sheets twitch in sync as the train jolts to a halt in Hanover station. Herr Vis-à-Vis, already on his feet, scoops from the luggage rack his very American attaché case; snaps case open; stows precisely folded *Frankfurter Allgemeine Zeitung;* snaps case closed; turns toward me at attention; combines farewell bow with a finally frank, long, searching glance; walks out—only to collide at the compartment threshold with the conductor walking in.

An exchange of *"Ach, Pardon!"* . . . *"Ach, Entschuldigung!"* Whereupon the conductor, who turns out *not* to be the conductor because his cap has a stationmaster's red visor—the stationmaster, then, comes straight toward me.

"Herr Morton?"

His right hand salutes, his left holds out a taped-together folded yellow sheet. Tape peeled away, it unfolds into a telegram forwarded by the *Times* Rome Bureau.

From her!

EMBARK TOMRROW CABLE ME C/O SS ANDREA DORIA IF PALERMO MEET STILL FEASIBLE STOP RAN INTO DENVLIND WHO JUST FINISHED PROOFING TRANSLATION MANNS KRULL STOP DENVLIND SENDS REGARDS TO MAESTRO PLUS REGARDS FROM AT CORE SENSITIVE SPINSTER

IMMER NOCH DEINE

MARCIA

"Danke!" I stammer at the Red Visor and plump down into my seat to deal with this ambush. To sort it out.

And, amidst the station's *"Träger!"* shoutings, the luggage thumpings, the loudspeaker blarings, some sense begins to emerge. It makes sense that the *Times* Rome Bureau forwarded the cable not to my Travemünde hotel (unknown to them since Frau Mann arranged my lodging) but to the train for which the *Times* Bureau had procured ticket and seat reservation. DENVLIND makes easy sense because that's Denver Lindley, who edited my *Asphalt and Desire* at Harcourt, Brace and whom she got to know at the "Asphalt" book party. And since Denver came to translate *Confessions of Felix Krull,* Mann's latest novel, at least partly through my mediation, PROOFING TRANSLATION makes sense no less than she and Denver running into each other, what with his Plaza lunches and her meetings at the *Gourmet* magazine office in the Hotel Plaza penthouse.

As for AT CORE SENSITIVE SPINSTER, after a minute even that cryptic mischief makes sense. That's her send-up of Mann's comment on *Asphalt and Desire.* I still know by heart (who can blame me?) his praise for my "poignant and accomplished portrait of a tough, cynical but at core sensitive girl." And come to think of it, this very telegram has proved Mann right: she—my model for that girl—has become sensitive at last to the questionable feasibility of Palermo in view of all the travel involved for me. So her SPINSTER dig should be forgiven.

Fondly forgiven and fondly disregarded. A conclusion that grows clear as the wheels below me begin to click slowly against rails. The Italo-Scandinavian Express has begun to move out of Hanover station. Yes, fondly disregarded, that SPINSTER nudge, because what makes most sense about her telegram is the aptness of my receiving it on a train. I never really got off the one that rolled me out of Vienna in 1939. New York did not end my emigration. The parent house on 151st Street is not—as she thinks—a childhood nest on which I'm fixated. It's a way station for a traveler neither fit nor fated to be tied down, who'd lose his purpose if he reached a terminus. Let Americans keep rushing after fulfillments ever receding. I know that I'm beyond arrival. My mission may be to plumb the mirage of destination, the vainness and vanity of haven and home.

Food for discussion with her. Delicate discussion. But not in Palermo, whose infeasibility I'll cable her tomorrow, first thing after the interview.

Meanwhile I can tear up the Palermo schedule. I can and I do. I actually tear it up. It's cheap paper, ripping quite easily. Piece after piece flutters down into the wicker-shell wastebasket. Too bad Herr Vis-à-Vis is no longer here to watch my little spectacle. I'm no sooner finished than the stooped babushka'd Balkan slavey shuffles in to remove the scraps.

Faster and faster click the wheels. And behold! My notepad begins to fill up with questions for tomorrow.

•   •   •

"You mind," says Thomas Mann, "staying out here for a few minutes?"

"Out here" is the boardwalk of Travemünde, which rims a stretch of Baltic coast. On the beach three children are tumbling around a soccer ball. No one else disturbs a vastness of gray sea, white sand, blue sky. It is just after 9 AM, the time set for our meeting but too early for most ocean lovers and also for chambermaids to finish their morning chores. Some tidying up still needs to be done in the parlor of the Mann quarters at the Hotel Kurhof. Frau Dr. Mann, firmly in charge of setting the stage for her star, has asked us to enjoy the fresh air just for a little while: she'll call us when the suite is ready "for you two to do your duty for *The New York Times.*"

"I don't mind at all," I say. "That bracing ocean air!"

"A breath of youth for me," Dr. Mann says. "When I was small we used to summer here. On this very beach. It makes one feel young. And when I feel young, I get loquacious."

He has an august way of being impish. Draws himself up very straight, lowers his still dark eyebrows into a near frown, yet his hand passing across the gray mustache does not quite conceal the grin. "This," he says, "is a warning."

I'm so pleased to be joshed by him, I dare josh back.

"No, it isn't," I say. "For me it's a promise."

But the joshing is over. He points, serious. "That boy. The dark-haired one, running after the ball. That's me, seventy years ago. Running on sand with wet feet. You see him?"

"Yes."

"Running with that saltwater prickle between the toes. Exulting!" He rests both hands on the railing, muses into the expanse. "Sun and air and openness . . . the reprieve of it."

The dark-haired boy has thrown himself down on the soccer ball, the other two throwing themselves on top of him, all three screaming. So I'm not sure I heard right.

"Did you say 'reprieve'?"

He nods into the expanse.

"Before going back into the city. Having to bend over schoolwork again and walk nicely in stiff shoes."

He turns away from the ocean, back to me. "I suppose that comes in mind because we are on a reprieve right now." Again, his grin half disguised as a frown. "You heard my wife. We'll have to go in soon, to do our duty."

"Oh, I hope it's not going to be so onerous!"

"No, no. Of course not." He even pats me reassuringly on the arm. But the frown is still there, with the smile gone. "I just wish I could do now what I did then. My discreet little ritual. Just before we went back to the city."

He stops, turns back to the beach again, looks at the boys, who've suddenly abandoned their soccer ball. All three are bent over, legs apart, hands flailing away into a dune in a fury of hole digging, creating three little separate sandstorms.

He keeps watching them, silent.

"Discreet little ritual?" I say, as unproddingly as possible.

"Oh yes, the ritual." He turns back to me. "Yes, always on our last day here. That's when I filled my beach shoes with sand. But I made sure nobody was watching. And back in Lübeck, I hid them under my vacation gear in the attic. And when the teachers became nasty and the discipline oppressive, that was my solace up there. When nobody was looking, I took the watering can for the window boxes. And I put it under the faucet for a minute. And then I tiptoed up to the attic and poured some water on my beach shoes. Then I pressed my face against the moist sand. And all the wild scents of summer ran through me. Seaweed and salt and sweat, heady and careless. Marvelously delinquent."

"My God," I say, much struck. "I am thirty now. But I wish I had your beach shoes."

"I suppose that's what started my fascination with beaches," he says. "Their invitation to licentiousness."

"*Meine Herren! Fertig!*" Frau Mann calls. "Gentlemen! All set!"

He nods, waves back to her. But it's a wave with a slow back-and-forth motion, implying "Thank you. In a minute."

Which is great for me. I don't want this momentum interrupted.

"Licentiousness!" I say. "My God. Forgive me, but I can't help thinking now of your most famous story—*Death in Venice*! Is that what you meant by its beach setting?"

"*Death in Venice?*" He turns away from the beach, starts walking toward the hotel. "Oh, I don't know. I don't know what meanings I had in mind then. I try not to be too cunning about meanings when I work on something. It only gets in the way of the flow." He stops walking. I stop, too. "Looking back at that story," he says, "of course, licentiousness explodes in it. Even the role it played in my own life, well, a certain incontinence emerges there, too—no, no, please!"

He waves away the notepad I've taken out.

"No, this isn't for the interview. The interview will be literary. This is personal."

Again he pats my arm, this time with a plea I must reluctantly obey. Back goes the notepad into my pocket.

"Very well, then, *Death in Venice,*" he continues. As he pronounces that dark phrase there reappears—to my surprise—his underhanded grin. "I finished that story before the war—" He interrupts himself with another wave at Frau Dr. Mann, still standing at the hotel entrance some sixty yards away. Another slow up-and-down wave signifying "We're coming, but not just yet."

He turns back to me.

"Did I say, just before the war?"

"Yes. That would be World War One."

"Of course. I finished that story—it must have been 1912. But the incontinence involved came later. Let's see . . . ." As he contemplates how much later, the incongruous smile plays again across the gray mustache. "Oh, 1923 or thereabouts. By then I was paterfamilias of a huge brood, a wife and six children no less. Responsible for them all yet suddenly without adequate means to support them. Inflation, you know. The estate I'd inherited, the money from *Buddenbrooks* and so on, all melted away in that awful abrupt runaway inflation. Overnight we became villa proletariat. In fact, I used that term in a story—"

"Yes! Isn't that in—in 'Disorder and Early Sorrow'?"

"Very good. Thank you, my attentive reader. So, being villa proletariat, I must be very controlled about indulgences. Pleasures and amenities had to be sacrificed so that we could afford our daily bread and the basic upkeep of our house. I had to economize everywhere—"

He stops. His grin now is not underhanded but outright.

"You didn't expect to be bored like this, by money matters, did you?"

"Bored?" I say. "Fascinated! By anything you connect to *Death in Venice!*"

"Well, the connection is at hand. In the midst of all this scrimping, a cable from New York. Alfred Knopf is offering two thousand dollars for English-language rights to *Death in Venice*. Two thousand dollars. Do you know what that sum meant in Germany, at that time?"

"A fortune?"

"Well, not quite. Actually, that's the point. A *small* fortune. It would keep the wolf from the door for half a year. Maybe a little more. Enough to celebrate a little. My wife—she is waving again—I remember her breaking out a bottle of Mosel wine that night. But before that I took a happy walk. I passed my tobacconist—or rather, I didn't pass him. I went in. And this I hadn't done for over a year because I simply couldn't bear to smoke the cheap stuff within my means. But now I went in. And I bought a beautiful Havana cigar. I can't remember exactly how much it cost. Probably I don't want to, it was so irresponsibly expensive. Probably it burned up too much of the precious Knopf advance. But I do remember how delicious it was just to free my Havana from its paper sheath. And having it, bare, in my hand. And taking out my cigar cutter, which had stayed fallow in my pocket for so long, to make the cut. And then— the first puff . . . the magic taste, the luscious, sinful, wanton pleasure spreading into the palate, the throat, the nostrils . . . I've never savored the like of it before or since. Every time I remember it, I say, 'Thank you! Thank you, *Death in Venice!*'"

He watches me absorbing all this. Amusement moves in the labyrinthine wrinkles around his eyes. Then a brisk tap on my shoulder.

"Reprieve over. We had better go in."

Together we walk toward the hotel.

"Speaking of cables from New York," I say. "Funny thing, but I received one from New York just yesterday, with a message for you, and it also involves Knopf. I'm to tell you that Denver Lindley just finished proofing the *Felix Krull* translation for Knopf and that he sends his respectful best regards."

"You know Mr. Lindley?"

"I took the liberty of recommending him as translator—"

"Oh yes, yes of course—you see how old I'm getting? Yes, and he was the editor of your novel about that girl. He sent me the galleys with your compliments. He cabled you from New York?"

"No, actually the girl did—the girl of the novel. She'd just run into Denver."

We are at the hotel entrance. Dr. Mann takes his wife's arm, is about to enter with her. But he stops, turns around to me.

"Did you say, the girl in your novel? This fierce creature? She cabled you from inside the novel? That's more interesting than the translation news."

"No, I'm sorry, what I meant to say, what I should have said"—I try not to sputter—"the real-life girl on whom the novel is based, *she* sent the cable."

Dr. Mann and Frau Dr. Mann look at each other, both smiling. No doubt at the foolish color in my cheeks.

"And she also sends her best regards," I say, as evenly as I can manage.

"The girl of your novel," Dr. Mann says. "Then I know her, through your pages. A very interesting young woman. Why, in that case, send her my own best regards."

"Mine, too," says Frau Dr. Mann.

"Thank you, I will! I'll see her next week in Palermo—I'll tell her!"

They've walked into the hotel lobby, arm in arm. The bellhop who opened the door for them holds it open for me, too. And holds it open. And holds it open. Keeps holding it open. I'm still fixed to the ground.

I'll see her next week in Palermo.

I need a few moments to cope with what I've just said. With what I've just committed to, in front of such a witness.

My God, the world's best writer. Virtually my best man.

And then I do follow him inside.

1960

Christmas with the Rothschilds

Sometime somehow I've run away from my parents' Vienna home, strayed far into some strange grown-up land, some neon-lit seacoast resort where I can skate to tango music long after say-good-night time but when I do turn in the skates stick to my feet, I must wear them even in bed, and so I head home again in the subway, awkward with those blades on my shoes, but I manage to hobble up the station stairs, and sure enough there's the Thelemanngasse, our little cobbled street, with my tutor, Herr Goldner, waiting to forgive my long foreign truancy as adult, to unlace my skates and teach me childhood ways again, how to greet my mother with *"Küss die Hand, Mutti,"* how to shrink to a size small enough for me to ride on Papa's shoulders again, and smaller still so that once more I can slither under the dinner table and up into my seat without moving the chair, even how to keep Mutti from mixing yucky cough syrup into my farina by choking back my cough and so prove that my cold is over. But she insists because I can't help coughing anyway.

Coughing, I blink my eyes awake.

To see . . . is this reality?

On my night table, three tissue boxes to select from and cough into. This might be reality because I remember them from last night—mentholated tissue, rose-scented tissue, plain tissue, all three encased in sky blue velvet patterned with golden fleurs-de-lis. Next to them, this morning's papers—*Le Figaro, International Herald Tribune,* London *Times. Voom,* the door opens, and glory be, in pads barefoot this pretty one in tapered slacks and slim-tailored jacket, sunburst of hair still voluptuously unkempt, waving a pair of boots.

"Think I can wear them in a Rolls?"

I stare at her. Marcia, my wife, discussing Rolls-Royce attire. This is indeed reality. Château Mouton. We Mortons are spending Christmas with the Rothschilds.

"I mean, mud boots on that Persian rug he's got in the car? He said we'd be tramping through the vineyard in the rain—"

"God!" I reach for my clothes. "I'm late!"

She stops my hand. "You stay put. You're still coughing."

"My fever's gone, I'm okay."

"You're going nowhere. Not in this freezing rain."

"But it's the Christmas wine tasting—"

"What'll you taste with? Your drink-nothin' know-nothin' palate? With a cold yet!"

"But it's the experience, for the book—"

"So use mine. Anyway, Sire would just laugh at you. He's onto your dirty little temperance secret. Shut up. Bye."

She bends down to kiss.

"You'll catch my cold."

"Your common cold, peasant? Classy broad like me in a swank joint like this, I don't stoop to such bugs."

"Yeah, but you're embarrassed about the boots."

"Just for that I'm gonna wear them! Let 'em ruin the carpet! Drink lots of fluid!"

"You already had breakfast?"

"Babysitter fed me. He's outside with that wagon. Fifty varieties of brunch waiting for you."

"God. When I can't eat in the morning."

"Your problem. Drink fluids. Gotta get ready for Sire."

And she's gone.

"Sire" is Baron Philippe de Rothschild; "Babysitter," our personal butler. Just two of several code words she and I have invented. When we're by ourselves we play duh, punks-in-the-palace. We're resolutely (if covertly) irreverent in order not to be thrilled by the deluge of opulence here.

But I can tell from her hyper manner that she's thrilled just the same. Me, too. In the teeth of my lefty conscience. Is the deluge drowning my character? Resist!

Resist Babysitter right now. He's coming through the door (granted permission to do so by the push of the ivory button on my night table), rolling toward my bed a wheeled three-tiered vista of silvery kettles, embossed copper pots, chrome-belled chafing dishes, Sèvres plate, God knows what other too much of a muchness. His white gloves set off his black blazer and he's all solicitously stooped decorum even while smelling faintly of some no doubt impeccable vintage. The baroness told us his name is Dupont but to Marcia he's Babysitter because he reminds her of the Bronx one who sat her on her parents' night out—the Polish janitor snoring on the couch in a stench of schnapps. Of course, in contrast to the rank Polisher, Dupont babysits us with the most tender respect. Bows wine-scented little bows as he points out to me the many prodigies offered by his wagon.

"Eggs, Mist Morton? Two minutes, or three? Water is already cooking. . . . No? Ah, you wish hard. I have fresh hard right here. . . . No? I can also make poachèd? . . . Or coddlèd? . . . Or sunny sy? . . . No? Maybe café first. American? . . . Turk? . . . Café Viennoise! The baroness say Mist Morton is from Vienne! . . . No? Not even Café Viennoise? . . . So tea. Ceylon? . . . Earl Grey? . . . Andorra mint? . . . Camille? . . . not all here, but I can fetch—No? No teas. But then, what beverage with the croissants? . . . No croissants! Perhaps *pain au chocolat*? Or this sandwich *jambon*?"

"Please—no, thank you very much," I say. "But is that juice?"

"*Ceci*? Yes, jews, very healthy! Orange jews, fresh squeeze. Or apple? Or grape also fresh—orange! *Merci bien!* Very good! Perhaps with the juice, erring, like the English. We have in the Frigidaire kipper erring, I can heat in three minutes. . . . No? Ah."

An almost fed up "ah." Perhaps this was one negation too many.

Crisply he closes shut the cap of the orange jews bottle, snaps erect from his bowings, severely adjusts the glasses on his nose. White gloves or no white gloves, he's turned into Mr. Simonson, principal of Food Trades High, frowning at my torn baker's apron. Tough tittie. In the face of this sybaritic onslaught I must maintain my integrity: no breakfast. But it's an uncomfortable impasse. Of which the phone relieves me. Marcia calling from her room next door.

"Fred, I meant to mention—"

"*Ma chère,*" I breathe theatrically into the mouthpiece, then turn to Babysitter, pointing at the receiver, "Will you excuse me? Thank you so much for the juice."

"What?" her voice shoots out of the earpiece.

I wait till the door closes on the white gloves.

"That was just to get him out of the room. He wouldn't stop with the dishes."

"But you're drinking fluids?"

"Yes, yes, big glass of orange jew."

"Good. I forgot to tell you. You'll have to wrap our gifts this morning."

"*Me?*"

"Well, I can't do it, with this wine tasting. The gifts should be under the tree before four."

"But I'm so inept at these things."

"So make it charmingly inept. And drink up the whole jew!"

Click.

Like a good boy I drink up the whole jew, in bed. Then off to my bath-room, to use a select few of its myriad marmoreal facilities. Then I walk into Marcia's room, bon-jour the two maids implausibly ironing the fresh silk sheets spread on her bed, find the blue gift box in her big suitcase, return to my room of our guest apartment where another pair of implausible maids plies irons on *my* bed. I bon-jour them, stutter in my pitiable mongrel French (its New Yawk twang on top of an Austrian accent al-ways breaks up Marcia) to assure said maids that they are not disturbing me, do carry on, *s'il vous plaît.*

They do carry on, undisturbingly, their very vacuum cleaner muffled pianissimo. To that discreet sibilance I sit down at the Empire desk, red lacquer and gold scrolls. Time to start applying myself to what's in the blue box—the gifts that are our attempt to cope with a brute problem: What can one possibly bring a Rothschild for Christmas?

Well, one brings (a) a seven-franc gift certificate from Les Halles, good for a blue-plate special of *pot au feu*. That's for Sire: he once mentioned that as a child he'd been tantalized by the smell of *pot au feu* coming from the gatekeeper's house but never ever tasted even a spoonful since no Rothschild chef would condescend to such a plebeian stew. And as another Christmas present one brings to Château Mouton (b) the Upper East Side section of the Manhattan subway map, laminated and framed like a historic plaque. That's for the baroness because she'd let it drop that during her New York years as Hattie Carnegie's top designer she'd always meant "to adventure" into the subway but never managed to encounter a station when she had the time.

Joke presents for people who already own everything serious. Presents with an egalitarian innuendo; a bow, however subtle, to one's social conscience. Important, because of this queer turn in my career. Who would have thought that national magazine editors would be just fascinated when I ask for a Lipton tea bag to go with the rarefied Brie at La Côte Basque? Would suspect that my frayed pants cuffs might be an esoteric fashion statement? Would overlook my pinko novels together with all other expressions of a prole soul? It's the combination of Continental background and fancy prose style that hornswoggles them. Suddenly I've become the man to unlock the mysteries of *raffiné* high life to their readers. The dear idiots have been throwing champagne jobs at seltzer me which seltzer me has fielded, baroque expense accounts and all, as a sort of wicked joke. As a silken lucrative peccadillo to fund my return to seriousness . . . And so here I am in the château, wrapping our Christmas presents to the Rothschilds, struggling with Santa Claus paper, not even too ineptly.

But not too happily either. Why? A pang in the prole soul? Yes, but there's also something else . . . there's a longing, a downright pining for my parents. Curiously, not the Vienna *Papa und Mutti* of my dream but my current parents in New York, in fact, my precisely current parents on Christmas Eve.

Or maybe that's not too curious after all. Wrapping presents now in Mouton naturally conjures last Christmas Eve, when I was also wrapping presents, not for any Rothschilds but, on my parents' behalf, for Ramona, Juanita, Anna, Ophelia, Carmen et alia—Papa's Hispanic crew in his workshop at 800 Eighth Avenue. But why this sudden yen to be there with them now? I didn't enjoy it all that much at the time, last year. In fact, I remember that I resented being shanghaied into this wrapping thing by my brother. Usually that's his Christmas Eve chore, Henry being junior to me and much handier. But last year he called, please, big favor, sub for him at 800 Eighth, force majeure, Christmas party invitation from his Queens College dean, as fledgling instructor he couldn't ignore that summons.

Now, I also had better things to do with my time than cover geegaws with gaudy paper. My summons was to my daily labors, which haven't gone entirely unrecognized in the world of letters. But Henry is such a damnably nice bright guy. Hard to pull rank on him, nor could I last year. So, instead of refining nuances in my manuscript, I was squirming behind Papa's desk on Eighth Avenue, embroiled with scissors and tape. And to me, now similarly occupied at Château Mouton, those hours last year take on such a wistful warmth. What I was wrapping then, gifts for Papa's nine señoritas, those things were really jokes nicer and better than the subway map or the seven-franc gift certificate. Those things were napkin rings shipped to Papa from Vienna—part of the decimated inventory of his factory commandeered by the Nazis and restituted in shambles after the war. Of course, napkin rings are not optimal presents for barrio girls innocent of dinner parties. But exile has taught Papa to improvise. Buying, on top of nine Christmas bonuses, nine Christmas gifts substantial enough to come from the boss—*viel zu teuer.* Much too expensive. Yet each Christmas his paternalism demands a gesture beyond extra bills in the pay envelope. So last year he reinvented the napkin rings as nice bracelets for the girls. By day's end nine bright braided brass hoops gleamed on nine dusky wrists. And the facts that all hoops were identical made nine faces glow with a sense of privileged membership in an exclusive club.

And now, twelve months later, I find myself wishing I'd be part of all that again, in Room 211 of 800 Eighth Avenue, wrapping away at Papa's current reinventions; hearing from across the narrow hall, muted, mystically obscure, the German of my parents' voices as they fix up the stockroom for the big Christmas lunch; hearing behind me, on the other side of the workshop partition, the girls whispering in Spanish while they thread nylon filaments through little holes in fake pearls. And if, say, Juanita would come out from behind the partition on her way to the restroom (the only excuse Papa accepts), what fun to slam shut the open desk drawer on which I work to hide the nature of this year's gift. And how I'd love to see again today the other objects rattling in the desk drawer, those buttons declaring "I love Elvis" or "Sinatra forever" or "Tito Puente!," all collected by Papa every morning to be returned at the end of the workday: Papa's precaution against fan arguments' disrupting attention to the job.

Now this year my brother will once more sit at that desk. And me, four thousand miles away at Château Mouton, I wonder what in hell is now rattling in the desk drawer of Room 211, what new Elvis buttons Henry will be guarding, what Christmas ingenuities of Papa's he might be wrapping. . . . But at least I do know exactly what other largesse he'll dispense in Papa's name: those little bundles of silver-foiled Belgian pralines in gold nets, heaped on Papa's desk. This never changes from year to year, having become a tradition: sweets to be handed out to a rather prodigious parade of neighbors. Nothing like Christmas in this New-York-nutty, marvelously dissolute building where Papa runs his correct little Middle European boot camp. Take Akinu, the Japanese glassblower, who'll be dropping up from his ground-floor store. His specialty is tiny gossamer figurines. But admire them closely—they turn into Kama Sutra couples in full hump. A hot ticket with the Madison Square Garden crowd from across the street, the bookies and scalpers who like to dangle these diaphanous fornications above the dashboard to warm up whatever doll they're taking on a ride. For us, at Frank Morton Costume Jewelry, however, Akinu has a different offering at Christmastide. He'll bring a little translucent Star of Bethlehem, receiving in return his Belgian pralines.

And dear Mrs. Laseur from upstairs will make her Christmas appearance, holding out a delightfully aromatic sachet my mother will exclaim over and use to scent her clothes closet and which will confirm her brave belief that the young ladies of the Laseur Dress Shop on the third floor really do sew blouses. Papa, who sometimes works late, long after Mutti has gone home to cook, knows better; so do I. And maybe just because of that I'd love to see Mrs. Laseur hold on to her auburn wig as she bends down to kiss my cheek for the pralines.

I'd even love to see again the pockmarked smirk of Lou the Cop, usually rocking in potbellied uniform in the lobby, rocking while swapping boxing odds with Garden touts, rocking his chair between the grizzled potted palm and the RAIDED PREMISES sign. He'll drag his hulk upstairs to bring us nothing but a hearty bad-breath "Have a merry!" He'll collect his pralines before heading a floor higher to Mrs. Laseur, where a much more substantial bounty awaits him in legal tender. A Yuletide lagniappe, keeping the premises un-reraided for another year.

And last not least there's Bix, Bix of Bix's Swing Shop next to our glass-blower on the ground floor. Actually, he should be first because he provides the machine crucial to the celebration my parents are preparing in the stockroom. Good old Bix, he'll come up no matter how crazy-hectic Christmas Eve is for him; no matter how many strung-out jazz cats converge on his place to rent (special year-end rates!) practically undamaged saxes, traps, trombones for holiday gigs. Forget all that, Bix will take time out to stagger up all those steps, clutching a gramophone; panting, he'll emerge on our floor with his haggard cheeks and hallucinated eyes; he'll stagger on to my parents in the stockroom. And from there my brother will hear (as I did last year) Papa's and Mutti's smilingly protesting voices. Once more they'll lose the arguments they've lost on Christmases past. They haven't won since Bix discovered that Mutti's mother vanished at Theresienstadt, where Bix's granduncle also disappeared. No, Bix won't accept a penny for loan of the gramophone, though he will accept the pralines. And how I'd love to press them into his hand again and to sniff what he'll leave behind—a mixed mist of pot and sweat.

In fact, I'd also love to hear again the dubious compliment Papa paid me last year when he came in from across the corridor later in the morning. Ostensibly he was checking on the girls, to make sure they remained work-focused right up to the Christmas lunch at noon sharp. In truth he was quite sure of them, having trained them well. He was less sure of less trainable me. So he came in, cast a quick eye on the seven napkin rings I'd already wrapped.

"Good—good how you do this. I appreciate, because this is abnormal hours for you."

Now, talking to me in English always imposes a certain formal distance between us, a stiff space, a withholding of our familial German by way of a rebuke. He always does that when referring, however indirectly, to the unnatural life his elder son has chosen. And that's exactly what he did here.

"Abnormal hours for you" breathed his doubt that I'm able to do any work, including napkin ring wrapping, at any time of day normal for my brother, Henry, or for the rest of regular humanity. "Abnormal for you" suggests all my aberrations exceeding even those Papa might try to find understandable in an aberrant New World at an aberrantly newfangled time. It suggests the many years during which he had to witness my way-wardness, until I succumbed to wedlock at thirty-two. For until then I lived with him and Mutti (my "rent" check in an envelope on the kitchen table, the first of each month). To me, this was the simplest way of boarding in Manhattan between frequent long magazine assignments abroad. To my hip friends (lighting up their regulation joints in their reg-ulation rebel pads), it was a smirk. To Marcia, it was a case of chronic boyitis aggravated by inordinate ancestor worship. Whatever it was, for Papa it meant observing, with utter bewilderment, the abnormalities I've matured into: how I clack away at the typewriter far beyond midnight, pecking out polysyllabic, subversive, decadent whimsies my agent will peddle after I rise at noon. How, in brief, I stick to my nocturnal bakery hours while practicing a much less solid trade than baking. How I even let go of the one solid side benefit of my unsolid activity, namely, teach-ing the unsolid activity at first-class universities (this could only happen in America) . . . only to throw away such solid employment at the very point when there was added reason to hold on it, that is, when I finally settled down to marriage. That marriage in itself being problematic, though, involving as it does a woman whose good looks misrepresent opinions and morals not nearly as good, a woman, moreover, whose un-kosher personality I perversely assumed during my late-night typewriter clackings, pecking out a novel from her viewpoint and thus committing, so to speak, acts of serial wee-hours transvestitism that culminated in my wedding selfsame woman in Europe, on the sly . . .

Yes, all this, if not more, simmered in Papa's "Abnormal hours for you" last Christmas. But if I were there today, I wouldn't resent it. And I wouldn't do what I did last year. I wouldn't answer Papa's dig with "Abnormal hours? Maybe I should charge you overtime." I would not say that. Or, if I did say it, I'd add, with a smile, "Daddy." That always made him feel American, and he'd smile back with the crinkles of his bare-skin mouth which I'm still not quite used to, though it's been years since he's shaved off his European mustache.

Only now I'm at Château Mouton and it's not Papa who enters after a knock at the door. It's not Babysitter either but Pauline de Rothschild herself, and since I hadn't expected her I may have been a moment too late shoving her half-wrapped subway map gift under the *International Herald Tribune.*

Did she notice? If so, it didn't break the stride of long-legged *faux* blue jeans that are probably haute-coutured Levi's of blue velvet.

"Frederic! Good morning."

"Good morning, Baroness."

"No, no—'Pauline.' Please. Make me feel younger."

"Good morning, Pauline."

"That's better. Good news: you don't have to have lunch either."

It takes me a moment to absorb this.

"Oh, I'm sorry," I say. "Sorry about no breakfast. I hope I didn't upset your butler."

"Of course you did. Good for you. You helped break him in. Dupont's still a bit too stiff for us here."

"You're very kind."

"Grateful! He's already more flexible. No breakfast was a shock. But he's adjusting to your no lunch."

"How did he find out—"

"Me. I know you never lunch except when you must, with publishers. Thank goodness we're not publishers. Just vintners. No problem."

"You've been talking to my wife!"

"She's a delightful conversationalist. But, really, no problem because we've abolished lunch at Mouton. Everybody orders day food for himself. Or herself. Or whatever. Or whenever. Utter anarchy. It's to atone in advance for dinner." She sighs playfully. "Black tie, alas."

"Well, that's very charming."

"No, charming is the day meal you *do* have . . . what's it called, your Vienna afternoon coffee?"

"My wife is a blabbermouth!"

"*Yowser*—that's what it's called. Only she pronounced it much better. But for you, I understand, no whipped cream, no Sacher torte? How original. Really, just rolls?"

"Yes," I say. "She really ratted on me."

"Not enough. Philippe abducted her before I could ask what kind of rolls. So I must ask you now."

"Any kind will do."

"No, it won't. You don't know my patissier. Vague instructions irk him no end."

"Well, any kind he likes to make."

"But that won't do either. *Yowser* is all you eat all day, so if you don't get just the kind of *Yowser* you want, you might not even eat that. You'll faint dead away with hunger, just as we sit down to dinner. Collapsed in black tie. Dampens the holiday spirit. So, please, what kind of rolls?"

"Goodness," I say. "In view of all that—poppy seed rolls."

"Poppy seed. Good. Actually, still not good enough for the dread patissier. He'll throw a fit if he's not told what *shape* of poppy seed rolls, I promise you he will."

"Uh, braided. Poppy seed twists."

"Thank you! Saved from kitchen wrath! One more question: How is your cold?"

"Just a little cough. Mostly gone."

"It's not an allergy? We can't have another Dalí disaster."

"A Dalí disaster?"

"Three years ago, still a trauma. The poor man came to design a Mouton wine label. My luck to choose a jacquard table linen for a tablecloth. He nearly wheezed to death over soup."

"I have no allergy. Just a measly cold."

"Good. I want you well and functioning"—she cocks her head mischievously—"for the kind of advantage I plan to take of you."

Her tony banter reduces me to lumpish straight man. Me, the supposedly sharp wordsmith. But all I can counter with is "Gee, Pauline, I've been taking advantage of *you*—your hospitality, with all my quirks."

"Candid quirks! You're on the up-and-up about no breakfast! Me, I've been hiding my agenda. But I'm coming clean now."

A wispy butler had materialized by her side, hands her a thick tome. She puts it down in front of me, on top of the London *Times.* (Luckily not on the *International Herald Tribune,* hiding her gift.)

"My scheme all along," she says, "has been to pick your brains. On *this.*"

This, the thick tome, is the *Oxford Book of Elizabethan Verse,* of all things.

"I'll be damned," I say. "I used to teach that."

"Johns Hopkins?"

"How do you know? My wife again!"

"No, no. I tracked you down in *Who's Who.* Has Philippe told you of our Elizabethan folly?"

"No."

"I talked the poor man into it. We're having a go at a definitive French translation. Even Shakespeare—he won't be safe from us. We'll take on some sonnets."

"Well, hats off," I say. *"Formidable."*

"You see, the Elizabethans haven't been done justice to, in French. Ever. Kills me. And here's Philippe, who's already done a lovely Christopher Fry in French, used by all the Paris productions. And me, what can I tell you? All my insomnia has been Elizabethan. The dawns and dawns I spent underlining, annotating, from Marlowe to Jonson and back again. So there's some excuse for our insanity."

"I had no idea."

"We've been furtive about it. Of course, we can't do the whole Oxford—we still haven't finished the wine museum here, a madness in itself, it's threatening to dwarf the Louvre. So—I've checked off in red the poems we've picked. Could you possibly leaf through sometime and comment? Approve our choices? Disapprove? Reprove? Laugh us out of court?"

She draws her head in between her cashmered shoulders, in humorous timidity.

"Happy to," I say. "Not that my opinion is definitive. But I'm flattered."

"And me—I'm relieved!" A very light, expert cheek kiss, subtly perfumed. "Shriven for Christmas! Confessed my ulterior motive!"

Laughing, trailed by the wispy butler, she skips away.

I'm left, coughing, in the wake of her élan. Pretty goddamn clever élan. It comes to me that maybe, just maybe, she's just confessed one ulterior motive in the service of another yet more ulterior. Unmentioned in our little chat, the fact that I've been commissioned by major publishers on both sides of the Atlantic to do a Rothschild book as well as by a national magazine to write an article series. The reason why I've been invited here in the first place. Perhaps not even a sufficient reason were it not for something else, also omitted in our conversation but researched by me in advance: namely that Mouton Rothschild borders on the rival family vineyard of Lafite Rothschild; that in the official classification of Bordeaux clarets, Lafite ranks as *premier cru* above Mouton's *deuxième*; and that (as the baroness let it drop yesterday in passing) Mouton nevertheless tops Lafite in many wine auctions, amusing for Mouton, disagreeable to Lafite since it's run primarily as a business, absentee-owned by a collective of French banker Rothschilds busy elsewhere in their countinghouses.

Now, in view of all this, wouldn't a chat like the one just now help illuminate the contrast? Help me, the invited writer, discover how very personally, idiosyncratically, culturally Mouton is inhabited by its sole proprietor, Baron Philippe, in tandem with a consort equally tangy? Wouldn't that make it easier for the writer to decide which of the two cousin estates will yield more interesting copy and so deserve superior space in a Rothschild biography?

Probably it would. And probably Baroness Pauline has fine-tuned her tanginess to the biographer. Probably I strike her as quite a highbrow sort, with kinks of my own. Hence her sympathy for my no-breakfast, no-lunch, yes-*Yowser* bizarrerie, her casual weaving in of Mouton's aesthetic credits such as Philippe's Christopher Fry translations, the wine museum, the Dalí bottle label (the Braque and Picasso designs already woven into previous conversations), plus the news scoop of "the Elizabethan folly" delivered by way of soliciting my literary acumen and thus stroking my vanity.

But also depressing my spirits. All that *haute* kinetic cunning makes me feel sluggish in comparison. Sabotages my wrapping. The Christmas paper resists me. My cough revives and unsteadies my hand. Until it subsides I leaf through the Oxford Elizabethans.

Surprise. Edmund Spenser's famous *Faerie Queene* has nothing checked off at all. However, there is a red check on the October eclogue of his *The Shepheardes Calendar,* which I barely remember because I never assigned it in class. But I see now that as a translated excerpt it's better than any *Faerie Queene* canto because individually the eclogues are much less entangled in context than the cantos.

Impressive. Unexpectedly perplexing. Is Baroness Pauline's intricate artifice further complicated by genuine scholarship?

This makes me tired; drained beyond the cold; discouraged by the complexities to be mastered in this project. Familiar blues, actually, whenever I'm on the brink of a new book. But the physical fatigue is new. I'm gift-wrapping again, but my fingers are too weary to stretch the paper wrinkle free over the raised frame of the subway map plaque. How much easier were the napkin rings at Papa's on Eighth Avenue! What balm to be back there now! . . . Even to pursue the "normal" career Papa once envisioned for me, concocting a new generation of wafer recipes in the baking lab of the National Biscuit Company? Or better still, running a nice little store—"Ye Olde Vienna Patisserie"—near Papa's office? Right on Eighth Avenue because that's also close to Frosch's Bake Shop of my apprentice days. Frosch's is now a TV mart, but the customer base must still be there for strudel and torte. Why not invest my savings in a tranquil existence like that? And stop having to wrench out of my brain words, phrases, insights, ideas, day after day after day? Why not get out of this constant, and confounding scribbling stress? . . .

And into my confoundment barges Marcia.

"There's my Christmas wrapper!" she trills.

Behind her, butler Babysitter trundles his hedonic wagon, pulls it right up to me, presents it with a bow a shade more wine-scented than before, exits.

She lifts a silver bell from the wagon's top tier.

"Your poppy seed twists, sir. Hot! Fresh baked!"

Such high spirits grate on my low.

"You tattled on me!" I say.

"Aren't you glad?"

She lifts a smaller silver bell. Revealed, an astounding sight: on scalloped porcelain shells, butter patties that are not just patties but miniature sculptures carved in butter, tiny replicas of my poppy seed twists, down to a needlepoint of micro craters representing poppy seed.

"My God," I say. "I forgot to mention I never have butter with my rolls!"

"See? I should have tattled more."

Not just my spirits, my appetite is depressed. I can't stomach the idea of anything fatty, no matter how exquisitely carved. But then there's the carver, the dread patissier, who'll think I've snubbed his little masterpieces.

"Marcia," I say. "You like your rolls buttered. Have some."

"Please, not today."

"But the damn kitchen here, they went to all that trouble. I can't send that back untouched."

"So make believe you gobbled up the butter. Throw it away."

"Where? They clean our rooms so religiously."

"Throw it out the window."

"You saved my life."

But no. I come back from the window, the little masterpieces still on the porcelain scallops.

"Would you believe?" I say. "There's some maintenance type right below our windows, working in the rain! You've got to help me with the butter!"

She puts her hand against her stomach, bends forward in over-the-railing seasick position, smiling.

"Too full," she says, "for a very fancy reason."

If regular high spirits grate at this point, roguish high spirits grate still more. Plus I'm irritated by my own embarrassing, ridiculous butter-nervousness.

"Yes?" I say. "Fancy reason?"

"Too full of fish eggs."

"Are we being coy about caviar?"

"Tons! I couldn't stop him. He spoon-fed me."

"Sire spoon-fed you?"

"None but."

"Caviar at a wine tasting?"

"Oh the wine tasting was rained out. So he took me to his Bordeaux hangout."

"And he spoon-fed you. Uh-huh. *Droit de seigneur.*"

"Well, more like, let's say, *droit de connoisseur.*"

"Nice little repartee. Be proud of it."

"Oh, lighten up. He's funny, he claims he knows exactly how many eggs to get on the spoon."

"Bit of a cliché, actually. A Rothschild making out on Beluga. Or was it Sevruga?"

"What Sevruga. Local sturgeon eggs. He says he wants to support the Bordeaux variety."

"A Rothschild making out on a cheap date. Nice twist for my story. So what was his next move?"

"You don't want to know."

"Sure I do. Cuckolds want to know everything."

"He sniffed my armpit."

"Did he? Whereupon what? Premature ejaculation?"

"Goodness, so lurid. Actually he complained that he smelled nothing. He said that all American women do that to their armpits. They deodorize their femininity away. Hey, where'd you get the Oxford Elizabethans?"

"I see you're changing topics."

"The topic is exhausted. Nothing happened postarmpit. Honest. Just heading back to the old château in the old Rolls. So where'd you get that book?"

"From the deodorized baroness."

"A Christmas gift?"

"It's a loan, she says, with an ulterior motive."

"Oh. She still a good flirt at her age?"

"She just wants advice on what to translate into French."

"Oh right, he brought up the Elizabethans, too. He loves to translate them because they deodorized nothing. So their poetry is so pungent. You know, 'pungent' sounds even more pungent with a French accent?"

"I bet it does. Great Gallic foreplay."

"I think you're really jealous!"

"Amused. Maybe not as—as carnally sated as you. But amused."

"The man is fat! And fifty-eight! He told me his age!"

"Such lordly candor. Exciting."

"You really are upset!"

"Not particularly."

"Unmistakable. The way you get so goddamn clever."

"You get pretty cute yourself."

Suddenly she sits down on my lap, turns from crisp to soft, huge lovely brown eyes swimming fondness. Her finger strokes down my cheek.

"What's the trouble, Fritzl?"

"What trouble?"

"Tell me."

"Why?"

"Come on . . ."

"Ech. Boring trouble. Déclassé trouble. Dull."

"Fritzl, please? . . . Tell me?"

She can always make me melt. I take a deep breath.

"I'm coldy and dead tired. And childish. I miss my parents."

"So?" she says softly, to my relief because we've had arguments about me being such a Mama's boy. "So?"

"So I'm ridiculous."

"Okay." She's stroking my cheek again. "Now I'll tell you something. Last night I washed my panties."

"What?"

"You don't know because we have separate bathrooms. See, I'm ridiculous, too."

"But you have your own maid to launder your stuff—"

"That's why. It's not like in a hotel where it all goes to a laundry, so it's impersonal. Here, when they see . . . intimate secretions—they know it's me."

She looks down, her long dark lashes lowering. She's melted, too, into the most adorable embarrassment.

"That's a darling secret."

"No, not darling. I thought about it in the Rolls, on the way back from the caviar and the armpit and everything. It's such a damn middle-class secret. That's what I learned from Sire—"

"Leave the son of a bitch out of it!"

"But he's a son of a bitch aristocrat! Ashamed of nothing! Us, we're ashamed of everything! Secretions and not making nice about the butter and missing parents and so on. Us Bohemians! Deep down we're a bunch of prisses!"

I kiss her on the lowered eyelids. That makes her look up again.

"Are you listening to me?"

"Every word."

"Okay. Make a deal with you. I won't wash my panties and you don't eat the butter, you just send it back. And you'll drink more fluids like this Perrier here, and you'll enjoy your *Yowser* coffee, and I'll finish your lousy wrapping for you and put the gifts under the tree, so you can have a good nap before dinner. But first you'll have your poppy seeds."

All of a sudden she is feeding me a roll. And, coming from her long slim fingers, it's warm and crisp and totally delicious.

Dinner in the château's dining salon. Correction, in *one* of the château's dining salons, the Renaissancey one. Ogive windows arching between classic pilasters, quattrocento sconces, candlelights glancing off white butlers' gloves, discreet swarming of stewards and sommeliers, high-voiced choiring of French Christmas songs: children of Sire's vignerons serenading us from the front hall. And all of no particular cheer to me. Nose less stuffed, cough under control, but soul drooping once more, smack in the middle of a paradisical soirée.

I can't seem to cope with my neighbors in Paradise. On my left, the lady introduced as principal stage designer for the Comédie-Française—

smooth sheath of iron gray hair matching her presumable Balenciaga. Exudes the *dernier cri* in austerity, a chic abbess of a personage and monolingual to boot. *"Pas anglais,"* she apologized over hors d'oeuvres of *huîtres de Marennes.* Which would be all right if her *français* would not zoom past me, unintelligibly, at supersonic speed. Nor does she slow down after hearing my snail-pace French, which of course fails to connect with her. Clueless but courteous, she nods before I come to the point of my remarks. Soon we resign ourselves to mute industrious smiling as we pass the pepper mill.

On my right, the young, rather pretty and almond-eyed culture reporter of Bordeaux TV. Speaks almost Oxonian Brit and has a ruby butterfly fluttering toward me across a scenic décolletage. Her game is golf, I'm still a tennis buff, and at first we have fun teasing each other about our sports. But soon the jolliness founders on an emerging difference. She appreciates, copiously, each new exalted vintage served with each new exquisite dish. I manage little more than token nips. She makes no direct comment but starts clinking glasses with me aggressively, followed by sharp side glances at my feeble sips (as she bottoms-up), then puts down her empty goblet with a glare at the barely lowered liquid level in mine. Does she feel that her overconsumption is pointed up by my under? At any rate she soon turns away to talk with the ruddy portly Comte de Whatever on her other side and simply never turns back.

Okay, let her. Let her remain averted so that I can inspect with leisure the triangular mole at the top of her spine. Let the ruby butterfly flutter toward de Whatever. Let the chic abbess continue to ignore me, except when in need of pepper mill. And let Pauline, argus-eyed hostess of this superbly congenial *souper,* observe the depths of my pariahdom. Probably no surprise to her. I see that she's taken some advance precautions to deal with my particular leprosy, i.e., my reverse drinking problem.

That's why she must have seated the president of the Confrérie des Chevaliers du Tastevin so far away, at the other end of the table. However, the minister of culture is to her right, which is almost opposite, and he's begun knitting burly gray eyebrows at the varieties of preciousness left in the glasses before me, none of which the sommeliers will remove unless at least half emptied.

"Frederic!" the baroness intones pleasantly, "do share with my illustrious friend here what you told me about T. S. Eliot. I would never have guessed!"

Obvious, the subtext of that request. To make up for my slighting France's glorious viniculture, I am to laud the power of her literature.

"You mean Paul Verlaine?" I say obediently. "That he was such an influence?"

"Exactly!" She turns to the minister. "Would you believe? Eliot, the greatest living poet in the English language—and his inspiration was a French writer!"

"Yes, I do believe this." The minister nods a brief smile at Pauline. "I was happy to learn of this years ago." Smile vanished, the burly brows resume knitting at my derelict goblets.

For an instant the practiced brightness of Pauline's face dims, the brio of the little wrinkles sags. Damage control didn't take. And I, the damager, get a perverse kick out of that. For all her bull's-eye flair, the baroness can miss, just like me. I don't even mind her second failure tonight, even if this one involves Sire's leching after Marcia again.

Pauline must have a hard time controlling her baron—this smart, handsome baldie, the sort of sovereign creature of impulse he is, headlong with smooth unpredictability. One moment he plays, for my benefit, brilliant Monsieur Mouton Rothschild (leaving by implication Lafite Rothschild in the dust), inscribes an eighteenth-century edition of Montaigne to me, entertains me with French/English punning, acts oblivious of my poor alcohol intake. Next moment he's not oblivious to it at all but seems to consider it a eunuch's trait. Only this can explain his blithe coming-on to my wife, in my plain sight.

Clearly the baroness couldn't prevent the baron from sitting next to Marcia. Just as clear, her countermove, which did work for a little while: she placed on Marcia's other side the tall French general quite receptive to feminine charms. Bent toward her, he was amazed, in broken but stentorian English, by her resemblance to a young lady he met while military governor of Morocco, the king's niece—the same petite nose, the same large Mediterranean eyes, etc., etc. . . . Yet et ceteras and all, he can't glom onto my Bronx princess for long. Sire—ashamed of nothing—

reclaims her simply by pulling a bit on the tiny hairs of her arm and then proceeds to whisper at length sweet nothings to her, while pointing at the table's centerpiece. Which doesn't bother me too much either because Marcia, though ostensibly listening, has extended her arm just an inch across the table toward me, her hand moving slightly, slowly, in an up and down motion, an unobtrusive "Let him . . . let him . . ." signal.

Now, since the chic abbess to my left zooms her French in every direction but mine and since I'm tired of contemplating the mole on the back of the TV nymph to my right, I decide to join Marcia and the baron, at least in the sense of directing my attention, too, at the centerpiece that absorbs them so. I must admit it's a fine pretext for making out, an extraordinary creation, this miniature woods of tiny-needled pines wrought (no doubt by the dread patissier) of spun sugar and set in a snowscape of candy crystals. And the green white of this diminutive vista echoed delicately by the embroidery—pastel citron on alabaster—of the tablecloth, by the pale leaf patterns on the Wedgwood plate, by the verdant shadings of the damask napkins.

Yessirree and hot diggety, some recherché mis-en-scène. But, except for the big-shot stuff, a bash not too different in principle from the one at 800 Eighth Avenue where I'd ordinarily sit today and get a lot more conversation from my table neighbors. Indeed, I'd get it this very minute—due to the time difference, the Mouton dinner synchronizes with my parents' famous Christmas lunch. Certainly I'd have arrived there by now (it's no longer morning in New York and therefore not "abnormal hours" for me). I'd be sitting at the 800 table which, by the way, will also have a centerpiece, a traditional one. No question, it'll be our stuffed-cloth Rudolph the Red-Nosed Reindeer again. Papa bought him years ago on the theory that a non-Christ Christmas icon would not compromise his Jewishness. For 365 days Rudolph hibernates (or rather estivates) on the top shelf of the broom closet until Papa hauls him down for three hours of Noel glory. And so what if this year Rudolf will look yet a tad more faded than last. This year, just like last, his huge red nose will still harmonize with the pink swirls of the paper tablecloth, the crimson paper napkins, the rosy-striped paper plates and paper napkins, all carefully assembled by my mother even though that means combing through several Woolworth stores.

But color orchestration is not the only aspect Château and Eighth Avenue have in common. At Mouton the gold-rimmed menu card by my place setting lists six courses: *huîtres de Marennes, foie gras à la gelée, consommé girondin, filets de sole Dnieper, faisan rôti, glace flamande.* Eighth Avenue usually also features six gastronomic highlights. I remember them well since on this occasion I override my no-lunch habit and make a show of nibbling at them all: roast beef, pastrami, corned beef, bologna, Genoa salami, Swiss cheese, each kind displayed on its own paper serving plate in slices lovingly arranged by Papa in fan shape.

And then the potables. Okay, at Mouton the menu card tonight boasts Veuve Clicquot 1921, La Tour 1938, Heidsieck 1947, Mouton Rothschild 1910, Mouton Rothschild 1880, Sigalas-Rabaud 1919. On Eighth Avenue we feature 7-Up, Pepsi, Coke, Seagram's ginger ale, Doc Dock's root beer, and Berger's two cents plain—all with safely unexpired expiration dates.

Granted, on Eighth Avenue we have nothing like the Mouton Christmas tree, this towering Judeo-Christian pine with a hundred electric candles flickering artfully under a double pinnacle of silver Star of Bethlehem and golden menorah. However, what we do have on Eighth Avenue is an equivalent for Mouton's lush cornucopia of gift-wrapped goodies heaped under the tree: what we have is two tables standing in the corner of the stockroom. One table will hold this year's successor to the napkin rings, wrapped by my brother, Henry. On the second rests the gramophone from Bix's Swing Shop. Otherwise this big table (covered like the others by the pink-swirled paper tablecloth) will be empty, a temporary, fraught emptiness awaiting the climax of the celebration.

And fraught, too, on Eighth Avenue, is the lunch table itself, as richly charged with undercurrents as this dinner at Mouton. As always, Papa will have made sure that Hyacinth sits far away from my mother. Underlying his tactic is a byzantine reason centered on Hyacinth's gums. Several times a year these require treatment, to which Hyacinth will not submit— for fear, apparently, that somehow she'll be decapitated in the process. That's where Papa comes in. Without even asking her, he goes straight to the phone. The appointment he makes with Dr. Mueller, our family dentist (formerly the best in northwestern Vienna), is, of course, after 5 PM so as not to conflict with working hours. Papa himself will firmly escort Hyacinth to Dr. Mueller's office on 156th Street, ignoring Hyacinth's whimpered protests, which will diminish somewhat after he buys her a chocolate ice cream on the way. And Papa will keep vigil by the chair, holding Hyacinth's hand while Dr. Mueller wields novocaine needle and periodontal probe. After the ordeal Papa will buy her a second chocolate ice cream as painkiller and take her home to Brooklyn by taxi since she might be too groggy for the subway (and at the end of the week will deduct only half the fare from her pay). As a result he never gets home before half past nine, delaying dinner horrendously. This happens almost every three months. But Mama would still forgive Hyacinth were she not also South Seas pretty with a passion-flower hairdo and a never-confiscated plastic white carnation in her midnight locks. As such she constitutes in Mutti's eyes an assault, however futile, on Papa's fidelity.

No wonder, then, that Mutti sits to Papa's right while Hyacinth is all the way down the table next to Ramona, who presides facing Papa, at the other end.

But even more fraught is this placing of Ramona. True, it's a prestigious spot, befitting Ramona's dignity as forelady. Indeed, until year before last that was the chair of my mother, who outranks any forelady as Mrs. Boss. Nevertheless she ceded the location to Ramona as a sop much needed tonight. For at a certain juncture on Christmas Eve our forelady will be sorely tried by a ghostlike resurgence of her rival and predecessor, Lucia. Lucia—here is Ramona's problem—was not just Lucia. She was Lucy, and more than that. She was Our Lucy, even to Papa, who doesn't easily unbend. To Mutti she was Our I Love Lucy for all her many winning ways, like the Congratulations! cards, crayoned in multicolor, she'd send to my parents on their birthdays whose dates she usually almost got right, or the amazing plaster bust of the Emperor Franz Joseph she'd dug up at a Lower East Side flea market and brought to my parents' apartment, a surprise all the more endearing since the doors of the IRT had sliced off the All-Highest nose. Her coworkers clustered around Our Lucy at lunch, giggling over Peter Lawford's drunks or Ava Gardner's hanky-pankies, inside stuff straight from Our Lucy's film-set carpenter cousin in Hollywood. Nobody has ever clustered around

Ramona, her long-embittered number two in the 800 hierarchy, a bitter-ness lingering even after Our Lucy returned to San Juan to take over her uncle's grocery store. Ramona ascended to forelady, but she never be-came Our Ramona.

Yet she deserves the anointment for her very solid qualities. She has the spinster's virtue of punctuality, often waiting for Papa mornings when he arrives to open the workshop. She is a Republican, which Papa, a Habsburg Democrat, respects because it contrasts with the others' giddy ignorance of politics. (Her never-confiscated button says I LIKE IKE.) Though she's a few years older than her colleagues, you could call her an almost pretty Republican, if you disregard the harsh fold down her fore-head and her ramrod posture, which becomes even more pronounced when she sits down to work. A drastic straightness announcing that if Mr. Morton should absent himself for any reason, she'll be there to pre-vent chaos.

Papa's appreciation of all this shows whenever a new supply salesman calls. He'll introduce Ramona as "our good forelady, Miss Perez, she has the power from me to sign shipment receipts." A prerogative exercised de facto by Our Lucy but which she was never so formally awarded.

Such are Ramona's consolations. They will all come to naught at a cer-tain stage in our Eighth Avenue Christmas luncheon. Ramona, privileged as her position at the end of the table may be, knows that. That's why she'll soon stop eating in order to appear engrossed in a very slow con-stant straw sipping from her 7-Up cup. This deepens the fold down her forehead, but it also distances her from the babble and proceedings around her. And the proceedings will proceed. (Watching them from so far away at Mouton with my mind's eye, they're much juicier than the gilded jabber from which I'm still so kindly excluded.) Papa will wait until most of the cold cuts have been polished off. He will clap his hands twice, stopping the hubbub; rise; give a Central European bow; and point to the table loaded with gifts; "Please, over there, maybe you will find some little holiday mementos."

And there'll be a happy rush to over there (except for Ramona, who follows slowly, warily), a zestful tearing of wrapping paper, a crying of "T'ank you, t'ank you, Mista and Missis Morton!" for whatever might be this year's napkin rings. Ramona will go through these motions, too, but with eyes half closed against what happens next.

What happens next is that Our Lucy's best friend, Anya, who is still with us, this Anya will suddenly produce the plastic-enclosed disc Lucy has mailed her from Puerto Rico. She will present it to Papa in a formal gesture, using both hands. And Papa will throw his head back and let his jaw drop a little, in ritual surprise. Then, with ritual solemnity, he'll pull the disc out of its sheath to display the white label in the center, on which will be scrawled in red crayon, "To Mr. and also Mrs. Morton, married cupple on their 37th aniversary, with sincere love, Lucy."

At this there'll be much ritual oohing and aahing (Ramona's eyes closing even more above her frozen smile). A circle will form around my parents. At its center, Papa, with somewhat stage-conscious, heightened emphasis, will place the disc on the gramophone's turntable and apply the needle. Shouts will go up: " 'Anniversary waltz'—dance, Mista and Missis Morton! . . . Dance!" And it won't matter a bit that my parents' wedding anniversary is not today, Christmas Eve, December 24, but yesterday, the twenty-third. No more than it matters that the scratchy yodels emanating from the disc aren't "The Anniversary Waltz" at all. Lucy sang that song only the first time. In each following year she's performed a different new operetta air and continued the variation even after her return to Puerto Rico. God knows how she manages to dig up in San Juan yet another period Vienna love ballad complete with German lyrics. But manage she does. I have every confidence that this Christmas, too, 800 Eighth Avenue will resound to something like

> *Dein ist mein ganzes Herz,*
> *Wo Du nicht bist, kann ich*
> *Nicht sein . . .*

rendered by Our Lucy's thin, ardent soprano intermittently in tune. And my parents, still standing in the middle of their girls' circle, my parents will nod and smile at the smothering of German consonants by Hispanic passion. And all around them the shouts will continue, "Dance, Mista and Missis Mortons! 'Anniversary Waltz'! . . . Dance!" Mutti will put her hand on Papa's shoulder. Papa will just smile, immobile, until Anya gives him a little nudge (in Lucy's name, so to speak), and that will do it.

He'll place his arm around Mutti's waist and take her hand into his . . . and, look, they're turning, slowly at first but then faster, swaying, swerving, swiveling, as if it were still Vienna 1937 . . .

Enormous applause crescendoing still further to the end of the number. Mutti will make Papa take a bow with her, kiss him theatrically, then rush to the eats table to lift her paper cup of ginger ale.

"To Our Lucy!"

Everybody will follow suit, including Ramona, for whom this is the hardest moment of them all. She'll smile along with all the others, but with a root-canal grimness of lips.

However, relief is at hand; at this very point she can legitimately remove herself from this Our Lucy delirium. Quietly she'll steal out the door together with my brother (and if I were there, with me). The fold down her forehead will smooth with relief, she'll look downright handsome as we hurry down the stairs to Bix's Swing Shop. Bix, of course, has been expecting us. His store is already closed, everything locked away, except for what's waiting for us on his counter. As always, he's let us his place to hide our anniversary gifts.

Ramona will take the Macy's shopping bag for whose contents all the girls have chipped in: the inevitable embossed tie for Papa, and for Mutti the inevitable shawl with spectacular long fringes. Ramona will lift this Macy's bag with a certain weighty slowness which very shortly will also inform her presentation of these offerings to my parents. This year her role in the ceremony will once again terminate those Our Lucy sentimentalities. This year she'll be affirmed again as the one-and-only forelady of Frank Morton Costume Jewelry. The only difference this year is that my brother will have to grab not only his bouquet of lilies but also mine of roses.

My God.

There'll be no roses.

In Mouton the realization catapults me to my feet.

Too abruptly. The waiter about to serve *fromage* has the plate nearly knocked out of his hand.

"Sorry!" I say. "*Pardon!* Apologies, excuse me for a minute."

I'm out of the dining salon and halfway up the stairs when I hear the footfalls and know who, but can't take time to stop.

I'm in my room, by the phone, when Marcia catches up with me.

"What's the matter?"

"Calling my brother in New York. Do the operators speak English here?"

(So far they speak only beeps, in response to the "0" I've dialed.)

"Why?" she says. "All of a sudden?"

"I meant to do it yesterday, but then my fever or whatever, I forgot, just totally forgot! I've got to ask him to buy a bouquet for me—Hello?"

"Your parents' anniversary?"

"You know! Why didn't you remind me?"

"I just guessed. Remind *you,* of all people?"

"Yeah, Mama's boy forgot! . . . Hello!"

Her lips on my cheek.

"As long as you're all right. I'll explain downstairs."

She's gone, replaced by butler Babysitter, summoned, apparently, by the commotion. He's still chewing his own dinner but already pulling on his gloves.

"Please!" I thrust the receiver into his hand. "Long distance, the international operator!"

"Yes, yes, monsieur." He nods vigorously even while swallowing. "You wish New York?"

"Please!"

And as he starts dialing, wine-scented, white-gloved, it sinks in—the uselessness of calling Henry. No point even trying. There's not even a phone in the stockroom where he is together with the rest of them. Nor will they hear the ringing in the empty workshop. I must get to a florist direct, my only chance.

"I 'ave New York operator, monsieur. What number?"

What number? I don't know the number of our local store, only the name.

"Riverbloom Florists, in Manhattan. R-i-v—No. No, wait."

No point either. I've no charge account there. No charge account, no delivery. And anyway, by the time flowers get down there from 105th Street, too late. But then a place jumps into my mind, not far from Papa, a florist on Fifty-second Street with orchids in the window, down the block from "21" . . . But what in the world is the name? I simply don't know the blasted name . . .

But I do know "21."

By God, I even remember the number, having called there a few times just before this Rothschild trip about a possible story for *Holiday*. I think I actually remember the number.

"Gotham 874-1000," I say to Babysitter, "A person-to-person call, please, Frederic Morton at Château Mouton to Mr. Robert Kriendler at '21' Club Restaurant, Mr. Robert K-r-i-e . . ."

Babysitter repeats these imposing instructions with a *distingué* crispness which, I hope and pray, will enhance their urgency. In fact, I wish that whatever switchboard he's addressing could somehow *hear* the white gloves holding the receiver.

And behold! That butlerian authority seems to have bestirred operators as well as electrons into high speed. Within seconds he nods at a voice in the earpiece.

"One moment, please." He hands me the phone.

"Kriendler."

"Bob, it's Frederic Morton from Mouton—"

"Uh, let's see . . . Frederic Morton from Mouton—"

"From *Holiday* magazine. We talked about a '21' story last month."

"My God, Frederic, of course! You really at Mouton?"

"Yes, doing a Rothschild book and article series, hip deep in deadlines, God help me."

"Not bad. Morton-Rothschild! Going to send me a case of that stuff for Christmas?"

"I think I had better. Because I need to ask you a favor."

"Shoot."

"Any florist near you—would you have his name and number?"

"Aw, don't send me flowers. A case of that stuff will do."

"Seriously, it's for my parents, Bob, it's their wedding anniversary and it plumb slipped my mind, and they're in their business place right now, near you, so I've got the gall to ask you, this florist down your block, if you'd lay out the amount—"

"Nothing doing."

"No? Two cases?"

"Nope. Mucho Mouton in the house already. We've got the classiest drunks in town. You'll see when you write your '21' story."

"Then I'm out of luck."

"Says who. We got tons of roses, vases full, standby for table decorations over the holidays—"

"Bob, not your flowers, please—"

"All right, how many years are your parents married?"

"Thirty-seven—"

"Thirty-seven roses. We'll send a busboy. What's the address?"

"Now wait a minute, I said, not your—"

"Want me to start messing with a florist Christmas Eve? So what's the address?"

"Eight hundred Eighth Avenue. But listen—"

"What cross street?"

"Between Fiftieth and Fifty-first. You can't be serious—"

"And the room number, please."

"Second floor, room 211, Frank Morton Costume Jewelry, it says on the door. But they're all in an unmarked room directly opposite. Bob, I owe you a big one."

"Nah, just biggish. Okay, and I guess with a card saying 'Love, Fred' or something like that?"

" 'With all my love, Fred' would be just great."

"Right . . . See, you're a much better writer than me. But I tell you, the busboy who's going to write it, bet he's got a better handwriting than you."

"Let me know which one, and I'll send *him* a case."

"Just wish him a Merry Christmas, and wish me one, too."

"And how, Bob! Merry Christmas! And—and goodwill toward '21.'"

"Hey! That's our Christmas card next year!"

"You got the copyright, my compliments. Least I can do."

"See you in New York, my friend. And be kind to the Rothschilds."

Click.

• • •

A moment's hush in the dining salon as I reappear.

"Hallelujah," Pauline says. "Our Frederic is well enough to join us again."

She claps her hands. A small round of applause. I bow and sit down.

"Your madame," Baron Philippe says, stroking Marcia's arm from wrist to elbow by way of identification, "she has ordered therapy for your estomach."

Goodness, there on my place setting is a Gothic tea kettle and a tea cup topped by a beveled tea sieve and five varieties of tea in little paisley tea tins and even a hot-water decanter—Marcia must have told them that I like to dilute.

The chic abbess smiles at me. And she of the cleavage butterfly is suddenly full of sympathy. "Myself also," she says, "when I have a poor stomach, I cannot have wine. But perhaps you would like a little of my cheese, very lean?"

And she cuts me a piece. And, best of all, Marcia puts her forefinger to her lips and then points it at me just long enough to hint a kiss.

Altogether, I have a right to feel pretty good. Her lovely secret kiss, the table swindled into forgiveness, the flowers delivered in the nick of time. The big-shot-to-big-shot lingo I performed pretty damn well with Bob Kriendler.

Then what in hell is the problem now? So I forgot my parents' flowers but remembered the "21" number. Remembering that number and knowing Kriendler, that's what righted things again, right? No small feat to fulfill an Eighth Avenue obligation from the stately remove of the Rothschilds, right? My abnormal hours, and the aberrations of privilege they wrought, were what saved me, right? Almost makes up for not seeing my parents' reaction to the gifts, which must be happening this instant. Mutti caressing the shawl's long fringes to emphasize her thrill to the girls while swooning to the perfume of her sons' flowers, and Papa knotting the embossed yellow-and-crimson tie—he'll never touch it again—directly on top of his plain brown one, all to enormous Hispanic giggles . . . It almost makes up for missing all that. Right?

Right?

March 1967

St. Moritz Blues

Not until the fourth day after my arrival do I snap on my ski boots. No leaping onto the snow right away as in winters past. Kept my promise to respect jet lag and altitude adjustment. The only skiing I've done so far is après, through the Palace lobby, slaloming past Alfred Hitchcock's table, snaking around Fiona von Thyssen's, sometimes collecting drinks invitations, sometimes mere nods, the latter leaving me more reading time for Sartre's autobiography in my suite.

And so far so good. Three days gone without needing to phone la Shrink even once. When I do reach for the receiver it's to call home, but never in a panic—as Marcia confirms at the other end: how good I sound, how together, how definitely right it was for me to accept Andrea Badrutt's platinum invitation as long as I don't attack the slopes like a twenty-year-old idiot, so let's not fret about it because she herself is fine, too, as fine as any nonskiing snow widow of a downhill maniac deserves to be, in fact, eat your heart out, she's having the greatest time watching sprouts budding on a tiny head . . . when I'd left last Monday our Rounzipussy had still been a wee baldie, having lost all the black hair with which she barged into the world four months ago—now it was growing back as auburn locks! Tough on me for missing those first silky little shoots!

Touché. First thing to do when I'm back in New York next week, stroke those darling sproutlets. Meanwhile, everything is really fine here as well. Kept my insomnia at bay, except for last night, when I twitched awake at 3 AM. The Placidyl I finally take at 4 AM tastes down-right exotic on the tongue; it's been so long since I had to give in to a pill. At any rate, one queasy night can be discounted, especially this one, preceding as it does the morning on which I'll resume my sports-manhood at last.

And what a morning it turns out to be, tourist-brochure ripe, the fa-bled Engadin winter sun striking a thousand sparks off Saint Moritz Lake's blue fluting. A pricey panorama savored from a window table of the Palace breakfast room. Yes, breakfast, due to another pledge exacted from me, namely to cut out my "vice" of foodless mornings.

So I do submit to rolls and tea, no more. Rolls, I admit, as crisped to a golden brown, as delicately ridged as I ever greased pans for in my salad days as baker boy. Rolls kept toasty under an artful fold of linen napkin. And, natch, tea ain't just tea around here but some arcane elixir a bit too jasminey for me. Defying a high-flown career, my tastes have remained stubbornly plebeian; perhaps they're the sole remnants of my purity. An almost Rothschildean work of art, the Palace *petit déjeuner,* and to me less treat than medication.

But outside the world is a glory of peaks, the sunny breeze exquisitely chilled as if in a champagne bucket, just cold enough to massage the cheeks. As for Bernd, the ski guide waiting for me at the hotel en-trance—instantly *simpatico.* A priori *simpatico,* truth be told, because he is free like my suite, both courtesy of Andrea Badrutt, Mr. Palace Hotel. But Bernd would be *simpatico* regardless. He's a huge blond with a bru-tal sort of good looks tempered by a high-pitched voice and an engaging gaucheness.

He stands at attention, shaking hands with me with his right while his left balances on his shoulder his skis as well as mine. The intonation of his *"Guten Morgen"* is unmistakably Austrian. To loosen him up, I answer with *"Joh, grüss Ihna,"* in drastic Viennese dialect. The surprise throws him into giggles that shake his bulk, skis and all. He's the only Austrian, he tells me, in the otherwise all-Swiss Saint Moritz ski school. Hm, I think to myself vaingloriously, how the great Badrutt tailors his hospitality to little me. Just because I sent up the Palace's velvet follies in presti-gious pages.

But vainglory (no news after what I've been through), vainglory is no panacea for nerves. Said nerves suddenly act up at the funicular, when I find no ski pass hanging from my neck nor purse in any of my pockets. Stupidly I've forgotten them both, either out of a stupidly prolonged jet lag or out of my stupid latent jitters now oozing moist out my palms. Lucky the turnstile attendant breaks into a big smile at the sight of my gray old-model parka, uniquely shabby in Saint Moritz, with rusty pocket zippers and stains from sunscreen ointment. He's recognized me, as he actually should, because this craggy grin of his beams out of a photo-graph illustrating my Saint Moritz piece in *Holiday* magazine. *"Gruezi, Herr Morton!"* I'm waved through with a bow.

Such Big Shotry shocks Bernd into his Attention! stance again. In the funicular he refuses to let me hold my skis, grips them in an outsized hand together with his own while our car scampers like a chamois up white steeps to the Marguns plateau. I try to relax him (and maybe me as well) by explaining that my rather raw Vienna accent comes from the scruffy backwater district where I was brought up. Not too different, it turns out, from the Linz streets of Bernd's childhood, of which he begins to speak, or rather mumble, addressing our skis more than me, except for a quick glance at my parka—same type, he says with a grin, as the one he inherited from his uncle as a graduation present.

But the kinship between us soon develops quite unexpected depths. At the Marguns chairlift—next leg of our journey upward—the toothy grumpy turnstile warden there has no idea who I am and very little pa-tience with explanations about forgotten ski passes and purses. Bernd, however, leaps to the rescue, hauls out a five-franc piece to pay for us both, gets four francs in return—when something odd happens.

He stares and stares at the four coins in his palm. And stares some more until Toothy grumps, *"Noh? was ischt los?"* And Bernd stutters, *"Nichts, nichts, danke,"* and pockets his change just in time for us to jump into the next double chairs coming around in the lift.

"Sorry," he says as we float up side by side, "but was that—that was four he gave me back, right?"

"Yes, four," I say, startled. "I owe you a franc. Plus interest."

He doesn't smile at the joke, too embroiled in his difficulty. Just mumbles that he hasn't gotten his "figuring" back.

Did I hear right? Yes, I did. I busy myself with readjusting my seat belt, wondering how to respond to this disclosure of a weird handicap.

Lucky something comes into view just then that helps to gloss over the awkwardness: the group far down on the Marguns run, stick-figure distant but unmistakable to a student of Saint Moritz fauna . . . seven skiers, one after the other, the first five curving smoothly, the last two wobbly, teetering through desperate turns, toppling again again and again, so that the deft ones ahead must pause till the clumsies flounder to their feet again.

"Look," I say, "the shah."

"Who?"

"The shah of Iran. The reigning emperor."

"Down there?"

"Yes, he's the second, the very slim one. And the one ahead of him, and the four behind, they're all Swiss detectives, they all ski great, see? But the last two are his Iranian bodyguards—oops, there's one in the snow again."

Very briefly Bernd chuckles along with me. Then his finger points down to the shah group, tentatively, puzzling out the numbers. "Four . . . and two . . ." And adds, "See, Dr. Greiner, he's helping me catch on again."

"Oh," I have to say now. "There is a problem?"

"Yeah. From the explosion."

"The explosion?"

For a moment we float side by side, silently, in our chairs. When he answers, he pitches his sheepish, almost shamed high voice to the crow wheeling just beneath us. To this crow he starts confiding as if he were in a confessional airborne through sunlight, blue sky, black bird wings, and white peaks.

The explosion, that was on his regular job. Irregular, he did weekend ski teaching at the Tauern uplands near Linz. But regular, he cleaned the lab at the Voest steelworks in the city, and somebody had forgotten to turn off an oxygen valve. But he was all right after the explosion, not right away, but after he woke up after a week. He could move everything normally, even his memory straightened out, but not his reading and figuring. But the insurance took care of the nerve doctors, they cured his reading but not yet his figuring. And this great lawyer, Dr. Huber, got him a settlement to pay for the best ski-teacher school, the Arlberg one. Only he was scared if he was good enough. But he did all right, the certificate even got him into Saint Moritz last month. Only figuring, that was still trouble. So Dr. Greiner comes up from Zurich twice a week for exercises. But it wasn't a problem till now because everybody had their ski passes, so no money figuring till now. So he was so sorry it happened with me.

"No, no, I forgot my ski pass, my fault," I say. "And I had to sponge on you for cash. So I'm the one who is sorry."

"I mean, I'm sorry my figuring is still so stupid."

"Wait a moment," I say. "Everybody's got some sort of stupidity. I had to have a nerve doctor, too."

This makes him look up and face me, with amazement.

"Also an explosion?"

"No," I say. "Though, well, yes, you're right. Sort of an explosion inside. Mixed-up nerves. It's complicated."

We've floated into the top station at this point, must jump off fast to get out of the way of the chairs behind us. My left ski boot has clicked loose, and before I can stop the servility Bernd has bent down to fix it. But when he straightens up he face is not servile.

"Nerve things," he says, shaking his head with a smile at me that's almost comrade to comrade, sharing a common bafflement.

Whereupon he pushes off (myself behind him), carving into the snow long leisurely arcs of effortless perfection, his glide a fluid extension of the slope. Every other minute he slows down, performing for me an exaggerated tutorial hip shift as he turns, then glances back to make sure that I'm repeating the motion right.

After some initial bobbles my wedel reflexes begin to kick in, and I do just about right, all right. He speeds up a bit, shortens and tightens his arcs, glances back at me again, nods yes, I'm really getting into the swing of it, grins, zooms on down with exuberant yodels that echo through the valley.

I start crowing in answer, so that when he looks back next time it's not teacher checking on student but two mountain devils larking it up.

Cocka-doodle-doo! Who dares say I'm forty-two!

Of course, just then I would trip over a bump. Not a bad fall but enough to release the binding of my left ski, which only the safety thong keeps from scuttling down the slope.

Bernd stops instantly, though he's at least thirty yards ahead and I haven't made a sound. He turns around; shrugs a jovial "Oh well, happens" shrug; waits as I struggle upright and click in my binding. No move on his part to help. Senses somehow that such babying would be a letdown for me after our mountain-deviltry together. He just cleans his goggles until I'm operational again and glide right up to him.

"Oh yeah," he says with his upper Austrian gutturals, "That crazy bit of powder up there. It surprised me, too."

Off he pushes again, wedeling, yodeling, yodeling us back into our headlong camaraderie, and me so exhilarated, I'm startled by his sudden stop. We've arrived at the Corviglia Club chalet.

A bit too fast.

No time for adjustment from mountain high to high society. Sure, I've entered these sacred precincts before. Once at the Duke di Sangro's *clair de lune* buffet and then again at Henry Ford II's honeymoon supper, where I shouldn't have made a face at that strange candy-flavored smoked pheasant. Both were evening affairs I penetrated supposedly by dint of eminent pen, more probably through Badrutt firepower since Andrea escorted me. Both times a funicular car, specially chartered, rode us up the starlit dunes. And up there, at night, torches flaring on the eaves, rainbow candles flickering on the tables, the clubhouse really seemed a fata morgana of exclusivity, the Union League raised to the nth power and catapulted 7,500 feet high.

But now, today, as I kick my skis off before the oaken entrance, the Corviglia in the sunlight doesn't loom so formidably. It looks more or less like other chalets at this altitude. Something of a relief—which must mean that I wondered if they'd admit Bernd and me, Badruttless.

Foolish worry. Baron Erwein Gecmen-Waldek lui-même, the club's ruddy-cheeked, cashmere-crewnecked manager, left eye squinting slightly as if it missed a monocle—anyway, Erwein gives a convivial handshake, even insists on hanging up my parka. Inside, I'm again surprised how by daylight the place resembles other upscale ski restaurants. Oak furniture rich with rustic knotholes, panoramic windows, antlered walls. But— aha!—those little white cards on the tables. They speak the rigors of this Olympus. They say that the Corviglia, being an apex enclave, has nothing but supreme tables, except for the supremer ones. On the merely supreme tables the cards say MEMBER. On the supremer, LIFE MEMBER. Just the usual Theater of the Absurd, staged with painstaking invidiousness by the Beautiful People. That's what I think objectively as jaded chronicler of a wealth-warped world. Subjectively, I can't help feeling relieved when Erwein steers me to a supremer table in the corner, the Badrutts'.

Since Bernd seems to have vanished into the W.C. and my host, Andrea, is not yet here, I sit down by myself. The club steward (materializing fast in a Swiss green jacket) I fend off, saying I'll wait for my friends before ordering. This I announce rather audibly. Lunchers nearby needn't think that I'll remain companionless. In the unlikely case that they think about me at all. En route to this corner I've passed certain other supremer tables. One occupied by Gianni Agnelli, another by Konstantin von Liechtenstein. To both I've been previously introduced, and both were too busy to see my nod, tycoon chuckling it up with a racy blonde, Highness engrossed by a swarthy emphatic type, every inch an oil emir. Obviously I'm not among the celestials who may call Agnelli "Johnny" or Prince Konstantin "Tino." Okay, so a writer who has raised his share of eyebrows elsewhere is still safely invisible here. Okay, so Society is those people whom I know but who don't know me. Okay, so let them cultivate their ignorance. Much more important are my hamstring muscles. They ache from all the happy exertion. I need Bernd to tell me how to best relax them.

In fact, since he's still not here, I decide to join him in the W.C. The urinals there, alabaster clean, are all unoccupied. Nothing seems to stir in the paneled stalls.

"Bernd?"

No answer. Baffled, I exit, only to run into Baron Erwein.

"Have you seen my ski guide?"

"Oh yes, husky chap. Enjoying his goulash soup downstairs. You just missed Andrea's call."

"He's eating *downstairs*?"

"*Bien sûr*, had him shown the way to our ski dons' brasserie. Andrea's hopping the next funicular. Should be here in a jiff. Do have something meanwhile."

"Thanks. I'm fine."

I'm so fine, my hamstrings contract into sharp pain, my palms perspire. It's back to my table, and to hell with any possible social signals on the way.

I'm just stunned. Never in fifteen years of skiing, even in uppity places like Gstaad and Zürs, have I experienced anything like this. Never a ski lodge—regardless of snob rank—that cuts the bond between guide and ward by not allowing them to break bread together.

Probably I should have expected it here. But just here, just now, I need Bernd more than three Placidyls. Bernd is my fellow wounded, my brother, and he's spooning his soup alone downstairs. How face him after lunch, on the piste? I so need to restore our camaraderie somehow.

Perhaps the only way to do that is to bare myself to him the way he bared himself to me. Expiate his basement soup by putting him and myself on the same level. Tell him as soon as we're reunited, spill it to him unsparingly about my "explosion." Tell him that though mine didn't happen in a steelworks but in the foyer of Secker & Warburg, my English publishers, it was like his, as sudden and devastating. Me, striding in on the crest of prideful wrath, furious that always, always, always something will spoil the pleasure of success—number one bestseller on both sides of the Atlantic, National Book Award finalist, translations into thirteen languages, and all that's really changed in my life is the upgrading of my frustrations from mean to grand.

Will that make sense to someone like Bernd? Because for him to understand what was about to explode in that genteely carpeted flower-vased foyer, he has to understand what led up to it in London, the king-sized beaut of a frustration served me earlier that day in my suite at Claridge's: the Warburg sales director calling me to say that on this day, the last of ten days in the course of which I'd worn myself frazzled with print interviews, TV and radio stints, book signings, endless laborious posturings, the very day on which my *Rothschilds* finally scaled the top of the *Evening Standard* list, this was also the day when—sorry, old boy— the book would be out of stock, would remain unbuyable for almost a month. A month! When I'd warned Fred Warburg so often by letter, by phone, that 55,000 would be far too low a first printing for a book that had skyrocketed so spectacularly in the United States. Old Fred had an earful coming at our lunch.

And so, Bernd, I announce myself brusquely.

"Mr. Morton to see Mr. Warburg."

The receptionist doesn't even look up. Too busy with some bauble in front of her switchboard, a gold ring she plays with dreamily.

"Good morning!"

Like talking to a wall. She's still nudging the damn ring back and forth. Ignores me totally. On instructions from Fred Warburg? To take me down from my high horse before we have our contentious lunch? Unbelievable.

"Good morning! . . . Good morning! . . . GOOD MORNING!"

At last that makes her raise a round-cheeked freckled face.

"I'm so sorry, sir. Yes?"

"Frederic Morton to see Mr. Warburg!"

My words still don't quite connect. Her freckles, I see, are wet. Her eyes stare in my direction but are fixed on some void. Pale blue, ravaged, streaming eyes. Which look down at the ring again.

"My mum's, sir. I lost her last night. I took it off her finger."

"My God," I say, or try to, with suddenly failing breath.

"Frederic Morton. Yes sir, I'll announce you."

She reaches for a switchboard plug, but begins to blur . . . blurs and dissolves and fragments into a haze that darkens, strangles, expunges all.

What came next, Bernd, was white walls, white coats, and Marcia's taut white face bending over me, smiling hard: everything's okay, no heart attack, no stroke, just a slight psychosomatic EKG irregularity, just enough to teach me finally slow down, ease up, for God's sake . . .

My explosion, Bernd, only it was I who didn't turn off the oxygen valve. No "figuring" problem followed, not even any further EKG glitches in

New York, where we flew immediately afterward—but, my God, what woe sinking into me for many months and not letting go, the black dread in my bones, the midnight panics and the wee-hours shakes, the daily shrink and the near-hourly pills . . . How make all that clear to you, Bernd, now that you've seen me apparently so yodel-fit again? How get through to you that I'm your fellow walking wounded, your fellow skiing wounded? We're brothers, despite this terrible segregation here of soup in the basement.

Exactly why I shouldn't even wait until after lunch. The thing to do is to go down right now, eat something with him, since Andrea isn't here yet anyway, spoon soup at his side, and pop a Placidyl right in front of him, proof of *my* trauma as visible as his counting trouble.

I'm on my feet, heading for the pillbox in my parka. Ski pass and purse I may have forgotten, but I do remember taking my Placidyls, my crisis resource, zipping them into that handy little pocket in the left sleeve of my parka.

But—no parka. I saw Erwein hang it up on one of the clothes hooks on this oaken wall. Yet it's gone, vanished amid all the other garments. Simply not there.

There is, however, laughter behind me.

I turn around. It's Andrea who must have just come in, Andrea and Erwein, both their shoulders shaking.

"Hullo, Freddy." Andrea's Oxonian Switzerdeutsch. "Sorry I'm late. What's the matter?"

"I can't find my parka."

"It's right by you."

"Where?"

"On that hook. Right there."

"The blue one?"

"Of course."

"That's not mine."

"Of course it is."

"No, mine is gray."

"Believe me, it's the blue, Check if your things are in the pockets."

The blue one also has a left-sleeve pocket, though stylishly slanted.

But with a familiar little bulge. Sure enough, that's my pillbox inside. And my mittens, my sunscreen, and my goggles are in the other pockets. And Andrea and Erwein must practically hold each other up, they're laughing so hard.

"Well," I say, "enjoy your prank."

Their sides are too splitting. They can't talk.

"Why did you do this?"

Apparently they're still not composed enough to answer. But of course I know why. And so do they, and so do Agnelli and Liechtenstein, if they happen to watch this little comedy: my old parka was simply too squalid a scandal for these rarefied snows. Somehow I'm not up to saying that outright, not in the middle of my Bernd/explosion problem. Yet I have to say *something,* especially about the Placidyls they found in my pocket.

"With friends like you," I say with a small smile, "I need tranquilizers."

"Those wimpy things?" Erwein asks. "I say, we men take much stronger stuff." And collapses again. Andrea, perhaps sniffing my discomfort through his laughter, coughs out something about the cold forecast and the superior insulation of the new jacket.

"What happened to the old one?"

"Sent it back to the hotel," Erwein says, still rather convulsed. "Would you kindly donate it to the Moritz Historical Museum?"

"What fun," I say dryly. "How much do I owe you for this blue thing?"

"Oh, Fred," Andrea says, now sobered by my tone. "We owe *you!*" He comes toward me, arms opening. "We owe you for being a good sport, please! And now lunch?"

I let him hug me. But I'm not going to be all that good a sport.

"I'm eating downstairs," I say. "With my ski guide."

Andrea lets go. Erwein stops laughing.

"Oh, yes," Andrea says. "The Austrian lad. So you like him?"

"He's wonderful. Thank you for picking him. Will you join us down there?"

Silence, for a moment.

"Uh, I can send a steward down there," Erwein says, "for your orders."

"Not for me," I say. "I love goulash soup."

"Good lord, I haven't had goulash for ages." Andrea links arms with me. "Capital idea. And I've never been down there. Let's go."

And me, despite the risk of smoothing it all away into one big easy joke, I can't resist saying, "Well, as long as you're with me, they might let you in."

At which they laugh as if they really mean it.

No windows, no views in the basement, just a hearty smell of paprika and fried onions. Plus a whiff of hierarchy which seems to have seeped through the ceiling from above. Those deeply tanned hunks clinking beer steins must be all elite "seasonals"—ski guides hired privately for the whole winter—because I recognize the tall bushy-mustached one, that's Emilio Pucci's, the redheaded bull who is the duke of Alba's and the flaxen-haired giant of Fritz von Opel. All joking together at their table, whereas my own big Bernd, being just another ski school hand (only temporarily privatized for my benefit), sits all alone, slicing salami onto a heel of rye, already past his goulash soup.

At my sight he jumps up, rigid; stiffens yet more when he sees Badrutt, stutters that he'll be finished in a minute, ready to go.

Of course I tell him that far from having had my lunch, I've come to eat it with him here, and so is Mr. Badrutt, so please, let's all relax and sit down.

Sit he does, but with shoulders taut, half raised in high alert. He remains that way even when Andrea announces he'll get on the self-service line for his goulash soup and mine, insisting that he'll also bring Bernd tomato salad, it goes so well with sausage.

No chance, of course to squeeze into Andrea's brief absence my "explosion" confession complete with Placidyls. There's just enough time to swear to Bernd that had I known of this separate-eating silliness, I'd never have stopped here in the first place. No, no, Bernd says, focused on peeling his salami slices, unimportant, just interesting how things are done here. And on being handed the tomato salad he thanks Andrea formally, with a big, solemn head nod. Still entirely unthawed.

Whereupon Andrea begins to deploy the finesse he uses to soothe his difficult billionaire guests. He tells Bernd a Saint Moritz legend about the local mountain demon, who will unleash terrible spring avalanches unless a virgin strips off her clothes and jumps nude into the snow, right here on the Corviglia plateau—probably the reason why a lot of rich old farts picked this spot for their club!

Bernd stops chewing in order to exhibit a dutiful smile. Andrea doesn't give up. Says, speaking of virgins, how about deflowering a little cognac bottle? Someone managerial must have overheard him, for almost immediately such a bottle appears from upstairs. And when we clink snifters to Andrea's toast, "To virgins in the snow!," Bernd's powerful teeth become visible in what just might be genuine amusement.

But none of it really works in the end. That becomes clear after lunch, when we're on our skis again, Bernd and me by ourselves. Of course I appear in the blue parka I had to collect from upstairs, not the old gray one that reminded him of his own. The new parka, I explain, is another of Mr. Badrutt's jokes, but this one I could do without.

Very nice parka, good quality, he says and speeds away, down. He does keep looking back to make sure that my edging doesn't get sloppy, corrects my knee position. But no yodeling, no grinning, no mountain deviltry together. Just a ski pro being meticulously professional with his charge. Whatever else was between us—gone.

Not that I don't try to revive it. My chance comes when he stops to let me catch up with him for advice on how to better brake on icy patches. I suggest a breather before going on and am about to launch into the beginning of my "explosion."

"Excuse, please," he interrupts to point his ski pole at a sudden cloud over Fiz Nair. "Excuse, but before the weather changes, perhaps we should get down quick, please."

Indeed we get down quick, as the sun recedes and the breeze turns unfriendly. Back in Moritz, I've no sooner clicked off my skis than he snatches them up. "Tomorrow, please, same time if this is convenient?" Off he goes with a polite, quick *"Guten Tag."*

My afternoon coffee I take not in the hotel lobby as usual but in that nearby little bistro, Casa Something-or-whatever. After this Bernd thing, I'm not in the mood for Palace talk.

When I reach my suite—there it is, hanging from the clothes tree, my infamous old parka, gussied up with a red ribbon and a handwritten note pinned to a sleeve:

With apologies from the mountain demon who is behind this wicked parka prank. He promises never to do anything like that again if a second virgin will jump naked into the snow. Let's discuss how to find virgins at dinner with the Karajans tonight.

Your Andrea B.

Well intentioned, if a bit labored. Hardly increases my desire for more Palace talk. I may develop a sudden indisposition excusing me from social dinners. Same feeling applies to the message slipped under the door: please return Mr. Don Congdon's call from New York. Perhaps Don sweetened still further the already gorgeous Rockefeller-Guggenheim two-book offer. If so, he'll only have sharpened the contrast to the homely advance I'd get for the novel I'd much rather do. No, I don't feel like agent talk either.

What I do feel like—what I badly need—is Marcia's straightforward Bronx earthiness she's preserved in the teeth of the unstraightforward good fortune that's befallen us.

When I call home, however, it's Nanny Becker picking up, disgruntled, in the middle of mixing formula, while "Mrs. Morton is out with the pram in that windy Riverside Park." Which leaves me still lonely for some close non-Palace voice, for my kind of homey reality. Almost automatically I call Papa at his office.

But when the hotel operator gets through, something worse than disgruntlement comes down on me—an inhuman impersonal metallic voice. *Number GA-74633 has been disconnected.*

WHAT?

The panic lasts only a moment. Of course, disconnected—dialing that number is a reflex out of date. I should have remembered because I visited the Eighth Avenue office only last week to collect my travel blessing for the Saint Moritz trip. (Papa's hand, thinner with age, on top of my head: "Go forth in good health, return in good health, the Lord prosper your journey.")

A ritual I never neglect to undergo, mostly for the hard grip on my shoulders that follows it, which is as near as Papa ever comes to a hug. This visit, though, was a double sentimentality being a double farewell, the second for keeps. Good-bye to Papa's 800 Eighth Avenue place, those odd premises of which I've become so oddly fond. Business has shrunk badly (only three girls left of his old crew of nine) while the rent has gone up *schrecklich*. Frank Morton Costume Jewelry is moving to a smaller room off Herald Square whose phone number I don't know by heart.

So I have to read it off my address book to the hotel operator.

HE-34128 rings and rings and rings and rings and rings—and nothing. And rings in vain again when I ask the operator to try again.

And now I really am alarmed. Five PM Saint Moritz time is 11 AM at Herald Square, smack in the middle of regular weekday office hours, during which Papa and Mutti never ever leave the phone unattended! Sweaty now, I try their home number.

"Hallo?"

"Papa! Thank God!"

"This is Freddy? In Switzerland? You are okay?"

"Yes, but are you? I rang and rang at Herald Square—and no answer!"

"The phone is still not disconnected? Three days after I notify! I will not pay the extra charge—"

"Papa, what happened?"

"I cancel at Herald Square."

"You did!"

"They find another tenant, so I get back half the deposit. That's when I decide. It is over."

"Over?"

"I retire."

"My God."

"There is no point, with this Jap dumping. I know you wish me to say Japanese. But they are Japs because they kill business. America, the greatest country in the world, it has to be nice to the Japs after Pearl Harbor? Take away the import duties? Letting them kill everything with their prices?"

"Well, it's complex, Papa. But this is so sudden. I'm surprised."

"You are a big busy writer. You have no time to notice. But you remember my orders bulletin board?"

"Of course I noticed."

"Empty. Killed by the Japs. So I put up your bestseller list. You are the Morton moneymaker now. I inform Mutti you are okay. Thank you for calling—"

"Papa, wait. So—so what are your plans?"

"We live in Florida. Good for Mutti's sinuses."

"When? Not immediately?"

"I have to find a reasonable place. I have saved, but it must be reasonable."

"Gee. We'll miss you."

"You will visit with the family. The airlines don't charge babies. So your little Rebecca comes free. She was very cute yesterday. But we talk too much long distance. I will inform Mutti—"

"Wait, Papa—you saw Rebecca yesterday? Marcia says she's growing new hair."

"Yes, very thin, *delikat*. I tell Marcia this is like you, that age. And I comb Rebecca just like you, that age."

"I wish I'd been there with you!"

"I tell Marcia, Mutti was looking for a special thin comb for your baby hair, it was always standing up on your head in this thin way, but I said, don't bother, Rosl, look, I blow on his hair, and it lies down. I comb your hair with my breath. But really, enough long distance. I inform Mutti you called—"

"Papa, hold it! You never told me any of that!"

"I never tell you many things. Your stomach troubles are okay, with all this skiing?"

"Yes, fine. I enjoy sports again—"

"Enjoy, good, this is important. And important for your business up there, these high-up people, the millionaires. This is your field you write about."

"I don't know if it's my field, Papa, but I do know I can't wait to come back next week—"

"Well, we understand you stay longer, you must find out the latest in your field. We have pride in your success in this field. This field the Japs can't kill—"

"Papa, what counts for me is the sport and the mountains—"

"Good. I will inform Mutti. We talk too much expensive long distance. We send love. Have a nice day."

Click.

I hang up, still somewhat shocked. Also a bit amused. His English (he hardly talks German with me anymore) always becomes more formal and therefore more fractured on long distance as if the fancy connection called for black-tie language. But I'm still shocked—and envious. He's so goddamn together in his stoic stodgy stingy way. So much better at handling change. He may not have done as well as I in America, but he sustains exile better. Not only our particular exile in the '40s but other later inevitable banishments, like just now from career to retirement, from midlife into old age. Better than me—never felt at home in the U.S.A., don't feel at home now in the winners' circle. Sometimes I actually miss failure, as if I'd been cast out of snug confines into some blazing vertigo. Haven't assimilated success, haven't assimilated my time of life. Still trying to yodel myself young. But, my God—*forty-two!* How did that happen? What an alien, unnatural age for a natural twenty-three like me, someone not meant to be adulterated by maturity. Where does Papa get off, being such a resigned, sensible sixty-eight? Preparing such a pragmatic, factual landfall on Miami, those grotesque, blue-haired shores?

But what I envy Papa for is not just his skill as exile. It's the baby-hair-combing thing. Suddenly I wish he'd never told me, just as I never told him about my shot nerves (explained them away as stomach troubles). I envy Papa because he had it both ways at my age: managed to make his Vienna factory flourish right through the worst depression but at the same time knew how to comb my baby hair with his breath. Will I know? In fact, will I have the chance? Maybe Rounzipussy's sproutlets will have thickened beyond breath combing when I return?

It occurs to me that Nanny Becker must have information on the subject. Again I call home. Only the answering service responds. Nanny (with formula) must have joined Rounzi and Marcia in the windy park.

And so I decide to dine with the Badrutts after all. For baby lore. Because my friendship with Andrea isn't merely utilitarian, it's also based on us both sharing belated papahood, joking together about being such oldish novice fathers. And if Papa Andrea doesn't know about baby hair, certainly Mama Cappie will.

The maître d' in the Grill Room, however, greets me with the news that M. and Mme. Badrutt will be a bit late. (Second time today, Andrea! Are you busy combing little Hans's hair?) We are asked not to wait with ordering. So we order, "we" meaning myself and the von Karajans, already at the table, whose two daughters, incidentally, are well beyond infant age, hence not useful for my purpose. Nor am I on the kind of footing with maestro and madame that would allow me to solicit schmaltzy reminiscing about baby hair.

And there's no chance to ask anything anyway because Eliette Karajan comes at me instantly with a question of her own about "something that's just a tiny bit of an outrage." Blonder, Frencher, prettier, even younger than most third wives, she has a flair for being vivaciously upset. She begs an answer from me, fast, before Andrea Badrutt arrives, for with him she might lose her temper and never find it again, she appeals to me as a Moritz specialist, a published scholar of the milieu—how is it possible that the table in the corner over there, which has been the Karajan table for years now, a spot where you can watch everybody coming or going—how can it be that it is now forbidden! *défendu! verboten* to her and Herbert! Reserved for some ghosts! Yes, ghosts! Because, look, nobody there, invisible! And if not ghosts—for whom? Nobody here can say! *Personne!* Not even that maître d'! I am her last hope!

Well, even her last hope can't offer an explanation. And with baby hair on my mind, I'm not much inspired to mimic sympathy. For which there'd be no time, for maestro directs at me a different inquiry of his own: Do my publishers insist on an insurance policy that forbids downhill skiing? No? Then why do concert managements and recording companies? Doesn't a conductor deserve the same sports freedom as a writer? Cross-country skiing, very nice, very charming, but on a beautiful day like today nothing like downhill—voom! No schussing allowed with gray hair? He still has plenty of control in his legs! If he's good enough to fly planes, isn't he good enough to ski downhill?

I nod vigorously, thinking that with the Karajans so candid about their concerns, perhaps I could be, too. Why *not* ask them about their daughters' infant coiffures? I may do just that once their irritations subside.

Toward that end the grilled salmon is a help. Ordered by all three of us, it is simply *ravissant,* as Eliette puts it. Yet just as the mood improves she discovers that a waiter has placed a RESERVED card on yet another table in that critical area over there, this one rightfully belonging to Drue Heinz of the 57 Varieties: another empty RESERVED table, deep into the dining hour! Or are there invisible specters munching away?

Maestro smiles at his wife's wit along with me, but he turns serious quickly. He asks if I have seen Leonard Bernstein ski at Moritz? No? Well, Bernstein does, and he, Karajan, understands that Bernstein skis well *and* downhill. Now, with all due respect to his eminent colleague, a fine, fine musician, this raises an issue. Bernstein is only a few years younger than he, Karajan. Yet the insurance does not prevent Bernstein from enjoying himself downhill, whereas he, Karajan, is prevented. Why?

Good question, I admit.

Well, he, Karajan, may have the answer. Vienna just may have a hand in this. Yes, Vienna, whose politics have tentacles everywhere, including music—precisely what caused his recent break with the State Opera there. So as revenge those tentacles may well have wriggled their way into insurance. And the reason why he is mentioning this to me is that I, too, had had a brush with Vienna politics, causing my family to leave that city. What do I think?

I'm thinking that the tentacles afflicting my family back then were of quite a different nature, 1930s tentacles which at that time were a lot cozier with the young maestro than with us . . . As I'm wondering how to phrase this thought less explosively, Andrea finally appears.

Not with his wife, Cappie, or with their little Hans, whom they occasionally produce evenings, if only very briefly, to show off the sole Palace heir. My secret hope has been for little Hans as perfect bridge to baby hair. But, no, it's not little Hans whom Andrea brings into the Grill Room. It's the shah.

The shah himself, plus retinue. Four fairly mountainous bodyguards, strapped into tuxedos, encamp around the Heinz (57 Varieties) table. Majesty reclines in the Karajan spot with a strikingly violet-eyed young woman. Andrea Badrutt remains standing, chatting and smiling with his lofty guest for a couple of minutes, then bows himself away, to our table.

And now Andrea proves his adroitness under very delicate circumstances (which of course leave no room for baby-hair discussion). That corner table, he sighs confidentially to the Karajans, the usurped Karajan table, apologies, but no choice with an emperor—it's like eminent domain. Furthermore, he himself feels just as victimized. The shah isn't even staying at the Palace anymore, he's taken over the entire Suvretta House annex—the Suvretta, chief Palace competition!—because it's cheaper for his traveling court of seventy, he even had dinner there, he's come to the Grill Room merely for coffee, just "to do" the Palace! The kind of trick tried by German dentists! And by the way, the woman is a lady-in-waiting of Empress Farah Diba, preparing for Her Majesty's arrival—officially that is, in terms of protocol. At which we all smile knowingly, as we are meant to do.

The Karajans appear mollified. I'm not because it turns out that Cappie Badrutt will be detained all evening consoling the Princesse de Polignac, who is distraught over her affenpinscher's allergy attacks; hence Mama Cappie will not be consultable re baby hair. Meanwhile Andrea, unceasingly adroit re Karajans, suggests that the Grill Room situation being what it is tonight, shah-wise, we might feel more *entre nous* having our dessert in the King's Club downstairs. He understands the Newleys are down there—wouldn't it be fun to join them?

It would. Dessert is sent down to the disco under the Palace lobby. Fine with me because that means another chance: the Newleys also have a baby roughly Rounzipussy's age. On the Palace sun terrace I've seen Joan Collins Newley coo into her pram without losing movie star panache.

Downstairs, though, the Rolling Stones din is hardly conducive to baby talk. A minor problem compared to the Karajan-versus-Newley ballet to which the genial handshakes and the tender cheek kisses are but overture. Obviously Andrea has been unaware of the touchy chemistry between the two couples. Me, too, though until now I've seen them together only amid the diffusing murmurs and manners of the Palace lobby. In the smaller, more focused arena of the disco, drumbeats accent arabesques of a satin confrontation.

Newley's opening gambit is a request for advice. Advice, as he puts it, from one great musician on dealing with another, namely Yehudi Menuhin. Menuhin had called Tony Newley no less than three times for house seats to Tony's musical *Stop the World, I Want to Get Off,* and just when Tony told him he could finally oblige, *this* one—Tony stabs wife Joanie playfully in the ribs—had given the seats away. To her obstetrician! "Indeed," Joanie says crisply. "And my pediatrician is next."

"Now, tell me, please," Newley appeals to Karajan, "how can I explain that to poor Yehudi?"

Poor concert hall icon craving in vain seats to a Tony Newley show! The suggestiveness of that can't be lost on Menuhin's fellow icon at this table. To me, on the other hand, Joan's mention of a pediatrician suggests an opportune segue to baby hair. But Karajan is too quick with his return volley.

"Oh, tell Yehudi the truth," he says. "That's what I did with Niarchos after I stole his Rolls."

This stops the conversation, if not the disco din. Actually, the celebrity Rolls robbery has become a widely cherished Palace legend of which, however, novitiates like the Newleys are still innocent, as Karajan has guessed correctly. And so he tells about jumping into his car in the hotel garage at five o'clock in the morning, racing down to the closest airport at Samedan, ready to leap into the cockpit of his Piper 12 craft, to land in Milano in time for his La Scala *Tosca* rehearsal at noon. In other words, his customary routine. Except that this time two cops drew pistols on him, even as he parked. In his hurry he'd mistaken the Niarchos Rolls for his own. And since the Samedan police knew nothing about opera conductors or tanker fleet owners, only about license plate alerts, they handcuffed him and locked him up in a room smelling of stale fondue for two hours until the whole *bêtise* was cleared up. Not a pleasant experience, but Stavros was so amused he invited thief and wife to a cruise on the *Creole* next time he yachted past Saint Tropez this summer.

The Newleys, too, display amusement. Not thrilled amusement.

Comfortable amusement, shared among equals. After all, the Menuhin vignette proved that a Karajan peer considered the Newleys much more than showbiz tinsel. Conversely, Karajan's deployment of the Rolls Robbery punctured any delusions the Newleys might entertain about the Karajans lacking a young kind of glamour. Vroom! robber scuttled down in the pirated Rolls from high ski pistes to the plane with which to graze a dozen glaciers. Hardly the act of a stuffy gray podium classicist. No, maestro is a dashing hotshot with jet set credentials—complete with Saint Tropez villa—easily equaling the Newleys'.

At this juncture, with the fortification of vulnerabilities completed, a certain relaxation almost sets in. But now Andrea quietly says, "Uh-oh." He nods at waiters scurrying to push chairs about by the wall opposite.

The rock drums diminish by a few decibels, halfway toward a disco-hush. And the shah makes an entrance together with Violet Eyes, followed by the four bodyguards, who have generated ladies on their own, the latter with curt hairstyles and angular handbags signifying coed detectives. All eight bivouac in the rearranged seating around Majesty and his consort of the evening.

Newleys and Karajans turn into covert gapers. I, too, but with me it's no mere curiosity. A clammy tingling, familiar and feared, has crept into my wrists. I'm praying this spectacle will distract me from a new bout of jitters.

And for a while it does. When the rock sledgehammers resume full force, the shah rises—trim, darkish, jaunty in his dinner jacket like a slightly overage but still viable Neapolitan gigolo—rises and escorts Violet Eyes to the dance floor. Instantly his guards follow. Four man detectives start rocking protectively with their girl gumshoes around the emperor.

"Maybe I ought to prepare you," Andrea says sotto voce, "because he's done this before down here, when he sees very beautiful women." He lifts his glass at Eliette and Joan. "He may have a bodyguard ask you for a dance so that he can cut in."

"This table stealer!" says Eliette. "What if I refuse? Iran will declare war?"

"Coo!" says Joan. "I always wanted to create an international incident!"

"This would be nice for the Palace," Andrea says. "But it's not an abduction into a harem, anything like that. Just ten minutes on the dance floor. Usually he sends three dozen roses in the morning."

"Not enough!" Joan says. "I'll tell him he has to fund a film for me for each number. Starting with *Anna Karenina!*"

"Lucky Noël isn't here," Newley pokes his wife. "He'd say you have the soul of a taxi dancer."

"*Na ja,* force majeure," Karajan says. "For Adenauer I once had to delay *Fidelio* fifteen minutes."

"I'll force majeure him!" Newley has gotten up. "Excuse me." And is gone.

To do what? Fetch a bomb? Or Dom Pérignon laced with arsenic? The jokes keep flying at our table. Majesty's horniness has made things convivial. The shah has not pounced as yet but at one point rocks his way quite close (followed by rocking guards) as though reconnoitering prey. If I were a few years younger and calmer, if the palm tingling would leave me alone, if I hadn't turned down just last month yet another offer (this time by *Esquire*) for yet another Moritz piece—yes, I'd enjoy such good material. But my hamstrings are cramping again, almost as bad as up at Corviglia, and for good measure I seem to feel dizzy, maybe with my ridiculous unresolved baby-hair obsession or maybe just simply from the disco drumbeats.

Suddenly these subside. I look up, as does everybody at our table. There is Newley at the DJ booth, handing over a disc with a smart thank-you salute.

And now the plaints of a ballad inform the smoke swirls of the room. "*What kind of fool am I . . . that cannot fall in love . . .*"

"If he's going to put his arms around my wife," Newley says, back at the table, "I'm going to make him dance to my tune."

This the shah does, shifting from go-go to ballroom, obedient and quite gigolo-graceful, while the bodyguards fox-trot their stiff best around him.

Muted amusement at our table, Karajan excepted, for he has vanished. Dizzy me also excepted. To get away from my nerves I flee into a mind game, imagine myself doing a second Moritz piece—how would I phrase this scene?

The scene, however, keeps shifting. Just as "What Kind of Fool Am I?" ends, Karajan reappears, heading straight for the DJ booth. Again a disc changes hands, again a thank-you gesture, this time by Karajan. And now a rhythm rarely heard in a disco starts billowing past the King's Club's dim electric tapers: Johann Strauss's "Blue Danube," an opulent nostalgia of violins.

"I knew it!" Eliette collapses her face hilariously into her hands. "That's Herbert conducting the Vienna Philharmonic!"

"*Chère* Eliette," Herbert says, now standing by our table. "May I have the honor?"

"Oh, this is cute," Newley says, getting up again. "Let's make it cuter. "I've got the *Candy Man* LP somewhere upstairs."

"In the brown valise, darling!" Joan calls after him, then turns back to our table. "I'd love to see the shah hop to Tony's 'Candy Man.' Oh, we've got to keep him on the floor! Fred, waltz me close. I'll give him a bit of Sweet Eye. Come on, you're Viennese."

Some Viennese. A nervous wreck with vibrating palms and convulsed thigh muscles, desperately trying to relax by playing a phrasing game— *with an emperor for a puck it's 1:1 in Newley-Karajan hockey, and Newley off to score again. . . .*

Not bad, but no good against my hamstrings. They go right on spasming viciously. The electric tapers have begun to rotate between my temples.

"Sorry, Joan, cramps. I overdid the skiing . . . Don't bother, Andrea, I'll be all right, just need to stretch out, I'll be back . . ."

With an all-too-unfaked limp I make it to the door. Lucky no one to see me supporting myself against the wall while praying for the elevator. It comes, I stagger in, and my fiendish hamstrings let up a little. Let up a little more when I stagger out, so that I'm still upright at my door, fumbling with the key.

But once I'm inside, they cramp again without mercy. Absolute torture, and I'm just a few feet away from the bed. I clutch the desk, right by the phone—where they ease up again. Yet each time I try a step, they tighten murderously.

And then it comes to me, the wisdom of my hamstrings.

They don't want me to reach the bed now. They don't want me to stretch out, to recover, to resume the evening as before, to be sucked back into this gilded nonstop ego chess. They want to prevent another Moritz piece I'd probably do after all. They want to refute Papa's idea that writing about "these high-up people" is my true career. Even more, they want to make sure that I'll breath-comb Rounzipussy in time. They want to arrest me by the phone until I pick up the damn receiver.

So I do. I pick it up. To tell my Marcia that I'm flying home.

1972

Miami, Mutti, and Morton Rampant

Hello, Bum," Cop says, approaching. "Bum, wake up! No sleeping in the park."

Cop asserts police officer authority—not easy, since she is my five-year-old Rebecca—by marching up with maximum momentousness, with slow, heavy, if necessarily small steps, thudding down her little sandals against the tiles of the Roney Plaza poolside. She is swinging her nightstick, a plastic spade still a bit sandy from digging castle moats on the beach.

"Bum!" Cop says. "You hear?"

Bum hears nothing. Sleeps right on, manifesting his bumhood (nice pastel beachwear to the contrary) by a disorderly sideward twist of his sun cap. Bumlike, too, his slump far down on his seat, making his right foot dangle askew from the deck chair. A dishevelment which degrades the deck chair into a tramp's park bench.

"Bum!" Cop says. "No sleeping here!"

Bum not only keeps sleeping but roars out a snore so loud that the canasta players under the next sun umbrella, a foursome all silver hair and pink pool pajamas, look up; then carefully register a smile. After all, Bum is normally my quite respectable seventy-four-year-old father.

"Listen, Bum!" says Cop, and taps Bum on the shoulder with the sandy nightstick.

This does wake Bum. He sits up slowly, yawns a vast rhino yawn, rubs his eyes. "Ah. Ja. Yes, Cop," he says. "I am not sleeping. I am just taking easy in the park."

And to show alertly he is taking easy, he folds his hands behind his back, crosses his legs.

"All right!" Cop says, somewhat appeased but still quite stern. "But remember!"

Cop begins to march away, with heavy tread of tiny sandals against tiles. Within seconds Bum's hands droop down, his legs fall uncrossed, he slumps, eyelids closing.

"Bum!" Cop says, whirling around. "You sleep again!"

"Ah!" Bum mutters, startled into consciousness again. "Ach, no. Just really taking easy. Look." And to prove his case, pulls a wrinkled copy of *The Miami Herald* from the pocket of his beachwear, unfolds it with much pomp to focus a knowing frown on the stock market page that's upside down.

"All right!" Cop says once more, loading the word with misgivings, yet once more marches off. Sure enough, Bum once more degenerates fast into prostration, newspaper dropping to the floor. And just as Cop bears down again righteously—I get a wifely nudge from Marcia.

She points at her watch. Almost 5 PM. My appointment is at a quarter after. Though the Miami Convention Center is only a few blocks away, it's time.

"Excuse us, Bum and Cop," I say. "We must be off. See you at dinner."

Bum sits up and reverts to being Morton Senior again, though only provisionally: he taps his granddaughter on the little shoulder in a way that says, "Wait. Brief intermission." To me he says, "Yes, Freddy, you must write about your Mister McSocialist."

"Well, about the Democratic convention," I say. "And I have to do an interview."

"Grandpa!" Rebecca says. "Be Bum again!"

"First say bye-bye to your father. He has helped his friend win the convention. He will be a politics big shot."

"Hardly, Papa," I say. "And the convention won't even vote until the day after tomorrow."

"Oh, this is formality. Say bye-bye, Rebecca."

"See you at dinner, Officer," Marcia says, patting Rebecca on the head. "Don't forget your nap."

"Oh, sorry, yes," Papa says, reminded of my wife's presence. "Say bye-bye, Rebecca, to your father *and* Mama."

"ByebyeMummyDaddy—Grandpa, be Bum!"

"Interesting," Marcia says as we walk along Dade Boulevard toward Convention Park.

"What?" I ask, though I have a fair idea.

"Not a word to your father about whom you're interviewing."

"I just want a peaceful dinner tonight. You heard him—it was me who sewed up the primaries for McGovern. Let it out I'm doing a piece on his campaign chief, there'll never be an end of it tonight. I'm putting the Bolsheviks into the White House!"

"Oh sure. With your column in the *Village Voice*. Preaching to the converted."

"That's not how he sees it."

"Reds taking over great America, that's what he sees. Only his Freddy could pull that off. Fatherly pride, in a way."

"He's complicated. And we're going to be late."

"Because you couldn't tear yourself away from him."

"Not him, Rebecca. So absolutely absorbed, playing with him."

"Of course. Big Grandpa, everybody clicking heels before him, but with her he's all fun and games."

"Actually," I say, "it's not quite as simple as that. When I was a kid—"

A loudspeaker truck drowns me out. HUBERT HUMPHREY FOR PRESIDENT! HUMPHREY IS OUR HOPE! HOLD ON TO HUMPHREY! . . . HELP AMERICA WITH HUMPHREY. . . .

Loud, too loud, desperately loud, in view of the McGovern surge. Yet just as well it kills conversation. For how convey to her that when I was a kid he'd enthralled me as thoroughly and easily as he does Rebecca now? And there was nothing simple about it because with me he had to overcome so much resistance. Back then he was no sweet, playful Grandpa, but harsh towering Papa all week long; remote Papa who ignored me at the lunch table (except for slapping his newspaper down hard when I spoke one loud word); unmerciful Papa who sent me off to bed an hour early if I showed up at dinner with a single dirty fingernail. Yet forty years ago in Vienna this dread Papa could turn into the very Pied Piper he is in Miami Beach today. Every Saturday afternoon— without fail—he'd trick me into loving him again. Downright seduced me on our weekly trip downtown to the Schweden Café. Each time I swore I'd resist, even shoved both my fists down deep into my pockets, so that he had to ask for my hand when we crossed the street on the way to the bus tram, but of course it was the wrong way, and that's how the seduction began. He'd lead me to the Number 8 tram that didn't go anywhere near downtown. So when I said we needed the G bus, whose stop is over there, he'd slap his forehead and roll his eyes at his mistake; already he was melting from august all-powerful omniscience into goofy fallibility, into somebody much smaller, mixed-up, and comic. By the time he reached the right spot with me and looked for the bus in the wrong direction, he had become my playmate, hilariously clumsy yet all the more eager to romp.

"Race you to the front!" he'd challenge me as we boarded the rear of the G bus. The vehicle wasn't moving yet, but for Papa it already seemed to be in bumpy motion because he lurched from side to side so that despite his longer stride I got there first; reached the front seats right behind the driver, leaning back at my ease while Papa huffed and puffed up, a distant second.

He was still panting pathetically when our tickets were punched. In fact, he kept on wheezing something terrible while the bus tooled down the long straight Alserstrasse. Not until we rolled into the older part of town, with its angled little streets, did he regain enough breath to be frisky once more.

"All right," he'd say. "Bet you the right arrow lights up next."

This arrow-betting game I loved (and didn't he know it!). A right-pointing arrow would light up crimson on the right side of the driver's dashboard before the bus made a right turn; before a left turn a crimson arrow would glow on the left. The game was to guess in advance which arrow would flash.

"No, I won't play unless I win something big," I'd say insolently, knowing that Papa was no longer the weekday despot.

"Uh, all right. You get a cinnamon wafer at the Café."

"No, two cinnamon wafers!"

"Okay. But you lose, and no whipped cream with your hot chocolate. Okay? Bet you the right arrow now."

"Bet you left," I'd say tersely.

The left arrow lit up, and we turned left.

"Wait a minute!" Papa would say, furiously adjusting his glasses to catch the street signs floating by. "Where are we? Hessgasse? Oh yes, but now we turn right. Bet you the right arrow."

"Left," I'd say tersely.

The left arrow glowed up.

"I don't understand this!" Papa would say, staring wildly out the window. "This isn't—oh yes, it's the Rudolfsplatz. I see. So *now* we turn left."

"Right," I'd say tersely.

The right arrow would glow up.

"There's something wrong!" Papa would wipe his hand across his mouth in panic. "It's the wrong route. Driver!"

But the driver, insulated in his glass cubicle, didn't hear and went right on bewildering Papa.

By the time we entered the Schweden Café, Papa was so discombobulated, I had to pilot him to the family table.

"Kiss your hand, Onkel Hugo, kiss your hand, Tante Elsa," I'd say. "I won all the bus bets. I won six cinnamon wafers and an extra portion of whipped cream."

"No, not fair!" Papa would protest. "The G bus took a crazy route today."

"That's funny," Onkel Hugo would say. "Because we came here by the G, and it went the same way as always."

"Sorry, sir," said Herr Helmut, the headwaiter, helping Papa off his coat, "but the G *has* to take the same route. There is no other way."

"This is all a conspiracy," Papa would say, collapsing into chair plush.

And me, taking my seat on top of two telephone books prepared ahead of time so that I'd be on the same level as the others, I sensed it was a conspiracy, all right, but a very nice one which would also allow me to order my own food, just like a grown-up.

"Very well, Herr Helmut," I'd say. "Hot chocolate, please, with double whipped cream, and a big plate of cinnamon wafers."

And Papa would throw up his hands, defeated, and I loved him very much. Only to hate him all the more that very evening, when he'd banish me to bed half an hour early just because I'd done my multiplication exercises in pencil instead of ink!

But how convey this ever-betrayed, ever-reborn love four decades later on Dade Boulevard in Miami Beach? Hurrying toward the Convention Center whose gate, thank God, is open? With Convention Hall already looming up, we're within the no-electioneering zone and therefore the HUBERT HUMPHREY blare has veered away. Conversation is possible again, but still, how convey all that to her quickly, before the Mankiewicz meeting?

"When I was a kid," I try again, "my father—"

"What do you mean 'when'?" she says. "With him you're still a kid. But go on, interview! You're late!"

"Aren't you coming?"

"Give my regards to Mr. Mankiewicz."

"But he said fine, to bring you along."

"No, thank you. No intruding wifey."

This is *so* her.

"You," I say, "are too damn shy for a cynic."

"Shut up and go."

"At least have a bite meanwhile. The delegates' canteen—"

"You kidding? Come to dinner without a decent appetite? Set your Mama wailing she hasn't cooked American enough for me? God forbid."

"This might take an hour."

"Fine. Gives me a chance to nose around for you. You know, background color. Scrounge up an epiphany or two. *Now go on in!*"

• • •

No epiphanies around Frank Mankiewicz's command trailer, parked by Gate 5 of Convention Hall. Just empty beer cans, flashbulb casings, cigarette butts. Remnants of some media scrum earlier in the day. Inside, to my surprise, there is only a security bruiser, yawning, who checks off my name on a list. The place could be any cramped, depopulated office before the arrival of the cleaning woman. Littered top of the photocopy machine, TV monitors, a half-full ashtray between the electric typewriters, a small phone bank. Yet this is something of a sleeping tiger. In some forty-eight hours a whisper will start here, to turn into a roar of headlines coast to coast. With these eight white phones here, Mankiewicz will trigger a war dance on the balloting night of Wednesday, July 12. From here he'll issue the high strategy calls to a battalion of phones deployed throughout the hall, priming the floor captains of the McGovern army, setting off drum explosions on the bandstand, making those vertical state delegation standards bob like totem poles gone mad, start McGovern flags waving by the hundreds and a thousand McGovern balloons swarming to the ceiling.

But on this Monday afternoon all is quiet—till the door flings open. Enter Mankiewicz, followed by the somewhat worn Irish mug of Lawrence O'Brien, chairman of the Democratic National Committee.

"Hi, Fred. You know Larry. Sorry I'm late."

"No problem. I was late myself."

"Anyway, Larry's going to join me at the press conference tomorrow on the McGovern Vietnam stand. You know, show 'em we're not just a bunch of crazed peaceniks, but we're backed by a mainstream figure—"

"Please, no insults." O'Brien smiles.

"Yes, this despicable mainstream O'Brien"—Mankiewicz smiles back—"him by my side shows the entire party's going to back George if the nomination goes our way."

"I like your straight-faced 'if,'" I say. "Look, I can make this a double interview."

"Well, the problem is," Mankiewicz says slowly, "the damn press conference is very early tomorrow, in time for the wire services, and right now is the only chance for Larry and me to get away and huddle—"

"In other words, no interview at all."

"Hate to let you down. But I made room for you tomorrow, PM—let me look in my book—yes, five-thirty? About the only time possible. It's all so down-to-the-wire crazy now."

Understandable. Yet annoying. I let a beat go by before I nod.

"Beautiful. And to say thanks, here's a hot maybe. McGov might drop in on Flamingo Park."

"Hey!" I say. "That wild scene?"

"Wild, including some of our best young supporters. He wants to say hello."

"When will he do it?"

"If possible, today."

"Today yet!"

"Any moment, if at all. Soon as he gets through with *Newsweek* because at seven there's a Cronkite thing. He'll try to squeeze it in between. But, Fred—I haven't told you. No other press knows."

"I declare myself flattered."

"Listen, McGov loves your *Voice* stuff. But he doesn't show by half past six—forget it. Now get outta here!"

Flamingo Park, with its lefty encampment, is only four blocks south and four blocks west of Convention Hall. Yet the sky has clouded so rapidly that it seems much darker than almost six when we get there—and right away start running: in the distance TV lights are bearing down on someone in a playground. No. It's Jesse Jackson, sneakered, shooting baskets for NBC.

We cruise on, searching, searching . . . and, yes, another TV light. No, just Abbie Hoffman in starred-and-striped tights debating masturbation with Germaine Greer, a head taller and helplessly model-looking, headband notwithstanding. Onward again . . . Indeed, there's another promising cluster—not McGovern either. It's massive, huge-hatted Bella Abzug, Mother Courage to Capital progressives, and Gloria Steinem, our madonna in blue jeans. They seem to have improvised a symposium on postfeminism, but I can't quite make out what they are saying because a black-hooded figure rides a branch high on the eucalyptus tree nearby, stentorian megaphone raised like a trumpet: *"The words of Jere-*

miah who came forth from Anatoth in the land of Benjamin . . ." And as if to counter the Old Testament with the New, there's a tambourine-cum-cymbals eruption from a torchlit tent bannered RESURRECTION CITY—ROCK WITH JESUS! This is followed by sudden applause behind us. We turn around. The clapping is neither for Jeremiah nor for Jesus, but for a man in bathing trunks walking on his hands, a reefer dangling from his mouth.

"Too many crazies," I say.

"I don't know," Marcia says. "Kind of comforting to have them around."

"You're still a Village Bohemian."

"Well," she says, "say our man really makes it to the Oval Office. Does that make us the establishment? Yikes! But with those types here around, we can still feel far out."

"You mean," I say, "Bum wakes up as Cop, and how embarrassing. . . . You know, I just might steal that for my column."

"Do. I promised you an epiphany. But it's half past, and no McGovern. So let's go."

"Let's give him a couple more minutes."

"We'll be late for dinner. Think the Big Mortons will forgive?"

"The Big Mortons," I say. "Nice zingie. Tell you what I'll do about the Big Mortons. There's a phone booth over there. I'll tell the Big Mortons we're unavoidably delayed."

"Very brave."

The phone booth, however, happens to be blocked by a tall thin man with a Vandyke. Which is peculiar because his orange armband identifies him as a legal aide to the encampment.

"Excuse me," I say.

He doesn't budge. "One moment," he says. "Till that camera crew's gone."

A camera crew passes by, is gone. He steps aside, points down to the floor of the booth. The receiver lies there, with the severed cord curled around it.

"We don't want them to catch this," says the Vandyke, "you know that would wind up on the late news? McGovernite hooliganism!"

"My God," I say. "This is really out of control here."

"Maybe it's meant to look that way. You're Morton Rampant."

Morton Rampant is the heading of my *Voice* column. But it doesn't carry my picture.

"How do you know?" I ask.

"We met in Washington a couple of months ago."

We did? Thin, tall, Vandyke, orange armband . . . "Yes!" I say. "Right! The demonstration. Weren't you passing out caps and socks?"

He smiles. "You got it."

"Yeah, and we stuffed the socks into the caps to buffer nightsticks. And McGovern was still pretty much nowhere."

"We still have cop trouble," he says. He nods at the sheared-off phone cord.

"*Cops* did this?"

"I can't prove it. But all three booths in the park are like that. The cords cut exactly the same way."

"But—why?"

"To make us look like vandals. Christ, look! That idiot over there! He's shooting up! Now, *that's* out of control!"

Off runs the Vandyke.

"Look," I say to Marcia, "now I really want to wait longer. If McGovern does come, I want to point him to this phone thing. Because if it's really a frame, it deserves a bigger soapbox than the *Voice*—as you say, preaching to the converted. He might even want to work it into his acceptance speech."

"Okay. But what about the Big Mortons? It could make us way late for dinner."

"Do me a favor." I pull out my address book. "The Big Mortons' number is in there, and it's not under B either. Tell 'em we're unavoidably delayed. Meanwhile I'll keep cruising for him."

"Where are we going to connect?"

"Say, the same place we came in."

"That tall palm?"

"Right. I'm not there in, oh, twenty minutes, that means I found him and you find me through the TV lights. Otherwise I'm by that palm and we're off to the Big Mortons' and you can bait me some more on the way back. Deal?"

"Deal." She smiles. "Happy hunting."

The hunting is not happy. I do pass an inspiring sight in the two huge tents of the University Action Groups, both topped by spotlit streamers: COME HOME, AMERICA. . . . COME HOME FROM WAR AND GREED . . . No matter how often I see those words, they still tingle down my spine. This is McGovern's core constituency, though without McGovern's presence, at least not yet. I pass on to a throng gathering around a park bench. A woman reclines there, long silky gray mane cascading down her white gown, strumming a lute, chanting. "There once was a union maid, she never was afraid . . ." Ethereal apparition, worthy message, still no substitute for McGovern.

I move on, to some fuss further down the gloaming. A shaggy lad in a tattered army jacket pushes a shopping cart piled high with books. "Trotzky's *Revolution Betrayed!*" he shouts. "Buy the truth! First edition! Just one buck!" Not far behind him trudges a baldie, fringe hair tied into a ponytail, a stack of newspapers under his arm. *"The Catholic Worker,"* he says hoarsely, quietly. "Two cents for friends."

After that—I've begun to circle back to our entry point—something that makes me blink when it shouldn't; Morton Rampant, age forty-seven, ought to be more blasé by now about spectacles like this young woman sitting cross-legged on a candlelit rug; blithely topless with psychedelic nipples, she has tattooed green cobras wriggling down her white arms as she holds up a deck of cards. "Dude-o!" she calls out to me. "How about a tarot trip?" I just smile and walk on stalwartly. The rendezvous tall palm is already in sight, and Marcia might already be waiting.

She is not. But I'm accosted once more, again by someone sitting on the ground.

"Got a knife, man?"

This time it's an enormous black beard underpinning incongruously rosy young cheeks and specs on a rather small nose.

"A knife. I'm afraid not."

"Of course you don't. Nobody has anything. This whole countercultural bit is a scam."

"Just because I don't have a knife?"

"Well, you look at this, man! They snow you with this do-it-yourself jive, like, you know, fuck shoe-store capitalism, buy this leather sole, buy the thong, buy the goddamn awl to make the goddamn hole through which you put the goddamn thong—except this awl here, it's a fucking bust! It can't make a hole! No way! Impossible! Don't believe me? Try it! Go on, man, try it!"

"You haven't tried it in the right spot."

This is Marcia's voice—she has arrived behind my back.

"You're trying to pierce the sole in the middle," she says. "The hole is supposed to be to the left, by the big toe—see the indentation? That's the thin spot in the leather. Pierce it there."

The beard places the awl against the indentation, tries, pierces.

"Crazy!" he says. "Thanks! Right on!"

"Right on to you, too," Marcia says, and leads me aside.

"I couldn't reach the Big Mortons," she says. "Their phone's constantly busy."

"Constantly? But they never phone at this hour. My mother's cooking and my father's watching the 6:30 news. It's his religion."

"What can I tell you? Always a busy signal. And"—she lowers her voice—"he's not going to happen here."

"McGov?" I whisper back. "Who told you?"

"His scheduling people."

"When'd you talk to them?"

"I called the Mankiewicz number in your book. He can't squeeze it in before Cronkite."

"Damn."

"It's howl with the wolves."

"I suppose so," I say. "I guess he has to, to beat Nixon, up to a certain degree. Priority over Flamingo Park. He has to make nice with the Cronkites. Okay, back to the Big Mortons'."

But just before we get to the Big Mortons' residence in the Roney Plaza—in fact, just across the street from that retirement tower—Marcia suddenly stops under a canopy. A claret-hued, crenellated, silk-finished baldachin of a canopy, proclaiming a Real Classy Eats Joint.

"Let's go in a minute."

"But they confirmed our reservation."

"I know," she says, going in, "we just need to fix something."

Inside, the little Tiffany lamps on the tables light up a dense crowd of chewers and chatterers, most with name tags on lapels. The maître d' rushes up, professionally delighted.

"Ah, Monsieur et Madame Mortón; bienvenue again this year!"

This year, as in other recent years, the Mandelbaum-Mortons will have their family fest here at the Embers Restaurant with the sort of salad-fork-and-finger-bowl panache Mutti basks in and Papa grumps at ("Five dollars for this two wet potatoes? Criminal!"). Here we celebrate both my parents' birthdays (his on June 25, hers, July 5) jointly on a date near those two days. Which is my other reason—apart from the Democratic convention—for coming to Miami this week.

"But Monsieur Mortón, *tonight*?" The maître d's baritone rises in alarm, betraying a Cuban accent under the French varnish. "Tonight we are already full with very big political personalities—"

"No, no, this is about tomorrow," Marcia says.

"Oh, *tomorrow*, good! Yes, I have your reservation tomorrow, two birthday cakes, lovely decorated, also the special chair for the little mademoiselle—"

"That's it," Marcia says. "That's why we dropped in, to tell you she won't need the high chair anymore, in fact, she's become a little sensitive about that. If you'd have a couple of pillows ready she can sit on."

"Oh but of course. I make a note, two pillows very nice, very soft, early bird six PM tomorrow. No problem!"

But, my God, there is a problem.

That dawns on me as we walk into the Roney lobby two minutes later.

"Wait a minute," I say. "Six PM tomorrow—my Mankiewicz interview is at five-thirty. I'll never make it!"

"So change the Mankiewicz time."

"Are you kidding? With his frantic schedule? Tomorrow's the day before balloting!"

"Then make the dinner later at the Embers."

"No, six o'clock is all they could give me, with the conventioneers flooding everything. And I couldn't have gotten even that without my bit of clout."

"So make the birthday bash the next evening. We can stay a bit longer."

"No good either. Next evening my father has something. Something he mentioned, some sort of function."

Actually, I know exactly what function. A B'nai Brith fund-raiser. But if I told her that, I'd feel funny not also telling her that Papa's contribution that evening would be two opening-night tickets to the Miami production of the *Rothschilds* Broadway musical based on my book; and how Papa came up with the idea, calculating that the two seats would cost him less than the average check expected by the B'nai Brith yet might well fetch a good deal more at an auction; and that I'd brokered his transaction with the Coconut Grove Playhouse; and that she, Marcia, was unaware of all this simply because I hadn't thought to tell her yet; after all, it had happened prior to her and Rebecca's arrival here (the *Voice* having sent me down early to cover preconvention maneuvers). Going into all this right now would take too long; would also fuel the irony in my dear wife's sidelong glance, those dark tropical eyes she knows how to narrow into a WASP sort of amusement when combined with a certain slight smile curving her lips. Damn it, she can even press the elevator button ironically.

"Well, we've got a Big Morton problem on our hands," she says, linking arms with me. And then, elevator door opening, gives me a push in, an oddly fond push, even if she goes on, "And of course with the Big Ones you've got no clout at all."

And I, for my part, I'm oddly fond of her needling even though it expresses her favorite dogma that Morton Rampant, mordant polemicist, scourge of the Nixonoids, is a Mama's boy. She insists on being amused by that no matter how often she's told that perhaps I was once a closet *Papa's* boy, but am now long emeritus, basically. At any rate, the issue at hand is not my clout with the Big Mortons but an abrupt change of date of what is after all the birthday dinner for both my parents. A matter to be broached right at the right time.

• • •

And the time isn't right at the Roney dinner *en famille*. Certainly not at the start for the simple reason that even if I wanted to, I couldn't get a word in edgewise. It's not Papa's who is holding forth; in fact, he hardly opens his mouth. Yet I suspect right away that he's the covert impresario of what's going on: conversation consists entirely of Rebecca's monologue—one long, happy police delirium.

She has had a police conference! A police conference with Sam, a real-life law enforcement officer! A conference about cop things like real-life bums who sneak into the Roney Plaza pool at night to sleep the night away on the deck chairs there! Yes, real life! And about chasing the bums off not only through nightstick prodding, Rebecca's method, but Sam's: using the pool hose to squirt water on the offenders, the very thing she might do tomorrow. At which my father, the once-and-future Bum, goes through tremendous wincings and warding-off gestures, Rebecca watching him gleefully as she talks and talks.

And talks, hence still no chance for me to bring up the birthday dinner problem. Rebecca's tale, far from over, expands into details suggesting that Sam is not exactly a Miami Beach cop. He came along (shortly after we left for Convention Hall) patrolling the Roney grounds when Papa stopped him for an introduction to Rebecca. Sam seems to be simply a Roney Plaza security guard. A drab detail compared to further lustrous facts, radiantly recounted by Rebecca: though Sam had to resume his rounds, he promised to report back to Rebecca on their completion. And this he really actually did after she returned with Grandpa and Grandma to their apartment! He really telephoned Rebecca!

Papa listens to all this, spooning his soup in all innocence. Occasionally he sways his head from side to side to indicate awed astonishment at Sam's call, which of course he himself must have instigated. No doubt Sam was as happy to oblige him as others of the Roney Plaza personnel. Papa charms them the way he once did his Eighth Avenue neighbors in New York. Here, too, he distributes gold-netted silver-wrapped pralines to his favorites so that they'd do him favors like "the police conference" in return. Probably the length of that "conference" accounts for the busy signals Marcia kept hearing when she called my parents' number. Probably the "conference" was long enough to let Papa watch most of the 6:30 news in peace. And quite possibly the length of the "conference" affected something Rebecca had promised us she'd do before dinner in order to get permission to stay up afterward, for one dance at the Roney Monday Night Senior Hop. This thought occurs to Marcia, too.

"Rebecca," she says, "with all this great phoning, did you have time for the nap you said you would take?"

Rebecca, absorbed in retailing Sam's way with litterbugs, seems to have missed the question.

"Rebecca." Marcia puts down her spoon rather hard, with a sharp glance at my father, who is suddenly claimed by the husbandly duty of scooping up the soup plates and marching off with them to the kitchen, rather fast. "Rebecca, answer. Did you have your nap?"

"I wanted to," Rebecca says blithely, "But it's not nice to hang up on the police."

"In other words, you broke your promise."

"So tomorrow," Rebecca says, still blithe, "I take a nap extra long. Okay?"

Naturally this is most un-okay. The lowering of Marcia's eyebrows indicates that she is about to say just that. But just then my mother enters from the kitchen with the steamed rice and the sautéed string beans, followed by my father, bearing a platter of sirloin as well as "sirloin." Now, "sirloin" constitutes another unkept promise, only this time we are the culprits. Before this Miami trip we had to reassure Rebecca that she would no longer be stuck with "baby food" different from the adults', an embarrassment particularly painful to her at special dinners like those with her grandparents. However, on the day of departure one of her milk teeth became loose. So Marcia, an empathetic no less than protective mother, entered into a conspiracy with Mutti. To avoid baby food humiliation yet avoid uprooting the milk tooth and subsequent swallowing of same, Rebecca is being served a promise breaker. The "sirloin" placed on her plate has been as thickly sprinkled with paprika as that of the grown-ups' sirloin and therefore has the same red-stippled surface. But under the common camouflage, ours is the real thing whereas Rebecca's is milk-tooth-friendly ground beef.

Will our bright little Rebecca notice? Not at all. Marcia and I are exchanging grateful glances. Rebecca is too busy planning out loud how she'll help Sam tomorrow: make rounds of her own, for example, watch out for bad people and inform Sam of any need for action. Quite happily she talks and munches on and on.

But after the dessert of vanilla crescents—trouble. It starts when my mother excuses herself; she must get ready for the Senior Dance, she has to change to her dance frock.

"Me, too," Rebecca says. "I change to my dance frock."

"You don't need one," Marcia says. "Not for one dance number. Remember we agreed."

"That's not fair! I need a frock like Grandma!"

"Well, we didn't pack any for you. You look great as you are."

"No, I don't! Grandpa's going to dance with me, and I have no frock!"

All of a sudden she is near crying.

"See what happens with no nap?" Marcia says. "You get cranky."

"Rebecca, I tell you something," my father weighs in. "You have a dance hat. This is better than a frock."

Rebecca stops rubbing her moist eyes.

"Dance hat?"

"This hat you show me when you unpack."

"My sun hat?"

"Sun only during the day. At night you change this to a dance hat."

"Right!" Marcia says. "Grandpa is right. At night you pin the brim up in the back and a little down on the side, and it becomes very elegant, an evening hat for dancing."

"You see?" my father says.

"I'll show you," Marcia says. "Let's get the hat in our room."

And Rebecca accepts her hand, smiling.

That Marcia and Rebecca need to take the elevator only a few floors down to the hotel part of the Roney is another of Papa's accomplishments. When I phoned him our Miami dates and he heard that the *Voice* would spring only for single-room accommodations for me, his financial reflexes kicked in lightning fast. On Marcia's and Rebecca's behalf he instantly booked a Roney bed-and-cot studio at the fifteen percent discount granted only to building residents. Quite a feat, snagging this Roney bargain on such short notice despite the convention deluge. Trust the Belgian pralines to have played a role.

At any rate, with my family in their cut-rate digs and Mutti shut away in the bedroom, presumably agonizing over what shoes to choose—dressy or comfy?—it's just me and Papa now, and therefore time to come to the point. In the kitchen, that is, doing the dishes, him soaping and rinsing, myself drying. Yes, high time to tackle the postponement of the birthday dinner.

"Papa," I say, "you and Mutti can do me a favor. How about making the birthday dinner a couple of days later?"

"Ah, the Embers cancel. Good, we go to a place not so expensive."

"It's not the Embers, Papa. Tomorrow night turns out to be difficult for me. And of course on Tuesday you have the B'nai Brith. Is Wednesday all right?"

"You never mention tomorrow is difficult."

"Because it's just come up. Tomorrow is the only time I can do a very important interview."

"Ah. Otherwise *The Village Voice* will not print you."

"No, the *Voice* prints my columns regardless. But with that interview I'll have material beyond the *Voice,* like a convention piece for the *Times.*"

"The *Times* will print your Red stuff?"

"Don't be so surprised. You've seen my byline on the op-ed page."

"You'll get extra money from the *Times*?"

"Of course."

Extra money is my leverage. But it might not work. He is scrubbing the steak pan too hard.

"Op-ed page," he says. "Ah, I remember. Big *New York Times,* all they pay you was a hundred and fifty dollars. Maybe they pay more if it's not Red stuff."

"Papa, you scare me." I grin; I'm trying to lighten things up. "Your dollar memory is terrifying."

"A hundred and fifty dollars from the *Times* is a *Schande.*"

"At least it's a nonpartisan *Schande.*" (I'm still trying.) "They underpay Republicans just as much."

Not a trace of a smile on his face.

"From *Holiday* magazine," he says, "you get three thousand each article. For the Rothschilds book many thousands."

"Papa, the writing I do now means so much more to me."

"How much you get from *The Village Voice*?"

"Oh come on, Papa! You remember the *Times* fee so well, surely you remember the *Voice*'s. You've asked me often enough."

"You get a hundred and thirty dollars for attacking America that saved us from the Nazis."

Here we go again. Just what I didn't want to get into. However, there's no choice.

"Papa," I say, "we've been through this before. I am not attacking America. Only the Nixon administration, which is devastating a whole nation in Vietnam and is also very bad for the American people."

"Aha. A question. Our Rebecca is an American, no? A real American born here?"

"Of course."

"Okay, you want to take good care of our own American in the family, no? Send her to a nice school, a fine university, good education. You can do this on a hundred thirty dollars from *The Village Voice*?"

"Papa, you know I have savings."

"From the Rothschild book. But you don't write that anymore. And Mutti and I, when we die we will leave you everything, but you must give half to your brother. And you have many years ahead paying graduate and undergraduate college, she's already so smart, and nice dresses when she is a beautiful woman, and when she meets the right person, you will need for her—how do you say *Mitgift*?"

"A dowry. I appreciate all that, Papa. I appreciate how wonderfully you play with her, better than I ever could, but for me the most important thing is the kind of America in which she'll grow up, and I don't want this to be in a country where all that matters is money and power—"

"Okay, okay!" He's interrupted me; finished rinsing, he turns the water off abruptly. But then he makes the interruption friendlier by holding out his hand, smiling, for the plate I've just dried. He stacks it in the cupboard for me. "All right," he says, establishing a cooperative drying/stacking rhythm between us. "But a question: Until your *Village Voice* America comes, money is still unfortunately important, no?"

"Unfortunately."

"Even for your wonderful *Village Voice,* money is important, or they pay you better. So we postpone the birthday dinner, you stay longer, they pay your hotel longer?"

"I'll take it up with them."

"They would be crazy to pay extra days, especially this fancy Diplomat Hotel they put you in, so far up in North Hollywood—"

"Papa, it's the only hotel they could get during the convention—"

"It costs more a day than you spend for the whole birthday dinner, plus the taxi you take so far back and forth, they will pay taxis extra days?"

"I'll submit expenses."

"Okay, you submit. They will pay?"

"Kindly let that be my worry."

"Even if you move to hotels less expensive, it's robbery prices everywhere during the convention."

"Look, the Roney can always squeeze in another cot for me downstairs on the hotel floor—"

"With Marcia and our Rebecca? The same room? You type all night. I remember the time you still live with us. In New York today you have a big apartment, but here, one room, you wake our Rebecca."

"Papa, please! First things first! What we have to settle right now—can we have the birthday dinner two days later? I'm not worried about finding shelter."

"Me also. I'm not worried."

To my surprise, he smiles as he examines the saucer I've just dried. "This is easy. The extra days, you move into our place."

"Your apartment?"

"The pull-out bed from the sofa, in the living room. Your brother sleeps there all the time. Very comfortable. And you type all night, fine. Mutti sleeps very well, any noise. Me, I don't sleep anymore anyway, even if it is quiet."

"You don't sleep anymore?" I say. "Since when?"

"Not important. Since even the time you still live with us. But your night typing that time, I think, okay, at least he is a good worker, a hard worker, a real Mandelbaum-Morton. Sometimes the typing was like— *ein Schlaflied.* How do you say this in English?"

"A lullaby. I never realized my typing carried to your bedroom. You never told me."

"Not important. Your interview tomorrow, this is important. Okay, I tell you something. We have the birthday dinner two days later. Meantime you move in here with us."

He's taken the last dish out of my hand, stacks it in the cupboard, closes the cupboard with a cheery, conclusive, almost ceremonious thud. We seem to have made a covenant. Somehow without assent. Working and sleeping in their living room? . . . God knows what that might do to my concentration or their comfort. But if I don't move in with them, is the covenant broken? Then no change in the birthday dinner date, hence no Mankiewicz interview compatible with my deadline?

There's no time to discuss it: Mutti enters in her pleated sky blue frock nuanced to her pale blue hair; her somewhat constricted gait hints that she's opted for dressy over comfy pumps. Moments later Marcia leads Rebecca in—mother in her usual dark slacks, daughter under a sun hat turned into a kind of soirée sombrero. Rebecca prances happily self-conscious, a bit of a midget model, swinging her future hips; her eyes, though, look a little pinched, possibly with naplessness. And the issue of the birthday dinner shift must hang fire because all the Mortons, big and small, are primed and primped for the dance.

Well, not quite primped, as far as my mother is concerned.

"Freddy!" She's staring at some felony bared below my Adam's apple. How can a personage like me, poised as I obviously am on the very brink of the Nobel Prize, appear at the Roney Plaza Senior Dance—tieless? And by extension how can the imminent Nobelist's father?

It's off to the bedroom for both of us, to the tie rack in Papa's clothes closet. Of course, he chooses more cunningly than I. After we emerge, decently knotted, he lifts Rebecca up to the hall mirror to touch his tie against her hat: its beige and white stripes are quite similar to the yellow and white ones of her brim, and her little grin unpinches her eyes.

If only all subsequent problems of the evening would resolve so smoothly!

The next Problem turns up almost right away. What surprise that it should involve nice Mr. Kahn. As on my previous visits I find Dave Kahn posted at the entrance to the Roney Social Affairs Room, whose *faux* Bourbon chandeliers shine on appropriately *faux* Currier & Ives prints along the walls. Mr. Kahn is sergeant at arms of the Roney Plaza Men's Club, which runs the Monday-night Senior Dances, but he's a sergeant at arms humanized by a hearing aid and by the palpable embarrassment with which he performs his duties. Standing in the doorway, he's bent his silver mustache into a fixed smile to sugar the fact that he must ask each husband or widower or single for a paid-up membership card. But tonight he also asks for a dollar.

This so shocks Papa, he lets go of Rebecca's hand.

"Yeah, sorry," David says. "A shame. What happened, our juke's still on the fritz, so till it's fixed we had to get one from outside. So the dollar is chip-in for the rental."

"Rental!" Papa says. "But we borrow the women's machine!"

"No more," Dave says, lowering his voice. "That's the real shame. Look at Sylvia."

He gives a quick, furtive nod in the direction of Sylvia, standing close to one of the two jukeboxes in the room. More than close: she's planted herself directly in front of its blue and gold plastic facade, blocking all access. Sylvia—sergeant at arms of the Roney Women's Club in charge of the other weekly Senior Hop, scheduled for Thursday nights—Sylvia's right shoulder is quite a bit higher than her left, but the straightness of the stance with which she keeps vigil over her juke is as uncompromising as the blackness of her dyed pompadour.

"It's crazy!" Dave Kahn whispers. "The women carrying on we broke their juke last time! Fantasy. Typical! So what can we do? A crying shame, but it's got to be one dollar per member family, two per guest family, I'm sorry."

"Fine," I say, but before I can get my wallet out, Papa has produced

three green bills with a speed and forbearance remarkable considering all
the wounded thrift in his soul.

Dave steps aside, letting us pass. Mutti touches her hand against her
pale blue hair wave, lifts her chin high, but not too high, into an angle of
demure pride. To the strains of Guy Lombardo's "I like New York in June,
how about you?" she puts her hand on my arm and struts both of us into
a public entrance.

At her side I'm not Morton Rampant but the author of a famous Bar
Mitzvah gift book. More specifically, I'm The Son Of The Mother Of *The
Rothschilds*. With us marches Papa, his hand cradling Rebecca's, a smile
pasted over his three-dollar trauma. I have no eyes in the back of my
head, but it's a safe bet that Marcia's wry WASP grin brings up the rear.

"Ho, the Vienna crowd, welcome!" says Milton Pinsler. He strides forward to greet us with a limp I haven't noticed before. But he still sports
his silver-buttoned crimson blazer that proclaims him host of this dance
as president of the Men's Club. His hand, gnarled, mottled, grandiose,
sweeps across five seats kept empty in the otherwise packed room "De-
fended them with my life, Rose." He bows to my mother. "Reserved exclusive for you and your gang!" The verve with which he manages to
bend down far enough to touch his lips to her fingers is impressive for a
man who ran Brooklyn's biggest liquor store for fifty years. From his
hand-kissing stoop he twists his face sideward to wink at my father. "Like
in the old country, eh?" Then he straightens up, wincing only for a second, and, with the same theatrical brio, folds his hand over his heart and
hangs his head. "Forgive this lousy juke," he says to Mutti. "It hasn't got
your Frederic's 'In My Own Lifetime.'"

Now, "In My Own Lifetime" is not exactly mine, being Sammy Davis's
rendition of a song from the musical based on the aforementioned Bar
Mitzvah book. Milton knows that my mother likes to have it played after
her arrival with me as a sort of trumpet blast celebrating my presence.

"No tragedy." I smile to make up for Mutti's stricken eyes.

"But!" Milton says, knobby index finger raised high. "*But!* Never fear,
Milty's here! Good news! Remember, Rose, 'Gaucho in the Night'?
Xavier Cugat? You and your ever-loving bridegroom danced it so beauti-
fully when Frank learned the tango last year? Give a listen!"

He nods a signal at Walt Golden, standing at the ready by the rented juke. Walt Golden, his vice president, similarly festive with ivory-handled cane, best toupee, and carnationed buttonhole, pushes a button. Xavier Cugat's trombones saturate the air.

"Thank you, Milton," my mother says and scoops me up, toward the dance floor, quite unaware that we're heading straight for the next problem.

She finds out soon enough.

Still, for the first two minutes of "Gaucho in the Night" her face holds on to its outward cheer even while our shoes keep bumping against each other. Then she breathes through her smile:

"Not a rumba, Freddy, a tango. A tango!"

"It's the best I can do."

"You don't know the tango?"

"I guess I've forgotten."

"Freddy!" Now she's hissing through her smile. "A man like you, you dance with the most famous people! And you do a good rumba, but not with a tango!"

"Well, I thought at least it's also South American—"

"No, it's different! What do celebrities say when you rumba the tango?"

"Mutti, people don't much dance ballroom dances anymore."

"But here we do! And they are all watching us!"

"Not really," I say. "They're watching Papa and Rebecca. Look!"

It's true. Those two are drawing all the eyes: Papa, carrying Rebecca on his left arm, his right draped formally and solemnly around little right shoulder, she with both little arms around his neck, but hatted head held very proud and high.

"See how well Papa tangos," Mutti says.

Indeed he does for a man his age, walking briskly and correctly through all the dips and turns. But it's not he but his tiny partner who gets all the "ooohs" and "ahhhhs," which now change into outright applause, to which she blushes and hides her facelet against Grandpa's chest (like Marcia, she will turn enchantingly shy at unexpected moments), presses against him so that she squashes her hat—which of course evokes some more applause.

This does make Mutti smile. It also offers her an opportunity. With all attention focused on her granddaughter she can, discreetly, end her son's tango debacle and start his rehabilitation by rumba. She dances me straight to Vice President Walt by the rented juke.

"Hello, Mr. Golden, my son Frederic here, he would very much like a rumba next."

"Rumba?" the vice president says, squinting his eyes along tiers of titles on the juke. "Rumba. Let's see . . . conga, merengue . . . cha-cha, samba . . . lots of sambas . . . Sorry, no rumba."

"Ridiculous!" Mutti says, and steers me to the Women's Club juke.

"Sylvia, my son Frederic wants to say hello."

Sylvia and I nod and smile at each other. Sylvia, though, raises even higher her already unevenly high right shoulder, somehow conveying a heightened alert.

"Frederic would love to dance a rumba," Mutti says.

"Wish I could help you out, honey," Sylvia says evenly, immobile.

"I know we have rumbas in our women's jukebox," Mutti says. "Yes, you see? Look! 'Begin the Beguine.' Or there, 'Amour, Amour, My Love.' See?"

"Not at the men's dance, I'm afraid."

"But just one rumba—"

"Mother," I try to interpose, "It's not important—"

"Please!" Her hand motion silences me.

"Just one rumba!" she repeats to Sylvia. "As a favor to me! I'm a Women's Club member."

"Sweetie, all the rumbas you want at our dance, Thursday."

"But Thursday Frederic will be gone."

"It's our president's order, honey. From Florence direct."

"But this is ridiculous—"

"Sweetie, listen, the men already wrecked *their* machine. Last week they almost ruined ours. So this week Florence decided—enough."

"Sylvia, I have an idea: *you* operate the machine. No touching by men. I make them promise!"

"Promise?" Sylvia emits a curt derisive laugh. "Yeah. Like they promised about the coffee urn."

"What?" Mutti asks.

"The new coffee urn over there! The men use it even more than us. Sweetie, you were there at our last meeting, you heard Florence on the coffee urn. We advanced the whole entire purchase price. The men haven't even begun to cough up *their* half. Not a red cent!"

"But this is nothing to do with dancing one rumba!"

"It doesn't? Let me tell you, Sweetie, I'm on Florence's slate, and next election somebody's going to raise a stink about that coffee urn! Letting the men get away with it! Now, on top of that, let 'em wreck our jukebox? Florence says no, gentlemen, not on our watch!"

"Sylvia, darling, one second. I voted for Florence—for you, too, the whole ticket because it is very good how you protect our interest—"

"Exactly what we are doing right now."

"But I will protect, too! Any man coming near our machine—over my dead body! You just play one rumba!"

"No can do." Sylvia shrugs slowly, regretfully, inexorably. "Florence's orders."

"But just tell her what I said. Over my dead body! Tell her—where is she?"

"Her apartment. It's her gin rummy night."

"So please, telephone her! Tell her my son Frederic, he has so many important things to do in New York, but he has come especially for my birthday, he wants to dance just one rumba! Florence has read his book—"

"What she reads makes no difference," Sylvia says. She reaches for her handbag on top of the contested juke, slings the strap over her shoulder, the higher, right one, with an abrupt, emphatic motion. "No difference! That's what she'll say. I'll call her, but you'll see—no difference!"

She marches away. "Meanwhile, you watch our machine!" she shouts from the door.

"Don't worry," Mutti says to me. "Florence loves your book." Bravely she smiles, and both of us join the applause that started again: "Gaucho in the Night" has crescendoed to its end, and Papa is returning to our seats, grandchild on his arm. The clapping is for

Rebecca, her face still pressed so adorably abashed against his chest.

"Our Miss Morton!" Milton Pinsler claps his hands above his head for emphasis. "Our star of the night! Our megastar!"

"Wonderful. Thank you," Marcia says, receiving her from Papa. "And now we'll say good night."

But Rebecca's face, become visible, contorts with suffering eyebrows and trembling wee nostrils.

"It hurts!"

"What hurts?" I ask.

"My hat!"

"All right, we'll take it off."

"No!" Rebecca stops my hand. "I need it for the dance!"

"Now look, young lady!" Marcia says. "You had the most wonderful tango with Grandpa, everybody here just loves you to pieces, but now you are a little cranky, and I'm tired myself, so we'll quit while we're ahead and say good night."

"No, the Blue Dance! Grandpa promised the Blue Dance!"

"What Blue Dance?" Marcia asks.

We all look at my father.

" 'The Blue Danube,' " he says, offhand. "I just mention it by the way."

"We all agreed," Marcia says with thin lips, "one dance. No more. But Grandpa promised and what's done is done. So"—she holds out her hand to Rebecca—"we'll go to the mirror out in the corridor, where we'll make your hat more comfortable and you'll see for yourself that you still look ravishing, and then we'll come back and you'll do a couple of 'Blue Danube' turns with Grandpa, and then that's it! I'll be so tired out by all this, you'll take me straight to bed. Let's go."

A pout still purses Rebecca's little mouth, but she lets herself be led away.

"What a doll, your Becky," Milton Pinsler says. "Like my son's Amy. The thing is . . ." He sighs and shakes his head. "See, I knew you Viennese guys were coming, so I checked out the juke in advance. Would you believe this junk machine they sic'ed on us? A million cha-cha-chas—but waltzes? Zilch!"

Of course just then Sylvia would have to re-enter the room. On her way to her jukebox, she stops a moment for a shrug at my mother. "I told you, sweetie. Florence says sorry, no."

And as if that weren't bad enough, there drops into the between-numbers quiet a short thin sob from the corridor, harbinger of more robust wails to come.

"You hear that?" Mutti says to Papa. "Your fault! You promised Rebecca another dance!"

Her voice trembles with emotion. And this almost-whimper of my mother's punctures the detachment through which I've tried to filter all this into a minor comedy. But it's not funny anymore that her famed son has disgraced himself on the dance floor and that her enchanting granddaughter has turned into a bawling brat. The dance she's so looked forward to on the eve of the birthday dinner—its glitter lies in ruins.

"Milton!" Mutti turns to Mr. Pinsler, desperate. "Do something! Phone Florence! Official! Men President to Women President! Tell her you will pay the coffee urn half! But she should let Sylvia play music—just one waltz and one rumba! Please!"

"Excuse me!" Milton says. "One moment! Coffee urn half? Sylvia brought up the coffee urn. Hats off, that's world-class chutzpah! That's a beauty—that really takes the cake! *We* should pay up on the coffee urn? What about the chairs? A much bigger item! They still owe us on the chairs! And I bought those damn chairs for both clubs back in March. What am I saying—back in February!"

"But please, just for tonight," Mutti says. "For tonight forget the fighting—"

"Tell *them* to forget! I love you, Rose, but *they* brought up the coffee urn! They ought to thank their lucky stars we're not suing them on the chairs! Me, I ought to sue them! Emotional distress! There's guys talking impeachment over those chairs! Know what the Women's Club is doing to me? Makes me go to the men's room! Excuse me!"

He exits, the limp very noticeable now.

And Mutti still won't give up.

"Franz!" She turns again to Papa. "Your fault, with 'The Blue Danube'! So you make up for it—you go to Sylvia!"

She plumps into the chair next to Papa's, clutches his arm. "Because Sylvia likes you, she owes you a favor for her grandniece's interview with you on Dachau—remember, it won the school prize! Are you listening to me?"

He nods, but he's not really looking at her. His eyes are half-closed, lids tensing into many wrinkles. With his free hand, the one not clutched by Mutti, he's unbuttoning his collar which ordinarily he never does while wearing a tie. Nor do my parents ordinarily make such a spectacle of themselves.

"So go to Sylvia!" Mutti says. "Remind her of the grandniece! Just play one rumba and one waltz! Forget the Men's Club and the politics and the fighting! Just for two numbers, stop this terrible politics all the time!"

Papa's hand is inside the unbuttoned collar; he is looking down, shaking his head as if at some flaw on the parquet floor.

"Nobody can do this," he says in a peculiar hoarse voice.

"What?" Mutti says. "Do you hear what I am saying?"

"Nobody can stop politics."

"But you have to," Mutti says. "You have to stop it, here! Outside, okay, the convention, but here! Especially us! For us it's not just Democrats and Republicans—it was the Nazis! Life and death! And we survived it, and now we have the golden years before it's too late! Just dance a little without politics killing everything! Just—"

In midsentence she stops; lets go of Papa's left arm; clutches his right hand, the hand inside his loosened collar that's rubbing his neck. "No!" she says. "Not that again! I can't stand that! I can't watch it!"

She's gone, run out the door. In her bare stockings. In her distress she shucked off her tight pumps. Only now do I notice them lying by her empty chair. I notice, furthermore, that I'm not the only one embarrassed by all this. People near us are fleeing from the painfulness of the scene into the cha-cha on the dance floor. Worst of all, I now recognize Papa's neck rubbing. He used to do it often after Dachau, but I thought he'd gotten over the tic long ago. But now his hand is rubbing, again and again, the scar on his neck where the S.S. whip once cut through his skin.

"I get Rebecca too excited," he says in that hoarse voice, rubbing. He sits all alone in the empty first row of chairs, attended only by Mutti's shoes. I pick them up from the floor, looking away from him. The rubbing motion of his hand inside the collar seems in such perverse sync with the beat of the cha-cha-cha.

"Papa," I say. "Don't worry about Rebecca. But this isn't our night. Let's go."

"Mutti also," he says hoarsely, rubbing. "She gets too excited. She doesn't understand. Nobody can stop politics."

"You shouldn't rub your scar, Papa. Please!"

He pulls his hand out of his collar. But he still stares down to the floor. "Even Dachau," he says, hoarse. "We finish washing the dinner bowls. Ten minutes before lights out. But every moment, politics. Whisper fights: Only Russia can stop Hitler! No, only America! Even between you Reds, the Trotzky people—"

"Papa, please!" I'm still holding Mutti's pumps. "Let's not remember bad things. Let's just call it a night."

"Bad things?" he says, finally looking up. "Politics fighting? That was good. In the camp that was good."

"What?" I'm jarred within my disconcertment. "Never mind. Let's get out of here."

Suddenly he stands up. "Okay." His normal voice is back again. Briskly he takes me by the arm. "Come on."

But instead of heading for the door, he's going in the opposite direction. He's leading me (with Mutti's shoes still in my hands) to the dance floor, right through the cha-cha revelers.

"Where are we going?" I ask.

He doesn't answer, doesn't have to. We are walking in a straight line toward Sylvia.

"Wait," I say, "Mutti suggested this, but I'm not sure—"

We are already there.

"Good evening," he says, a bit loud since the cha-cha is rising to its climax.

"Good evening," Sylvia says, with measured cordiality. She lets her arm rest casually but firmly on top of her jukebox. "Sorry I couldn't oblige Rose."

"Oh, this I realize," Papa says. "This is understandable. But we have something for you. You know the musical show from my son's book—Freddy, where will it perform in Miami?"

I'm so surprised by this turn in the conversation that it takes me a moment to comprehend that he's addressing me.

"Uh, the Coconut Grove Playhouse," I say.

"Yes, beautiful theater," Papa says to Sylvia. "And we have two premiere-night tickets we can give to you—I mean, to your ladies' club."

Sylvia's arm drops off the jukebox.

"Beg pardon?" she says.

"Two premiere tickets, good seats. And what you can then do—" He turns to me. *"Wie sagt man 'verlosen'?"*

"Uh, raffle them off," I say.

"You raffle them off, the premiere tickets. Maybe this will make you more money than the coffee machine cost."

The lipstick on Sylvia's face parts, revealing four long capped teeth. "I don't quite understand," she says.

"The famous *Rothschilds* Broadway show," Papa says. "It was in the papers. It opens here in September, right, Freddy?"

"October," I say, still astounded. "The first week of October, if all goes well."

"It won the best awards in New York," Papa says. "There was a big article here in *The Miami Herald.* You remember?"

"Maybe." Sylvia crosses her arms over chest. "Now that you mention it."

"This will be the highest point in the theater season in Miami. And you get two premiere tickets."

"I'm trying to get this straight," Sylvia says. "What's your angle?"

"Because we want to have a nice dance evening, my wife, Rose, and me. We are celebrating our birthday week with my son and family. You just play some music, a waltz and a rumba. And then you get the tickets. It would be very nice."

Sylvia uncrosses her arms, crosses them again.

"Are you serious?" she says. "This is on the level?"

"Very serious," Papa says. "Very on the level. Right, Freddy?"

I have to nod, of course.

Sylvia heaves a long breath.

"I can't possibly phone Florence again," she says. "I just can't disturb her twice."

"Yes, this I also understand," Papa says. "This means it is up to you. You have the decision. It would be very nice for us and very good for your club. Thank you."

He takes me by the arm, leads me away.

The cha-cha is over, and so we traverse an empty dance floor. It's like walking on a stage, with many eyes trained on those egregious women's shoes in my hand. Probably I'd be even more embarrassed if I weren't still so astonished.

"When in the world did you get this ticket idea?" I ask.

"Mutti is very angry with me," he says. "It will make her feel better."

The incredible thing, of course, is that he started something that he knows might cost him money.

"If you give Sylvia the tickets," I say. "I'm not at all sure I can get you an extra pair for the B'nai Brith. You might have to write them a check after all."

"We see." He stops to rebutton his unbuttoned collar. "If she doesn't play the music, I give her no tickets. But I have tried. You can tell Mutti."

Not that he is actually grinning. But there seems to be a certain smugness to the way he reknots his tie around his rebuttoned collar. All his adroit little manipulations make me feel doubly foolish, carrying my mother's shoes before so many watching people.

"Papa," I say. "You're a pretty damn shrewd politician. Is that why you think political fights are good—even in Dachau between Jews, if I heard you right?"

"Yes. My tie looks all right?"

"Fine, great. So did I hear you right on Dachau?"

"Yes. The way a tie looks, this is very important to Mutti. Your tie also, you should fix it."

I do tighten mine. But he still hasn't answered my question. On purpose? Another manipulation?

"You have to clear this up for me." I say. "How can that be good, inmates fighting about politics in Dachau?"

"Oh, the fights," he says, still adjusting his collar, pulling it down in the back. "The politics fights. It makes us feel we are not finished in

Dachau. We are still connected to the outside. We will live and get out to the politics outside. Ah, you hear?"

Indeed I hear: music from one of the jukes—and by God!—it's the opening strains of the "Blue Danube" waltz.

"It worked!" I say.

"Aha." He walks on, smiling. "Here also," he says. "Men's Club, Women's Club politics. It shows we are not finished. We can still fight strong. We are not too old. There is Mutti."

My mother has come back into the room, naturally in her stocking feet. But her face is bright, brightening still more when she sees me.

"Freddy, you have my shoes!" she says. "Good! And look what Marcia has!"

Right behind her comes my wife, our little daughter on her arm in the same dancing position as with Papa earlier. But now Rebecca, hat askew and tiny long-lashed eyes closed, is angelically asleep. Mother and dreaming cherub are doing a waltz turn, and then another, and then dance out through the door again, toward the elevator, drawing more "oohs" and "aaahs" from their audience. The Mortons have redeemed themselves, thanks to Marcia, whether or not she smiled her famous wry smile.

"Sit down, Rosl," Papa says to his wife. "Freddy, maybe you help Mutti with the shoes."

"No, no," Mutti says. But I do, of course, knowing how tight those pumps are, bending down because that looks less undignified than kneeling. Especially for a near Nobelist.

"Very nice," Papa says. "Freddy, maybe you dance with your mother."

I straighten up, opening my arms for her and my heart to him. Who cares if he manipulated me on my kid Saturdays and on how many adult occasions for forty years thereafter? I love, I just love this reactionary penny-pincher with a diabolic pipeline deep into the human soul.

"Did Papa tell you?" I say. "I'm going to move in with you for a few days."

"No!" she beams.

And then Mutti and Morton Rampant launch into the waltz.

September 1994

Vienna, Bald Starlet

So long, soft haven. Slow, reluctant, but necessary, this separation from blanket, from pillow. The digital clock numerals glow 10:45. Already 10:15. No use setting the clock ahead—I'm still getting up too late. An old habit made worse by awareness that nowadays rising from bed means rising straight into ye olde morning angst. Relax by deep breathing (quoth Dr. Coleman), which you can start by yawning. Very well, I yawn my way out of the air-conditioning onto the terrace, to test the air.

Quite warm for mid-September. A sunny, humid day, familiar to me as a New Yorker. Unfamiliar, on the other hand, to an ex-Viennese. I can't recall such mugginess here during my childhood in this city. Perhaps, like so much else in Austria, the weather, too, has been Americanized during the many decades since.

Suddenly a quick, chill burst of wind that says "Take the exercise mat inside." The mat stays right where it is. Sure, these gusts could get shivery—on the other hand, there's a green subalpine tang to them, a pinewoods serenity I'll miss after my return to Manhattan tomorrow, and I need to suck in every single whiff of serenity I can get.

On the other hand. It's an on-the-other-hand sort of day. Old Fred is still no-breakfast Fred, in fact more adamantly so than ever, for with advancing age it's reassuring to keep at least one's crotchets intact. On the other hand, drinking orange juice is advisable for vitamin C, against whatever bug has felled some of the film crew I'll have to face again in a couple of hours. But what do you know, the door of the fridge in my sitting room is still stuck! A nice array of juice bottles remains nicely locked inside.

Now, grousing into the phone, waiting for the hotel technician to show up, would take too long; as would the languid room service; as would getting dressed, going down to the breakfast room, gulping, going back up. I have to get in my mat workout, stair climbing, shower, shave—and still make the car that'll pick me up at 11:30 sharp. Bottom line: no vitamin C. That'd be some annoying souvenir to bring back with me from my native city . . . the flu caught on my last day here.

Of course, also annoying is the fact that I complained about the fridge door already yesterday. On the other hand, I can't get too mad at the Hilton: not only upgraded me to a penthouse suite again but the concierge also filched on my behalf the exercise mat from the fitness center. A stuck fridge door doesn't undo so conscientious a make-believe of VIP-dom.

And out on the terrace I start with equal conscientiousness my daily make-believe of youth evergreen: sixty push-ups, fifty sit-ups, thirty lift-ups, thirty crunches, two-minute headstand. Often my tensions dissolve into my high breath. Lately they keep on simmering through my limbs. They sure keep simmering today. On the other hand, I shouldn't get too nervous about my stubborn AM nervousness when in Vienna there is a perfectly good reason: it's too early for relief by medical long distance. Midmorning Vienna is predawn U.S.A. An inevitably queasy gap when one's wife is an MS quadriplegic with a diabetic complication and one's ninety-four-year-old mother frets in a Miami hospital with a broken hip. Marcia's blood sugar level? Mutti's X-ray results? . . . can't pick up the phone for that until early afternoon. Only afterward is there a chance to mellow out for the rest of the day.

Yet some easing does come earlier when I've finished mat work and start stretching. By then the piney gusts have steadied and softened into a gentle, continuous, skin-stroking breeze; it speaks of ancient tree-climbing, strawberry-picking Tyrolean summers and breathes into my pores some boyhood peace.

However, here, too, there's an on-the-other-hand: the same pleasant wind delivers a nasty surprise when I'm all done. I reach for my glasses which I'd put on the balustrade—gone. Nor are they anywhere on the terrace floor. Damn. One of the earlier livelier flurries must have blown them down to the ground.

Certainly they've shattered into many pieces. No point calling the concierge to organize a retrieval. And no point trying to dig out my duplicate specs so stupidly buried somewhere deep in the big suitcase already packed. Not if I want to make that inexorable 11:30 car that must deliver me to location by noon, and still squeeze in some stair-climbing. Normally I walk up the Hilton's twenty floors four times each morning. Late as I am today, I ought to do it at least once to maintain the mirage of youthfulness required of a septuagenarian starlet.

Septuagenarian starlet, that's how I decide to think of myself, with a grin, on the theory that a grin should be as relaxing as a yawn. I'm making a hilariously hoary debut as leading man in a feature documentary based on one of my books. Daring a glamorous time crunch by doing at least one stair climb—that should be a distraction from morning malaise.

On with my gym shorts, tank top, sneakers; down the elevator and flitting bare-thighed through the fancy lobby (past reception desk smiles at the eccentric Mister Morton, past the white-robed astonishment of a sheik) through the side door that leads to the fire stairs.

Without my glasses I must negotiate the drably lit steps with care. The film crew about to assemble will have to go home again if the starlet breaks an ankle. Caution slows me down, tightens the time crunch. Can't pause to indulge my Hilton fire stairs hobby, namely looking for new graffiti. The porters, chambermaids, bellhops who pass up or down here like to vent their mood on the dusty white walls. These scribblings, mostly chambermaid or cook erotica, backstage tidbits peeking out from under the grand theater of a five-star hotel—they relieve the tedium of up, up, up, flight after flight after flight.

And just today, when I'm not looking for graffiti, there's suddenly one that seems to have been looking for me. Boom!—it jumps out from a wall on the seventeenth-floor landing: a swastika, smeared in brutal black garish thick ink . . . an evil comet attended by a tail of paler scrawls. On the instant I become the emigrant Jew recklessly returned to Hitler land. I stop, petrified; then step closer, squint: to the right of the swastika someone has penciled an arrow pointing at it with the words *Fuck youself;* further to the right is a second arrow pointing at the first, with the words *This is spelled fuck youRself.*

And so shock yields to chuckle. Here the Nazi remnant in the folk soul erupts—only to be obscenely rebuked, and then the obscenity is rendered impeccably literate. On the other hand, the whole thing might be a joke of that impish Irish waiter in the Hilton restaurant. At any rate, I trudge on upward with a smile.

Also pleasant, a consequence of my slower, more careful climbing: reaching the top, I'm a good deal less sweaty than usual. The shower can be skipped for a much faster upper-torso wash. Even so, I still have to shave and therefore make the car just barely in time.

Instead of opening the Toyota's front door for me as he usually does (so I can sit next to him), Tony opens the back. Without my glasses I don't see until I'm quite close that this isn't Tony in the first place. This driver is a lanky taut-cheeked much younger man who says in English, "Good day, sir. I am Walter instead of Anton, who has a cold of the stomach."

Hardly good news. So the bug against which I didn't take vitamin C this morning also hit Tony. Chubby, jovial Tony, who likes to start our ride with the latest Viennese political jokes, some better than others, all therapeutically diverting. But Tony also knows when to stop, namely the moment I open the script on my lap—a signal that it's time for me to go over the lines I'll soon have to produce on camera.

Today's script, though, contains only stage directions. This last day's scene is to be all body language and facial expression as I watch two people in a public vehicle rolling through the city . . . me, the watcher, as I'm now, a bald seventy, sitting behind my tousled child-self and my young father, both on the way to their Saturday coffeehouse hour together; watching those two attain a bright little island of Sabbath in the long gray week of toil. Little Fritz's homework toil to improve his dismal standing in the class; young Papa's toil to make his factory prevail in the survival race of the Depression. Young Papa and little Fritz will ghost up from 1936, and

I'm to observe them, sitting just a few meters away, across a distance of sixty years, silently. So there isn't a single line to study in the car today. No starlet chore to preempt my 1994 prephoning morning heebie-jeebies.

Nor do I have old Tony to entertain me with punch lines. Just this silent young Walter behind the wheel up front, with long black hair down the back of his head that seems to twitch tensely from time to time. Hardly a calming sight. I resort to looking out the window.

And that works for a while due to an interesting effect of nearsightedness sans glasses. Today's opulent Vienna blurs into the raw poverty I remember from the '30s. Along the Simmeringer Hauptstrasse the smooth asphalt of the sidewalk blotches, mottles, buckles, and regains its weathered cobbles; the shiny store facades swim in a dingy fog of disrepair. Amusing, how you can conjure a time warp simply by losing your specs.

But then the house fronts vanish, replaced by an endlessly long wall enclosing the Zentralfriedhof, Vienna's giant Central Cemetery—and all amusement vanishes. Not because my sense of mortality has been awakened (it never really sleeps). No, because very soon we will pass Gate IV, marking the Jewish section. Which means that somewhere close to the other side of the wall there looms a dark tombstone whose gilt inscription ends with that baleful sentence. Back in my little-Fritz Vienna it became a family scandal, exploding into arguments that could not be muted even "before the children." And now the drive to today's shoot leads ex-little-Fritz perversely right past the trouble cut into the stone, to reconfront me with it.

Actually, to tell the truth, it's a reconfrontation I've been experiencing for quite a while, ever since I finished the book being turned into a documentary now. Typing the last page, I realized that the epigraph to this manuscript was really a certain sentence on a certain tomb. With that realization came the hope that Papa would never catch the true import of what I'd written.

To tell the whole entire truth, I suspect that, consciously or not, I already began nursing this hope when I began that book, buckled down to the very first sentence. And so used a style too difficult for Papa to penetrate? And gave my polemic about the strangling of the Sabbath a title as innocuously obscure as *Crosstown Sabbath?*

Deliberate or not, those obfuscations took. To this day Papa seems to have no clear idea that what he considers my writing delinquencies, including my "anti-Americanism," might somehow relate to the sore words chiseled into the base of his father's headstone; unauthorized words that were not part of the previously agreed-on inscription; contraband words the stone mason had added after a secret phone call from my grandmother. At the unveiling, these words had shocked Papa almost as much as the accident that had killed Grosspapa, had so angered him that he had stomped away from the graveside ceremony.

ARBEIT WAR SEIN GANZES LEBEN say the gilt words on the black marble looming beyond the long cemetery wall. WORK WAS HIS WHOLE LIFE. A sulfurous eulogy summing up a marriage, smoldering with the heat of decades of quarrels. "Here lies my husband," my grandmother hissed with each syllable of that phrase, "a man who worked instead of lived. Work engulfed his existence, devoured all love, warmth, joy, leisure, ease, everything we could have had together . . ." That swart stone keeps exhaling her hiss at the corpse below, to echo through eternity.

Against this hiss Papa would argue whenever we took the No. 71 tram to visit the grave together. Don't mention this to Grossmama's face, he'd tell me again and again, but how unfair, how awful to speak badly of Grosspapa's work in a manner made possible only through that work! Without work, how could he have risen so mightily, how could he have provided for us so well? A blacksmith apprentice arrived in Vienna from Galicia, orphaned, unconnected, illiterate, penniless, how else could he have become an industrialist, except through work? Hard, dedicated work, which never stopped until the terrible morning when a hunk of exploded flywheel crashed down on his forehead. Without his hard work Grossmama would not survive him as a lady of means, means she used to have her slander engraved on the best marble in the most elegant golden calligraphy!

And surely, Papa would continue, surely my memory of Grosspapa showed how different he was from the person those words described! Didn't I remember how Grosspapa would take time out from work when I visited him in the factory, remember his kisses and his sweets?

And I'd say yes—yes, of course. And it was true, I did remember (and do remember) that Grosspapa Bernhard usually appeared quite soon after a secretary notified him of my presence; remembered him entering from the hall with the machines, opening a door through which motors thundered and pistons clanged and closing the door again so that I could hear once again the milder typewriter clatter of the office in which I'd been waiting. I remembered Grosspapa coming toward me, striped trouser legs moving fast under a smudgy hem, for he always wore a mechanic's smock over his pinstripes. And, yes, his smock had a pocket from which he'd pull a raisin-nut chocolate bar of just the sort I liked, and he'd drop it down the front of my sailor suit and say, *"Ah, unser junger Herr Fabriks-Kollege!"*—*"Our young Mr. Factory-Partner!"* and he'd lift me up for a hearty kiss, though he usually released me quickly again because again the piston roar would drown out the typewriters with the plant foreman opening the door about some urgency in the electroplating department. But even with the kiss so quick and Grosspapa gone again, the imprint of his gray mustache kept prickling on my cheek and the chocolate bar melted warm against my chest.

And so, yes, little Fritz always said yes indeed, he remembered kiss and sweets, yes, his remembrance confirmed Papa's fierce rebuttal of the gravestone accusation. But after little Fritz became Frederic, American writer, the day came when he said no. That day he defected from Papa's side to Grossmama's by starting his Sabbath book. And he didn't just repeat her accusation; he magnified, deepened, universalized its impeachment of the Western entrepreneurial ethos as poisoner of life; he enlisted Occidental history, religious as well as secular, to question the Judeo-Christian dynamic which had goaded unnumbered Grosspapas so formidably into the quicksands of success; used myth, psychoanalysis, sociology to document how the West's faith in individualist, do-it-yourself salvation sacrifices the warmth of "us" to the insatiable exactions of "me"; how the fundamentalism of the chosen ego promises milk-and-honey deliverance contingent on arduous infinite travail; how it embroils us in a fratricidal armageddon, a free-for-all of ferocious strivers intemperately contending for a payoff equally intemperate, such as a regal fortune or an imperial victory or planetary fame; how our supremacy-wracked, celebrity-ridden, joy-parched, never-enough culture initially created the Sabbath as a one-day respite from the grasping, aggrandizing, manipulating it demanded, and how the Sabbath inevitably withered as the Western enterprise waxed, technologized, accelerated in pursuit of a redemptive jackpot ever receding; how this process paved over lilies and leisure, morphed hugs into pixels; how the apparatus of achievement in chronic overdrive will break its own flywheel with excess momentum and come down on the achiever like that exploding press did on Grosspapa, buried on the other side of the Zentralfriedhof wall . . .

"Sir, excuse me," the voice juts into my thoughts from the driver's seat up front. "Excuse me if I ask, is this the correct street to the terminal of the Number 71 tram?"

"Uh, yes," I say, refocusing. "Yes, it is."

"You see, I am really from Salzburg, only one year here in Vienna, and I am not really a chauffeur. So excuse me."

"We're okay," I say. "I know the neighborhood from visiting the cemetery."

"Oh, this is lucky. Because I was worrying till now."

"No, no, we're already quite close."

"Oh, very good, thank you. Because I confess, I am in a different film business. I am a little bit out of line, location driving."

"No problem."

With that I want to resume my Grosspapa/Sabbath musings since they might apply to the scene ahead. But then it comes to me that there *is* a problem—one my driver has left hanging. That's why his long black hair is still twitching. He's "out of line"? "In a different film business"? Obviously this is meant to evoke a request for clarification, some further response from me he's awaiting.

"What film business are you in?"

"Oh, thank you for the interest. I am assistant lighting man. In fact I am shooting a Red Bull commercial right now."

"Right now?"

"No, no, I am sorry, sir, not right now but this past night and also a shoot tomorrow night."

"You're between night shoots?" I say. "Goodness, you should be home, sleeping."

"No, no, sir, I jump when I hear of this driving opportunity from the production manager."

"Aren't you tired?"

"No, excited, to work with an American production even if only driving—"

"Wait a minute," I say. "This is for Austrian television."

"I realize. But the production manager says you also shoot in English."

"Yes, in case some American stations want to pick it up."

"PPS?"

"PPS? Oh, you mean PBS. Yes, they said they'd like to see this when it's finished."

"I am sorry, my pronunciation, but I am studying English in Berlitz school."

"You're doing fine."

"Trying, sir. Intensive course. So it will be on Public Broadcast System?"

"We'll see. They've expressed interest, that's all."

"And I am so much interested, the greatest thing for me will be to work in America—"

"I appreciate that," I say. "Here we are, not even late."

"If I can just give you quick my card, sir, just in case an American production comes here, I have A-class references, thank you!"

"My pleasure."

And since he's jumping out so quickly up front that he's stumbling, card in hand, I can't jump out myself, youthful-starlet-like. I must wait for him to open the door.

A bear hug from director Curt Faudon.

"Hey, where are your glasses?"

"Would you believe? The wind blew 'em off my terrace. I'll try not to squint."

"Wait a minute. You wear glasses in all the other scenes."

"My God!" I say. "Of course! I forgot. That's terrible."

"Not necessarily."

"But what are we going to do?"

"Think of something. That's for me to do. And you, you relax your face. The makeup girl is in the trailer."

I know my Curt Faudon by now. The more trouble, the breezier.

"Curt, what else has happened?"

"Nothing. Just waiting to hear back from Hubert."

"He isn't here yet?"

"So you weren't here a minute ago."

"But I have no costume fitting. Doesn't he have a costume fitting? So he should be early."

"Good memory, Fred. That's why I put a call in to him. Tell you what we'll do about your glasses—"

"But no Hubert, no scene! He's my father!"

"So your father's going to drive up any minute. But about your glasses, we'll take glasses off some extra's nose and put them on you. How's that?"

"Fine. But Hubert's never been late before!"

"Fred, that's filmmaking, very exciting. Now will you go to makeup, please?"

"Yes, sir, director, sir!"

I muster what breeziness I can.

I share the trailer with Gábor, cast as my little-Fritz self, hence my costar; in contrast to me he's already a seasoned and composed pro. The makeup girl is powdering his mouth area as I enter, and since he must keep his lips closed he gives a playful military salute. Of course, if he did say something I wouldn't understand him: Faudon couldn't find an Austrian kid resembling photos of me at that age, but auditions in Budapest produced in Gábor an amazing, if unintelligible, look-alike. His mother, standing next to him with a solicitous thermos bottle, is also limited to Hungarian while Gábor's translator is outside, talking to Faudon.

And the linguistic barrier suddenly seems peculiarly apt. After all, the little Austrian boy who joined Papa in denying the gravestone charge would not have understood a word of the English the adult American writer used to affirm that very same charge amplified into a book.

And something else bizarrely appropriate about this little Hungarian, this strange-tongued reimbodiment of what I was six decades ago: when the makeup girl, her job done with the boy, puts the glasses back on his small face—glasses I've had to wear even before kindergarten—why, little Gábor looks more like my essential persona than I myself do now, glassless. Which confirms a certain long-standing suspicion—namely, that only my young self is the genuine me. Perhaps not quite as child-young as Gábor here; but once I strayed past the quarter-century mark I seem to have devolved (regardless of intellectual accomplishment) into a more and more imperfect copy of my intrinsic authentic twenty-three-year-old identity.

"Turn, please," says the makeup girl, whose powder puff is trying to dab off my cheeks some of these inauthentic crinkles.

Obediently I turn and face the trailer window looking out on the terminal's streetcar shed. When I squint I can make out a peculiar shape inside the shed, quite different from the other vehicles. The shape isn't a 1936 bus like the one Papa and I used to take for our coffeehouse trip: Vienna's Transportation Museum didn't have one. What it did have, what now bulks in the half-light of the shed, is a tram of the same vintage: a squat wooden thing with open-air platforms, much broader in the beam than the current ones, which are slimmer, sleeker, streamlined. Yet these, like later models of myself, seem less genuine; they just slump on the rails, dark, inert, inanimate. The 1936 tram, on the other hand, breathes, almost heaves with an interplay of glows and silhouettes. The cinematographer's crew is setting up in there.

And—amazing—a similar contrast holds true of the group assembling just outside the shed, the extras in their costumes. Their 1930s look, the smart snap-brim fedoras and compact small mustaches of the men, the mannered hats and styled permanents of the women—they appear so much more vivid and sentient (at least to my squints) than the faded blue jeans and the random manes of the 1990s crew. . . .

"All right, let's set now," director Curt says, charging into the trailer. He waves three pairs of glasses confiscated from extras or staff.

"How's this one? . . . No, too wide. And this? . . . Same story. But this? . . . No, same again. Fred, you've got such a narrow face!"

"There goes our last chance."

"Last chance, nothing. No such thing in filmmaking. But there is such a thing as an optometrist. I had an intern look one up on the Sim-meringer Hauptstrasse. He'll be back in a few minutes."

"What about Hubert?"

"Oh, we don't have to worry about him. He just called in sick."

"What!"

"The same bug."

"But then there really can't be a shoot today!"

"There better be. You're flying home tomorrow."

"But how—"

"I'll think of something, that's how. That's my job. And meanwhile your job—well, your job is, think cool and stay cool, okay?"

What I'm thinking, however, can't suddenly keep from thinking, is that the "Papa" actor is sick. A sign? How's the real Papa? It's 12:30 PM, 6:30 AM in Florida, and the real Papa gets up at six.

"Curt," I say, "my keeping cool will cost you. Can I use your cell to call Miami?"

"Hello? . . . Oh, Freddy!"

He sounds quite awake, his voice vigorous for ninety-six, though hoarser than it used to be.

"How are you, Papa? And how is Mutti's hip?"

"Oh very nice. The X-rays are very good."

"The ones from last night? You already know?"

"I call five minutes ago. Before I fix coffee."

"They open the room phones so early?"

When Marcia was in the hospital I had to wait till eight.

"I have the number of the night nurse station."

"But they don't give that out—"

"You are nice to them, they are nice to you."

"Your Belgian pralines! I should have used that in New York! So her X-rays are really good?"

"The night nurse says Dr. Klinger says maybe she comes home to-morrow."

"Wonderful! Me, too, I'm flying home tomorrow!"

"So your movie is finished?"

"My part of it is, except for the narration. We decided I'll do that, too."

"Oh, this is extra work?"

"Yes, but I can record that in New York."

"Good, so when can we see your film?"

"Well, there's editing and postproduction, but when I come down for your wedding anniversary it'll be ready for your VCR."

"Nice, that will be very nice, watching your coffeehouse memory."

Hoarse or not, his voice is really amazingly vital for ninety-six. And it looks like Mutti will come home tomorrow, and with luck the movie will strike them really like "a coffeehouse memory" unconnected to any gravestone malediction. And still, something about this conversation . . . there's something about it not quite right.

"How about you, Papa? Your voice is a little raw."

"No, just the morning. I feel as good as I feel a long time ago, when I was old. How are you?"

He's even making the same joke. But suddenly I realize what's wrong: he's learned about my doing narration, in other words, "extra work"; yet he didn't ask me as he always invariably does, if I get paid extra. A lapse of character? An erosion? A harbinger of Alzheimer's? Or maybe the money angle slipped by him too fast.

"I feel fine," I say. "Though this film stuff is tough work and we're on anything but a Hollywood budget."

"But it is prestige, no?"

"Yes. That's why the pay is so moderate."

He doesn't even ask me how moderate. "How is Marcia?" he asks instead. "She knows you are coming home?"

This is not like him, in view of the opening I just gave him; it's not at all like him not to remind me of my moneymaking obligations (reminders starting these days with "Since Marcia's medical bills, they are so high . . ."). It's like the failure of an essential reflex I've tried to stimulate in vain. Unless the stimulation was inadequate.

"Yes, Marcia knows I'm coming home tomorrow," I say. "And she understands that this kind of film work pays less than I'd get for a magazine article."

"You talk to her today?"

"Not yet," I say. "In my house they are much lazier than you. They get up much later." My tone mustn't betray my concern.

"But when you talk to her later, you tell the morning nurse, what is her name?"

"Camilla."

"You tell Camilla to put the phone right away to Marcia's ear. Because these nurses, they talk forever, they use up expensive long distance."

At last! That's my old money-money Papa!

"Don't worry, that's exactly what I'll do!"

"Because you are in very low income now."

"Papa, I love you! And I have wonderful news—this is a free call because I'm using the director's cell phone—oh-oh, he needs it now. Love to you and Mutti, call you from New York tomorrow!"

"Love also."

Click.

That's a relief. Unless, with that damn intuition of his, he smelled me out and quickly got stingy—just to make me feel better?

Faudon needs his cell phone because he has indeed Thought Of Something: call a theatrical wig shop to instantly messenger a dark brown wig resembling the hair of Hubert, my no-show movie father. Since the camera and I will watch young Papa and little Fritz from behind as they ride the tram, putting the wig on some extra should do.

No dice. The answering machine of the Hausner Wig Shop drips with efficient Viennese charm, delighted by your call, pleased to supply all your valued needs as soon as we open at 8 AM tomorrow Wednesday, today, Tuesday is our rest day and heartfelt thanks meanwhile.

"Christ!" I say. "Back to square one."

"Square one," Faudon says. "You know, square one can be a very creative place."

"Good luck!" I say. With a bitterness that turns out to be prophetic a moment later, when the intern bikes up, returned from the optometrist's shop. He brings five lenseless spectacles with wire frames similar to the ones I wore in previous scenes. Count 'em, five, and every single one of them proves ridiculously wide on my ridiculously narrow face.

Meanwhile, the 1936 tram has lumbered out of the shed, already connected to the overhead wire. Faudon's assistant director is shepherding the extras up the steep old steps. All probably for nothing.

"Let's forget today," I say to Faudon. "I can fly home a day later."

Faudon smiles. "I would have suggested that already. Except that our tram is committed for a week starting tomorrow. But that makes all this only more interesting."

"God, give me a little dullness!"

"It's just two little interesting things, no glasses and no father. For the no-father we just need one man with hair looking right from the back. Let me check out the extras."

"Good luck."

"Hey, I'm the director, I do the worrying around here." He holds out his cell. "Relax. Talk to your wife."

"It's too early."

It's 1:35 PM by now, 7:35 AM in New York. But—hold on!—7:35 AM *Tuesday!* In Vienna, Tuesday may be the Hausner Wig Shop rest day, but in New York it's the day Marcia's physical therapist shows up at eight in the morning, by which time her breakfast feeding, her medications and cleanup must all be finished and done.

"On the other hand," I say, "this is her early day," and take the cell phone.

"Hello," says Camilla.

"Hi, Camilla—"

"Fred? Amazing! I can't get used to it. You sound so near! You're still in Vienna, right?"

"My last day. How is she? Can I talk to her?"

"One moment."

"Good morning, Fred. It's one hundred and ten."

"What?"

"The sugar reading. That's always the first thing you want to know."

"A hundred and ten. I guess that's actually all right."

"Of course it is. How are you?"

"I'm okay. The shoot has technical problems. How was your night?"

"Dark. Wasn't yours?"

"Come on! No spasms?"

"Nah, just a couple of puny ones. Sort of punctual, woke us up in time, so we're done already. The dread therapist just rang up on the intercom."

"Actually," I say, "a hundred and ten is a little on the high side of normal."

"You want me to be eighty? That's so in-the-middle middling. You're a movie star now. You don't want a middling wife."

Since the connection has turned fuzzy, I walk away from the talk-buzz of the others, press the cell hard against one ear, stick my finger in the other. But it's not just the connection. Her voice sounds distinctly weaker today, which is probably why she acts extra feisty.

"Yeah, I'm some movie star," I say. "I'm an idiot, I let my glasses fall off the hotel terrace."

"So you'll look squinty like when I met you at the City College dance. Make it look like bedroom eyes, like James Dean when he starred without his glasses."

"I'll tell the director. So since I'm flying home tomorrow, what can I bring you from Vienna?"

"Oh, stay a couple of more days. Enjoy Alt-Wien."

"I don't enjoy missing you."

"Feh. What's to miss these days."

"Stop it. Anyway, I have to get back to the manuscript. I'm way behind and couldn't get down a single sentence here. So what can I bring you?"

"Forget it. You film today, you fly tomorrow, and in between you want to rush your head off with stupid gifts?"

"Look, I'm all packed, I have a driver—"

"So tomorrow have him drive you to the Vienna Woods."

"I have him only on shoot days. So what can I get you, for God's sake?"

"Okay. You know those chocolate chestnut hearts in Vienna? Rebecca loves them. Bring her a couple."

"Sure. Only they spoil fast."

"She's flying in Thursday. All you movie people move around like mad."

Rebecca is assistant to director Alan Rudolph, who is making a film in Toronto, and she, too, has to field "What's to miss" in her long distance.

"All right," I say. "Chestnut hearts for Rebecca. But what can I bring *you*?"

"Let's see. Those Hilton room service laundry bags."

"Seriously!"

"Seriously. Like the one you had your dirty laundry in when you came back last time."

"You're kidding."

"No. Camilla says they hold so much more than anything we have here, and I generate lavish amounts of dirty laundry these days. Steal some for me, Fritzl."

"Just laundry bags? That's all you want?"

"Maybe an extra chestnut heart for me. To make my readings even more unmiddling."

"You're wonderful."

"Sure. That's why the dread therapist wants to get his hands on me. Can't keep him waiting."

"You really are wonderful. See you tomorrow. I.L.D."

"Likewise, I am sure."

Click.

Wonderful doesn't begin to express her. She won't allow my emotions to brim over, remains stalwartly unpathetic even as prisoner of that harrowing bed. Always answers my mushy-romantic I.L.D. code (*"Ich liebe Dich"*) with her mock-Babbity "Likewise, I am sure." And yet the "Fritzl" from her dim voice still has that little catch in it that made it her love word for me when she was sixteen, half a century ago.

"Fred!" Faudon calls. "Ready when you are!"

I walk over to where he's standing with Gábor, Gábor's interpreter, and Gábor's thermos-bearing mother who has just given her boy a cookie. They're all gathered by the old tram, the extras already seated inside, as if the shoot were a go after all.

"Ready for an experiment?" Faudon says. "Everybody pay attention. Here goes."

With a flourish he scoops the glasses off Gábor's ears and puts them on mine.

Believe it or not, they feel right, even though the lenses are window glass.

"They fit!" Faudon says. "That's what I thought. You have a face narrow as a kid's!"

Smiles all around and Gábor claps hands with joy, then quickly stops himself to resume costar dignity and just nods graciously, chewing his cookie.

"Wait a minute," I say as Faudon gives him back his glasses. "When I wear his specs, *his* face will be naked."

"So what? You two are never going to be in the same shot. We'll just pass the glasses back and forth."

"Very clever. But we still have no father."

"No problem either. Instead of Fritz and father riding together, Fritz rides the tram alone and joins father in front of the Sabbath coffeehouse. That way we can still use the scene we already shot, Fritz and father entering the coffeehouse together. You'll explain in the narration."

"Curt," I say, "you are a goddamn genius."

"Tell Hollywood. Hanno!"

Hanno Fuchs, the cinematographer, sticks his head out a tram window. "How are you doing?"

"We have to reposition the overheads," Hanno says. "Another fifteen, twenty minutes."

"In other words, half an hour," Faudon says. "Okay, we can use the time for a voice sample. Can you spare Albert?"

"Sure."

Albert, the sound engineer, comes down the tram steps and leads us to the tram shed, the Gábor retinue included.

"Wait," Faudon says to Gábor's interpreter, "we're just doing Fred's voice sample for the New York sound studio. Gábor doesn't have to bother. Let him finish his snack in peace."

Hungarian chatter, back and forth.

"Gábor says he's finished his snack," the interpreter says. "He would like to come along."

And indeed he does, very close to me, star and costar shoulder to shoulder, right into the ice-cold shed, which becomes colder still when

Albert has the gates closed. Not only street noise is shut out now but the warming sunlight. Gábor's mother holds out the thermos to him, but he shakes his head and chatters in Hungarian.

"He will drink if you will drink," the interpreter says. "It would not be colleagues if he drinks alone."

"How nice of him," I say as Faudon has me sit on one of the toolboxes used by tram maintenance. Gábor's mother hands me a cup of nice hot lemony tea.

"Thank you," I say. "Excellent."

The sound engineer's assistant is lowering a mike boom toward my face. Gábor sits down on a toolbox exactly like mine before drinking from *his* cup.

"Eggsellend," he says, smiling, but he shivers a bit.

"Oh no, really, the boy doesn't have to stay in this icy place," Faudon says to the interpreter. "He'll come down with some bug, too. Tell him to wait in the sun outside."

Hungarian chatter, back and forth.

"Gábor says, please, he wants to learn about the voice samples."

"Isn't he something," Faudon says. "All right, tell you what. We'll give him some exercise to keep him warm. Tell him since this is a no-dialogue scene we can block out the physical action while they fuss with the sound. Tell Gábor to get up from the box he's sitting on and push it to the left."

Hungarian chatter, back and forth, while the sound people work boom and cables. Gábor gets up and kicks the heavy toolbox leftward.

"Good," Faudon says to the interpreter. "Tell him a little further left . . . yes, a little further still, until it's right in front of Fred . . . Right. Tell him, in the tram he's going to sit two rows ahead of Fred, which is about two meters. So he should push the box a little further away . . . Good, that's it. Now he should sit down . . . No, no, not that way, facing Fred. The other way, his back to Fred . . . That's it. Thank you."

"Mr. Morton, if you'll say a few words," the sound engineer says. "Please speak to the mike. Just one sentence."

"Everybody works too damn hard," I say, speaking into the mike.

"Thank you. There's some feedback. Plus the echo in this shed. We'll have it in a few minutes."

"Take your time," Faudon says, then turns to the interpreter and me. "Meanwhile, this is the physical interaction between Fred and Gábor. I'm going to do this slowly, interpreter, because you should tell Gábor as I speak . . . Okay? . . . All right, this is the interaction. Fred and Gábor, you are both in the 1936 tram with the 1936 passengers all around, everything is 1936 except for 1994 Fred . . . Am I going slow enough, because Gábor should understand this clearly . . . Okay? Okay, you are both riding along but on different seats, Fred sitting two rows behind Gábor . . . but after a while Fred leans a bit forward, to peer around the persons in between . . . because he's intrigued by something or somebody in front of him . . . and about ten seconds later, Gábor turns his head, looks over his shoulder . . . am I too fast, interpreter? . . . Good. So Gábor looks back, and for about five seconds the two are looking at each other. But—this is important, so I'll go very slow . . . But Gábor doesn't really understand that he is seeing himself sixty years later . . . but with Fred it's different . . . Fred realizes this is indeed himself as boy . . . Gábor follows all that, interpreter?"

Hungarian chatter, back and forth.

"He follows it," the interpreter says. "But he asks, if he doesn't recognize Mr. Morton, why does he turn around?"

"Good question," Faudon says. "Tell him, that though he doesn't recognize Mr. Morton, he somehow senses that behind him there's something important, you know, a presence that makes him smell the future . . . what's coming up, what's sneaking up on him in life."

Hungarian chatter.

"Gábor asks," the interpreter says, "when he turns around so he can react right with his face, what is coming for him in life?"

"Herr Morton, excuse me," the sound engineer says, "the mike is all right now. Can you say some more words? Perhaps a little longer than last time?"

"Okay, Fred," Faudon says, "tell the mike what's coming up for the boy later in life. Interpreter, you translate for Gábor. Go ahead, Fred."

"What's coming," I say. "What's coming up toward the boy later in life. Oh God, what's coming up is the Hitler darkness and the brightness of America, that hypnotic wondrous brightness that'll blind and burn the

Sabbath in him more efficiently than it was ever burned in Grosspapa, and he'll love Papa and betray him for good reason, and the girl he loves so, in the end she'll be brave about laundry bags—"

"Go ahead, Fred, please," Faudon says, because out loud I haven't said a thing.

"I'm sorry," I say, out loud this time. "But I guess I'm too damn cold in here to think. I'll tell Gábor outside."

"Thank you," the sound engineer says. "That is enough."

And his assistant opens the shed gates. And we all walk toward the tram that will roll us toward the gold letters on the dark stone.

Acknowledgments

Many thanks to my agent, Sandra Djikstra, and my editor, Geoff Kloske, for supporting me in my attempt to make autobiography as unauthorized as possible.

F.M.